FIELDS OF LIGHT
Book Three

ALSO BY LORI TOYE

A Teacher Appears

Sisters of the Flame

The Ever Present Now

New World Wisdom Series

Points of Perception

Light of Awakening

Divine Destiny

Freedom Star Book

I AM America Map

Freedom Star Map

6-Map Scenario

US Golden City Map

$\mathcal{F}$ields of Light

Lux in tenebris lucet et tenebra eam non comprehederut.

An Introduction to the Ascended Masters
of the I AM America Teachings

Lori Adaile Toye

I AM AMERICA TRILOGY: BOOK THREE

I AM AMERICA PUBLISHING & DISTRIBUTING
P.O. Box 2511, Payson, Arizona, 85547, USA.
www.iamamerica.com

I AM America Maps and Books have been marketed since 1989 by I AM America Seventh Ray Publishing and Distributing, through workshops, conferences, and numerous bookstores in the United States and internationally. If you are interested in obtaining information on available releases please write or call: I AM America, P.O. Box 2511, Payson, Arizona, 85547, USA. (928) 978-6435, or visit: www.iamamerica.com

Graphic Design and Typography by Lori Toye
Editing by Dawn Abel, Elaine Cardall, Betsy Robinson

Love, in service, breathes the breath for all!

Print On Demand Version

10 9 8 7 6 5 4 3 2 1

Cover Design by Lori Toye, cover illustration information follows:

Biblia Ectypa by *Christoph Weigel* (1654 – 1725). "The *Biblia Ectypa* is a fully engraved pictorial Bible, produced by the German artist Christoph Weigel and published in Augsburg in 1695. Instead of being an illustrated Bible (i.e. text embellished by illustrations), the *Biblia Ectypa* tells the whole Bible story entirely in beautifully-executed copper engravings."[1] The cover illustration refers to John: 1, "In the beginning was the Word, and the Word was with God, and the Word was God. He was in the beginning with God. All things were made through him, and without him was not any thing made that was made. In him was life, and the life was the light of men. The light shines in the darkness, and the darkness has not overcome it." (English Standard Version Bible) The excerpt in German, "Luxin tenebrisducet ettenebra ean non doprehederut," refers to the creative word and its relationship to God's light.[2]

1.   "Biblia Ectypa: Christoph Weigel's Remarkable Engraved Pictorial Bible (1695)." *Https://scolarcardiff.wordpress.com*. N.p., 28 Mar. 2013. Web. 29 Dec. 2015. <https://scolarcardiff.wordpress.com/2013/03/18/biblia-ectypa-christoph-weigels-remarkable-engraved-pictorial-bible-1695/>.

2.   "Biblia Ectypa." *Pitts Theology Library*. N.p., n.d. Web. 27 Feb. 2014. <http://www.pitts.emory.edu/DIA/detail.cfm?ID=6440>.

"*Let nothing dim the light*
that shines from within."

- Maya Angelou

Contents

CONTENTS

Introduction

We have reached the last book of the I AM America Trilogy and a stunning conclusion.

In the first book, *A Teacher Appears,* our connection to I AM THAT I AM is revealed within the individualized I AM Presence within our hearts. Focusing upon this Presence becomes the quickest path to the Golden Age and our Ascension, for this alignment with the Divine Plan brings forward our inner light and renews us with a childlike trust. The Violet Flame and many heretofore untold truths come forth to set us free.

Next, in *Sisters of the Flame,* the fiery warmth and cleansing passion of the Earth Mother fills our hearts with love and healing. The feminine intuition and consistent nurturing bring us to a point of conception. Aligning with Love, we fill with Grace, removing blockages and awakening our cells. Moving beyond ourselves into a Oneness with the Earth Mother prepares us for a global Ascension. Unwrapping a large thesis of Truth, followed by the antithesis – which disengages the mind to find the Heart of Love – a bold synthesis can then emerge to create a New World. In *Fields of Light,* our Father Spirit combines equally with our Mother Nature, giving birth to the Perfect Child. This child is our true Self, cradled within our hearts. This child emanates directly from I AM THAT I AM and longs to come out and play in the Light that Never Fails.

In *Fields of Light,* we learn how the Universe mirrors back to us our own thoughts so we can learn responsibility. This creates a powerful incentive to align our will to our I AM Presence, beginning a rejuvenating life of service. The work of the Ascension brings us freedom based upon the premise of choice, where decreeing the Light expresses the choice to return to the Light of God that Never Fails. This also returns us to our original DNA of perfection. Mother Mary explains how she has placed the Eight-sided Cell of Perfection in each of our hearts and forever holds the vision of our Immaculate Conception. She gives us a Swaddling Cloak to hold, carry, and protect us. As this Perfect Cell duplicates, our thoughts, feelings, and actions soon can only reflect the love that we truly are. This Divine Blueprint recognizes our Brother and Sister as our self.

My simple Quaker upbringing had not prepared me for seeing Mother Mary. But a few years ago when I took a recuperating friend to his Catholic Church, I waited for him in a small Chapel at the entrance. I sat in quiet contemplation in the first row. Upon opening my eyes, to my complete astonishment, I saw Mary floating outward from the altar toward me! She reached out and touched me. Within my body, an enormous healing welled upward. I was both stunned and elated. She vanished as gently as she had appeared and I soon left to rejoin my friends. I was so overwhelmed with emotion, I cried all the way home. She was resplendent in a way I had never imagined. Throughout this Trilogy, I have come to know the closeness of Mother Mary, by finding her within my own heart. With this kind of personal love and caring, how can we deny her vision of our perfection? Can we all surrender to such a Divine Plan? Why not!

Entering into world service activates our eighth energetic body. Purifying our thoughts activates the ninth, opening us to the presence of collective thought. Being aware of the state of the world makes it all the more important to take responsibility for our choices and to follow the guidance of our I AM Presence. Compassion is needed for the world to restore its will, and the Law of ONE allows the Divine Will to stream forth into our hearts. We are softened with Grace, dissipating our boundaries, until our hearts beat as ONE. Eternal peace and gladness then can come to every man, woman, and child.

The history of the Color Rays follow the Races that have been taking embodiment upon the Earth, giving us a fresh perspective on our own path of evolution. Each Race holds the purpose of Mastery and Ascension and all reach the same conclusion, that in order to arrive in a world of harmony and abundance, we need to find those qualities first within ourselves. As we give out, that is the measure in which we receive. When Unity Consciousness, seeded within all hearts, manifests, the Earth will emerge as a glorious Garden, cared for by a true Sister/Brotherhood. Beholding light begets light and the acceptance of our eternal freedom becomes a great celebration.

This third book is no "walk in the park," as many changes are necessary to purify the body and mind. A diet in harmony with our Divine Blueprint is essential. We need to face our fears and purify our thoughts from all lifetimes in order to stay connected to our I AM Presence. We need to make different choices if we have not aligned to universal laws, and ask to see the Divine Plan when we feel confused or disrupted, so we can participate step by step. We are given techniques for dispelling anger and fear and for purifying the body from lower-vibrational energies. Only by disciplining the focus of our attention can we reach our true heart's desire. By demanding and commanding perfection, creation adjusts itself accordingly, and this discipline becomes the joy of eternal freedom.

In conclusion, *Fields of Light* walks us through the Ascension process. By following energetic patterns of harmony, beauty, and balance, we will attain our freedom. We can ask our I AM Presence to come forth in perfection. Ascension allows the opportunity to create in a peaceful, expansive wave. We are told that when we stay focused upon our Immaculate Conception, all else will become as a soft spring breeze. With ways to renew ourselves, sounds to sustain our Heart's Desires, and decrees to fulfill our material wants, we can literally step forth as the identity we most desire to be, fashioned anew. So much wonder is ahead of us in the *Fields of Light*!

OM EANDRA
(a special blessing for the Earth Mother),

Elaine Cardall

Elaine Cardall is a study group leader in the Golden City of Malton. She is a vegan, mystic, teacher, healer, and writer of songs, prose, poetry, and plays. She lives off the grid, collecting Power from the sun, Love from the rain water, Wisdom from the wind, and Oneness from the Earth. She gives classes with her books *Angel of Joy*, about healing with the Elements in the tradition of the Essene Gospel of Peace and the *I AM Tarot*, which answers questions, reveals Truths, and stills the ego within a reliable system of Inner Dialoguing.

Preface

The following chapters contain lessons and vital information from the Spiritual Teachers. This information is being published for the first time. In fact, we never released this material before in either written or audio form. These transcripts, like the first introductory lessons that you might have read in "A Teacher Appears," or in the follow-up book, "Sisters of the Flame," sat for years in a blue cloth binder that I'd often pull out to research the underpinnings of certain Ascended Master terminology or techniques.

It wasn't until 2009, after we had published "Points of Perception," that I sat with my editor in my living room while she perused these transcripts. "Yes, this material definitely needs to be published," she stated. In fact, she was emphatic. Her concern was that it might be difficult for readers to fully comprehend or understand the messages contained in the *Golden City Series*, or in any other subsequent publications, if they did not have the original, seminal work that defined my entrance into the ethereal world of Spiritual Teachers, Ascended Masters, Archangels, Nature Spirits, Earth Changes, and Golden Cities.

So I organized the transcripts into three volumes. I pressed review copies of the first two books and then sent them to my literary agent for comments. She replied, "I think this information needs more." I had no idea what she meant. Then she added, "If you insert a small, descriptive paragraph or two in front of each lesson, I think it will help the reader."

"What do you mean?" I asked, still a bit foggy. She responded, "Like . . . 'we all got into the car and went to so and so — and then the Masters said,' . . . you know, the background information that can help the reader to understand just *why* the lesson was given."

With her words, my memory floated to a magnificent sunset scene of Kamiak Butte, and a night I experienced during a full-moon meditation with about a dozen or so spiritual seekers. Then the setting morphs, and I am scrambling down shiny basalt boulders in the hot, summer heat to view thousand-year old petroglyphs on the bank of the Snake River. This landscape segued into cool mountain moonlight and then I am hiking on a path at the foot of Mount Shasta.

I knew that I could add this background information, and understood that the rich complexity and valuable details would add to each lesson. I spent four weeks writing the first set of introductions, emailed the new manuscript to my editor, and after her polishing, re-input and re-indexed the entire book. I mailed a freshly pressed copy of the new edition of the book to her, "Is this what you had in mind?" "Perfect," she responded, "This is just perfect."

It was a risk. In fact, I was a bit uncertain if I wanted to bare thoughts and feelings that would likely reveal my reservations regarding the Spiritual Teachers' presence, let alone expose some of the events of my life that likely provoked their intervention. "I don't think I could have done it," my friend recently remarked. Then she added, "I don't think I could have so openly shared information about my personal life . . . but I know that it is helpful in order for people to relate to it." She added, "Sometimes this information can be misunderstood."

Letters and comments began to appear online. One reader wrote, "This personal account of her journey [Author note: "my" journey], speaks to each and every one of us." Another reader left these comments, "The book is intimate, and understands the personal questions and challenges we all face moving forward on our respective journeys." A book reviewer perceptibly wrote, "A story about a life interrupted by a spiritual mission."

Throughout my experiences in both "A Teacher Appears" and "Sisters of the Flame," I secretly yearned to find the most special and extraordinary person with whom to share my life. In the beginning of "Fields of Light," the fulfillment of this desire eluded me. I aspired for someone who loved and accepted not only me and my lifestyle, which at times was both simple and complicated, but who could also love my three children and share my spiritual path. Ideally, I wanted someone who accepted my mission as a trance channel, and who could sit with me and monitor sessions. Also, I wanted someone who, if needed, could ably work with the public and teach the material with both compassion and strength. In simple terms, I was not seeking an ordinary, conventional companion. I was striving for a unique comradery – a *spiritual partner*.

Spiritual partnerships are legendary in Ascended Master teachings. Each masculine Spiritual Teacher has a complement of feminine energy, and together the two often unite the paradoxical forces hidden within a single Ray through mirroring or expanding its potential of light and sound. There is not a lot of this in the I AM America material, however, much of the older, traditional Ascended Master teachings are rife with the energies of twin forces. Saint Germain's alchemic force is tempered by Portia's sense of ethics and balance; Archangel Michael's power expands his Divine Presence through the Archeia Faith; and even the Mighty Elohim Hercules becomes more powerful when his *Divine Complement*, Amazonia, is present.

The *Twin Ray* describes the genesis of the identical souls, split away from one another at creation, who later unite in their mortal journeys as eternal *Twin Flames*. In some accounts, as the Twin Rays enter the path of Ascension, they are absorbed through the Flame of Consciousness and reappear as Divine Complements. Here they exhibit the celestial perfection of their Ray's qualities — assisting, serving, and supporting their partner's equal light and spiritual vibration. To some degree, this spiritual union is described by many as the union of *soul mates*, but I'm not certain this portrayal says enough. These unions are definitely fashioned through a higher order, and demonstrate an intensity of light and a devotion of love beyond the restraints of Earthly action and reaction. These souls are the divine fusion of Heaven and Earth, graced with impunity and the gift of immortality. *That* was what I wanted. I chuckle a bit at this now, as this was an innocent desire at the time.

When the potential of this love left my life in the last chapter of "A Teacher Appears," I licked my wounds in the follow-up book, "Sisters of the Flame." Through the sanction of the feminine, I basked in the glory of raw emotion and its potential for spiritual growth and renewal in *Cellular Awakening*. And when the inner changes took hold, I emerged anew. I had recalibrated through love and light, and my spiritual evolution would be challenged, yet again, by entering another relationship — this time hopefully a conscious, evolved *spiritual partnership*.

My autobiographical journey in "Fields of Light" is about the arduous journey into higher love and the soul's development of acceptance, detachment, sacrifice, and forgiveness. And it would seem, to some extent, these lessons are magnified when you are in a relationship, whether spiritual or otherwise.

Each lesson from the Spiritual Teachers develops and reinforces the inner quest for spiritual growth and development — the liberation process better known in these teachings as *Ascension*. They literally describe how to see this light and how to define the subtle link between creation and creator; they explain how to enjoin both breath and sound to initiate Ascension; and they define the divine energy and the light of our aura with its numerous layers and rainbow of color. Apparently, our spiritual evolution is both characterized and calibrated by these distinctive bodies of light, and we can train our inner vision to see and "feel the precious radiance," of the I AM Presence. This invaluable light potentiates healing, both for ourselves and for the Earth.

When Lenard Toye and I first met, we always knew that our future destiny was likely in the Golden City of Gobean. So we literally moved over a thousand miles, from the Pacific Northwest to the high desert of New Mexico. We relocated our business, left those that we loved, and likely changed the trajectory of our lives for Spiritual Teachers who only we could see and hear. Were we outrageous? Perhaps a little, but it takes this type of commitment to fully immerse yourself into this teaching. I later learned that indeed we were following the venerated tradition of *Spiritual Migration*, a common theme in indigenous culture. In Abrahamic religions this is a form of asceticism and allegedly induces spiritual purification. In reality, I learned how to let go of the unessential, how to feel comfortable in unfamiliar surroundings, and to accept that my home indeed was *where the heart is.*

Looking back, it would be untruthful to deny that I didn't ask myself, "What if I had never moved?" It is only human to second-guess our choices, especially as we mature and realize the impact of certain events in our lives. However, now I can't help but think of all that *would not* have happened. If I had never taken this journey, it is likely you would have never held this book in your hands, or read its words. The choices that life offers inevitably transform the student through vital knowledge and experience. When offering a new spiritual technique or a new teaching to a student, I remind them of my guru's insightful words, "Don't believe anything I say! Take it unto the laboratory of self."

According to the teachings in "Fields of Light," the dimension of our inner light is alleged to radiate an "acre of light." Remember the song we sang as children, *This Little Light of Mine*? I'd change one thing – your light *is not* little. It is bold, and it is bright. Let your light shine with the effulgent "Light of a Thousand Suns." Saint Germain reiterates this request in the final chapter of this book, "The world is in need of your light and your love . . . come forth in your light and expand to all around you."

Yours in constant, recalibrating, and wondrous *Fields of Light,*

Lori Toye

1

Learn to see the light, and you will become light.

Creative Reflection
Saint Germain

While attending the Global Science Congress in Denver I perused several of the many tables of products and books with topics ranging from UFOs, conspiracy theories, and new technology. I was drawn to a table, attended by a lovely young woman, which featured stacks of recently printed books. She looked like she could work at the local bank or Chamber of Commerce, not as an extraterrestrial contactee and assistant. At the table was an unassuming man, with sensitive eyes, who reached his hand forward to me. "Hi, I'm George Green. I saw your presentation and am interested in your [Ascended Masters] information."

Before I could respond, I remembered his name. My friend Sherry had mentioned him before I left Asotin, WA, and suggested that he might be a perfect publisher for my book. "Oh yes," I responded, and I reached my hand out to his, and said, "I understand that you publish new authors – especially those with channeled material." He nodded, and before he could reply I added, "I have about 400 pages of unedited transcripts and around 100 pages of new material . . ." He handed me a business card and said, "I'm very interested, and perhaps I can help you out. Can we meet later?" "Sure," I replied. I was surprised that I wasn't nervous.

Before I could turn away from the table, Dean, the event organizer, tapped me on the shoulder. "Lori, I have someone I'd like you to meet." I turned to yet the other friendly face. The young woman, possibly a few years older than I, who was wearing a business suit and carried an elegant, professional ambience. "This is Dr. Norma Milanovich," Dean continued in a matter-of-fact voice. "Norma is a channel for the Arcturians. Since you are both channels, I thought the two of you would enjoy getting to know one another."

We greeted one another and, again, I was impressed at how "normal" she appeared, considering she was a channel for ETs aboard a starship that was allegedly orbiting in space within close proximity to Earth. Dr. Milanovich was a former college professor, with a background that was poles apart from my once conventional role as a stay-at-home mother and farm wife. "We The Arcturians," the book she channeled, carried a similar tone and message to the I AM America teachings; that of raising vibration and awareness of both the Fourth and Fifth Dimensions.

I looked at my watch and excused myself – I had almost forgotten! My friend David would call in just five minutes. Before I had left home he had telephoned, and I had bared my longing for a spiritual partner to him. I shared my secret aspiration for both a companion and spiritual equal – I longed for someone who would understand both me *and* my spiritual work. David had repeatedly assured me, "I promise, I will be there for you."

I opened my hotel door and the phone was ringing. I answered it. "Hi gorgeous," he said. His voice was comforting and soothing to my ears, yet I heard a subtle reserve in his tone, "I'm sorry I can't make it. I'm still tied up in court for a few more days. You know I'll make it up to you." We chitchatted for several minutes, and then I ended the conversation.

I sat alone for about an hour in my room, a bit furious, yet surprisingly, somewhat relieved. For several months I had sensed that David was not too enthusiastic about my spiritual work. Funny, but one of my channeling partner Dan's favorite sayings, "Actions speak louder than words," resounded in my mind. Now I clearly understood David's intent, and even though he generously offered me financial security, I could not compromise my dream of living in a spiritual partnership.

My hand reached toward the telephone, and almost unconsciously, yet deliberately, I dialed my newest friend Len's phone number. Surprisingly, he immediately picked up. "I've been waiting for you for several hours," he said. It was uncanny how connected we were. There was a drift of mirth mixed with astute affirmation in his voice. "I want you to know that I'm packed and willing to travel to Denver . . . that is . . ." he said, and his speech trailed for a minute, "Do you want me to?" Without any indecision, whatsoever, I respond, "Yes."

Len arrived in time for my afternoon workshop. It was a good attendance, with about twenty people, and I began the slideshow and lecture. He sat toward the back, quiet and somewhat reserved throughout the program. And it wasn't until dinner together, alone, that I finally got the nerve to ask him "Is anything wrong?"

After a moment of silence, Len reached across the table and touched my hand. His eyes ignited a profound light into my soul, and my mind drifted back to our first meeting on the sandy, ethereal beach of Asotin. "To be honest, I'm a bit intimidated." Len's frank and honest response immediately shifted me back to reality. I nervously budged in my chair – had I made a mistake in inviting him?

"Don't misunderstand me. I want to help and to be of service." And Len explained that before he had traveled to Asotin earlier that summer to meet me for the first time, Saint Germain had appeared to him and had succinctly stated, "Go to Lori." Len said, "It took me awhile to figure out that 'Lori' was the name of the person who had authored the I AM America Map…and I wanted to know – why? So the next time I was in meditation, Saint Germain responded, 'For Lori . . .' so, here I am!"

I was undoubtedly intrigued by Len; his connection to the inner realms was as real as the hotel dining room we were now sitting in. I said, "Well, what do you want to do from here? I fly out tomorrow morning for home. And I really appreciate you coming here . . ."

He interrupted me, "Stop. I am here as I was directed to be. I would like to fly back with you to Asotin and help you in whatever way I can. That is . . .," and he hesitated, as a hint of boyish shyness surfaced, "If you want me to?" I answered back, with a bit of improvised bravado "You've come this far – why not?" Yet, inside me there was a swirl of polarity and questions – who was this self-assured and knowing young man?

We sat in the back of the small aircraft, ready to land in the Lewis-Clark Valley. The small craft jostled like paper blowing in the wind, navigating pockets of turbulence. Len's eyes were closed for part of the flight and he awakened out of a half-conscious state. "Does flying bother you?" I asked, and he quietly spoke, "I've been in contact with Dan's higher self. I want to make sure that he doesn't feel threatened by my presence in your life."

His statement gave me pause. Since my friend Dan had left my life, I had uniquely redefined my heart's desire to manifest just the right person who would love me, my children, and above all, share devotion to the spiritual work. A month after our break-up, I had visited a psychic in Snoqualmie, WA. The spiritual teacher that had channeled through her was fatherly, wise, and loving in his guidance, and told me that I would have several opportunities for a lasting relationship, but it was best that I write with pen and paper the specific, exact qualities I was seeking in a partner. To finalize my petition, I was to deliver my request *by light* in one of two ways: by keeping the paper under a candle for seven days, or by placing my request under an electric light for, again, seven continuous days.

I spent days writing and refining my petition, and then placed the four-page letter under the prescribed light for a full week. Now, as I sat in the plane next to Len, I recalled several poignant phrases from my request to the universe: spiritual, yet grounded; loving and compassionate; devoted; dedicated to self-development; sensitive and hardworking . . .

Len's gentle voice trailed in the background and my focus transitioned from memory back to present reality, "I wasn't completely honest with you last night at dinner," he confided. "Your slide presentation blew me away. The two of you [Lori with Dan] worked so hard, and I am in awe over the work you two completed." Before I could respond, he added, "I'm uncertain if I have the skills that Dan has . . . but I know that I have been sent here to help you, and that's what I intend to do." Then I remembered one of the first entries I had listed on my petition to the universe: *must love my children.* I brushed his cheek with a kiss and said, "Well, soon you'll meet my kids. Then we'll see if you stick around!" After we loaded the luggage into the car, Len announced, "I want my first meeting with the children to be fun – let's have a Happy Un-Birthday Party!" We returned home to the little house in Asotin with cake, ice-cream, and root beer.

The next week was filled with our daily schedule of picnics and swimming trips to the beach, and Len seemed to fit right in. A few days remained until the children were to return to school, and I wanted these last days of summer vacation to be fun-loving and memorable.

The leaves on the sycamores and the backyard walnut tree transformed to hues of brilliant red and orange, signaling the children's inevitable return to their father's farm for a new school year. Our little home, which was once filled with the bustle of board games, laughter, art projects, sand from the beach, and piles of laundry, was abruptly and vacantly quiet. Len sensed my maternal void and suggested a backpacking trip to Mount Shasta – an adventure and spiritual retreat. We spent an afternoon at the Army-Navy store where Len purchased backpacking gear, hiking boots, and every possible supply we would need for about two weeks. Before we left Asotin, I quickly telephoned my friend Andrew, who was spending the next month in Ashland, Oregon. We made plans to meet up and hike the mountain together. We headed out in the early afternoon and before long we were traveling down the Columba River, following its silver course to Portland, OR, and onward to the California border.

The hike presented us with an array of extradimensional communications. Len, who is inordinately psychic, was constantly in tune with the many forces around us. I'd never met anyone quite like him, as he had fully integrated his extrasensory nature into his everyday life. The Masters, especially Sananda, continually surrounded him, and once we arrived at the mountain, the whispers of ancient Lemurians greeted us.

It was twilight, but the light from a full moon brilliantly lit the trail. We snapped our backpacks into place, and began to walk the trail, trekking in the mystical moonlight. We hiked for a little over a mile to Panther Meadows, and found a suitable site for our tents.

Panther Meadows is the metaphysical Mecca for Ascended Master students. This is the same location where Guy Ballard, an American mining engineer and founder of the I AM movement met his spiritual teacher Saint Germain. After filling his canteen with water from a stream, Guy stood up to meet the sublime Master who offered him a life-giving nectar from his golden goblet and revealed, "I can offer you a much more refreshing drink."

I sunk into my sleeping bag later that evening, and entered a peaceful, yet profoundly deep sleep. I was aware of my light bodies traveling to dimensions normally impenetrable –both hidden and secret. The morning light revealed a campsite filled with perhaps a dozen other packers, most of them nature lovers and spiritual seekers. The meadow was imbued with a unique comradery. At night we'd all gather around a central fire and cook together; sharing food, our unique experiences on the mountain, and friendship.

After a three-night stay, Len and I decided to venture into Washington State. We traveled up the interstate to the Olympic Peninsula – stopping at metaphysical bookstores and centers along the way, and selling a few maps. The Hoh River trail, a thirty-one mile trail into the rainforest, was our destination. After a stop in Port Angeles, WA, for supplies, we ventured west, and before long we were scrambling along another magical trail into the feminine rainforest.

We journeyed for three days along the trail. There was a comfort in walking among the majestic trees alongside the streaming river. At night, we'd find secluded areas where we'd pitch our tent and build a small, crackling fire to cook supper, and to heat water for a welcomed cup of tea. My feet had held up well, and I was, perhaps, in the best physical shape ever.

I marveled that less than ten years before I had lived on the Olympic Peninsula, and I had never hiked or even seen the Hoh River trail. In fact, I wouldn't have even recognized the person that I was back then compared to the person I was at this moment in time. The spiritual work had literally transformed me: body, mind, and soul.

Len and I sometimes walked for hours without speaking, yet we were still linked in a unique telepathic comradery. When the stillness broke between us, we'd engage in intense and sometimes philosophical conversation. I learned more about his life experiences; plentiful, for someone only thirty-six years old.

Len was raised a conventional Catholic in the suburbs of Philadelphia. Early on, it was apparent that he could sing like a songbird, and by the time he had entered preparatory school, he was floating between roles in musicals and plays in the community. Upon graduation, he was offered a scholarship to the Yale School of Music. However, family obligations prevented him from attending, and inevitably he received his undergraduate degree in music education. Like me, he married young, but he pursued his ambitions for the stage. He traveled extensively throughout Europe performing and singing opera. It was a strenuous schedule that took a toll on his marriage and family life, so he returned to the trade of his father and uncles – carpentry, construction, and contracting.

"I love to sing on my jobs, and I allow *only* classical music to be played," he affirmed. And then he broke the stillness of the forest green with his angelic, tenor voice. A chipmunk stood still as we both listened to the Mozart aria, sung in perfect German.

We hiked out on the fourth day, anxious for a hot shower and a non-freeze-dried meal. Sitting in a diner in Forks, WA, over chocolate milkshakes and french fries, Len asked, "Do you want to marry again?" A bit startled, I replied, "I don't know – maybe." I dipped the hot, salty potato into the sweet ketchup, and paused to savor the moment. Good food, warm feet, amazing company, and – a warm heart, too. We returned to Asotin and noted it was autumn. The garden had received its first freeze, and I found a few zucchinis hidden under foliage. Walnuts covered the ground and I gathered them into large paper grocery bags. At night we sat together, cracked walnuts, and watched television, interrupted by occasional conversation during commercial breaks.

On one of those autumn evenings, Len mentioned his automatic writing ability. This is a form of written channeling or communication, where ethereal knowledge is downloaded, usually through teachers. Instead of speaking the information aloud as some channels or mediums do, the information is transmitted via handwriting, a typewriter, or by inputting directly into a computer. The source of this compelling process is an alleged spirit or spiritual teacher, who conveys energy and information from conscious planes beyond our Earthly dimension. Interestingly, the medium functions only as a conduit to receive the material, and is not considered the author. Some scientific circles refer to this automatic writing phenomenon as the *ideomotor effect* – a physical movement that is independent of the conscious mind. Of course there are many variations and subtleties of this form of mediumship.

After our days together on the hiking trail at Mount Shasta, Len and I fervently debated the difference between discrimination and judgment, and just where one draws a line in perception, opinion, or conviction of someone's actions. "Perhaps you could ask Saint Germain?" I asked.

The next day Len retreated to the sanctuary of my home office for the afternoon. Later, a channeled lesson appeared on my computer monitor; a guidance on the power of thought, ending with a decree that was to be spoken on an exact pitch. [Editor's Note: Musical note A, above middle C 440, refers to a frequency of 440 hertz (Hz). Hertz is a measurement for sound – one cycle per second. So 440 Hz conveys a specific frequency that vibrates to a measureable 440 cycles per second.]

Greetings, Beloved chelas, I AM Saint Germain. Dear ones, when you think a certain process or thought, this universe is bound by the law to mirror or reflect any thought back to the one creating the thought. This is because you are made in the image and likeness of the Father/Mother God. All of you are creative beings and your thoughts and focus are your creations. Your thoughts are part of that which you sew into the fabric of your conscious personality.

Many teachers through the ages have taught the concept of discrimination. But have you considered discrimination to be judgment that keeps you distant from each other? So what is this discrimination based on? It is fear! There are only two choices: love and fear. Take note of your discrimination of self and others; is it ever based on love? Or is the unconscious motivation fear, fear of being wrong or wronged? Love is not an emotion. It is a state of being; the state of allowance; the state of pure creation; the first law of this universe and the reason for all existence in creation.

Love, that which binds all creation together, is the reason for creation, the reason you and I exist.

The focus of your creation—your thoughts, desires, hopes, and dreams—must be mastered for transmutation of Karmic imbalance and your Ascension. See light in all around you and you become more lighted. Your release from your own Karmic darkness makes space for more light in all realms of creation. Minute by minute, you are thoughtfully creative and this universe reflects this thought back to you. When you discern darkness in another or another's work, you are then on the frequency of darkness by your very thought and the darkness is gladly attracted to you and surrounds your auric bodies and precipitates down into your physical bodies. Allow all of your Brothers and Sisters to be where they are in their thoughts and outlooks on life. You and they are ONE in this creation. Focus instead on your own creation and allow others their own. Be not in discrimination, be not in judgment, for you will only be discerned and judged by this universe and the laws, for you have broken the First Law, Love. Love is tolerant and allowing and does not bind another to any fear, thought, or discrimination.

Why do I tell you this? You are all of the opinion that Princes of Darkness have free access to your world. Well they do not! They have been removed, so the Children of Light may grow in their light and ascend. The darkness you see around is created by the human beings after 1952. The begetters of darkness are gone. The only evil, or backward living, is all created by humankind, out of the Karmic memory you all have. Give up the memory of darkness and choose the memory of light!

You were all ascended before the Time of Lemuria, but you have all collectively chosen to forget and recreate the darkness in embodiment after embodiment. The time is now for transition! Choose now for self-transition! Decree the Violet Flame three times per day, seven times seven each time. Sunrise, noon, and sunset are the times of clearest, precise alignment. Decree:

> I AM THE VIOLET FLAME,
> TRANSMUTING MY KARMA TO DHARMA.
> LET THERE BE LIGHT!

Do this on the pitch A-440 for the first set of seven. Then for each set of seven, move up one pitch on the scale. For deeper voices, start one octave below this.

2

Creation is both disorder and harmony.

Pleiadian Ancestors
Saint Germain

Len was eager to get to work. He thought that a new I Am America office was in order. From the time my assistant Sherry had taken over the I AM America office operations, she had been running everything in a spare room at her home. We worked out an arrangement that she would continue to mail out maps and newsletters from her home. Then, on a fall weekend, Len and I began to paint a small, one-room office we found in an old brick building in downtown Lewiston, ID. The rent was affordable, and Len excitedly began to build office cabinetry, moved my office desk and computer, and purchased a transcription machine.

With Len as my partner, readily available at almost any moment to monitor sessions, this convenience proved invaluable. My channeling became prolific! We'd hold sessions at night or in the afternoon, but more commonly – first thing in the morning. Then we'd organize the rest of our work day together. I must admit that I missed my sessions with Sherry, Glenda, and Lynne – the "Sisters of the Flame." But Len's masculine energy complemented my otherwise overwhelmingly feminine dynamic, and made the energy flow balanced, and for lack of a better and more descriptive word – "complete."

Contrarily, even though I had desired to move into a spiritual partnership, now that it had manifested, I had moments when I truly missed being alone. Len sensed this, and suggested that I take time for myself, especially while the children were with their Dad for the school year. On our days away from one another, I'd often pack a lunch early in the morning, bike into the office, and spend the day transcribing channeling sessions. I'd return in the late afternoon, pedaling along the river's edge with the sunset shimmering on the water, with a new transcript stuffed in my backpack.

Len networked with our spiritual community, and he was invited to lecture for an evening at the metaphysical bookstore and center – "The Eagle's Nest" – in

Clarkston, WA. I was eager to listen to his presentation, which included his insights of auric vision, a brief chronicle of his time spent at the Barbara Brennan School of Healing, and his own spiritual experiences and teachings from the Ascended Masters. His talk was engaging and inspiring, and his experience as a teacher was visibly evident. He readily connected with his listeners. During the break, several attendees came up to me to ask if we taught any classes, and asked that we please notify them when they were available.

Autumn swiftly morphed into winter, and we'd often wake to frosty ice patterns on single-paned windows, or to a skiff of snow on the front yard where I had planted summer flowers. The Spiritual Teachers welcomed Len's presence as a monitor, and hinted that they would dispense a series of lessons that they designated the "Twelve Jurisdictions." This sequence of teachings was apparently important. The Earth Changes information that I was working on, for both Canada and the rest of the world, was intentionally paused so we could absorb and grasp the content of the new lessons.

On a late November morning, Saint Germain telepathically read me a list of topics we would cover in the Jurisdictions. I quickly wrote them down. They included: Harmony, Abundance, Clarity, Love, Service, Illumination, Cooperation, Charity, Desire, Faith, Stillness, and Creation. The Spiritual Teachers had yet another revelation regarding this body of information; apparently, I would not receive all of this material. Saint Germain explained, in detail, that masculine energy was needed for portions of this spiritual knowledge. Thus, Len would receive some of the lessons via clairaudient channeling and I would monitor these sessions; that is, if we agreed to do so.

I handed the list to Len, shared Saint Germain's explanation, and I could tell he was a bit intimidated. "Exactly what are the Jurisdictions?" he asked. I quickly replied, "They are a series of lessons, based on specific spiritual precepts, which prepare consciousness to receive the Earth Changes information." It was evident to both of us that to clearly understand this vast body of information, which included detailed Earth Change prophecies for the world, a spiritual preparation of consciousness was vital and essential. I reminded Len to personally ask Saint Germain for guidance regarding this, and to request that I receive the first channeling sessions specific to the Jurisdictions – that way, the energy would already be conditioned and easier for him to adapt to and access.

This is an important point that most seasoned channels can understand. Channeled information comes through a certain frequency and vibration, which fills a room and then, afterwards, this energy is present for several days – sometimes weeks. This ambient life force creates an environment that supports inner peace and natural relaxation, but, more importantly, it creates an imprint, similar to a footprint in the snow. This psychic footprint is detectable for about two full days, sometimes weeks. Sensitive humans and developed psychics can readily access and read this information.

The next day Len opened a package of new microcassettes for the tape recorder. "I've communicated with Saint Germain about this and I'm ready and willing to serve in any capacity," he said. During the next several days we received three amazing lessons, "Expansive Completion," "Jurisdiction One – Harmony," and "Jurisdiction Two – Abundance." After listening to the tape and reading the transcripts, we both agreed that the *Twelve Jurisdictions* were, indeed, twelve laws or virtues designed to guide human consciousness through the turbulent Time of Change, onward into the New Times, and then forward to Co-create the Golden Age.

Len immediately identified nuances and subtleties that past monitors would often miss – allowing for unique questions and answers on many new in-depth topics. This included a distinct bantering and discussion on spiritual topics between the two of us. Yet, sometimes our conversations led us into exhaustive debates, filled with passionate idealism and differing points of view.

The following channeled lesson addressed harmony – that is, the accord and synchronicity found to exist innately in the natural world. Ironically, such beauty is constantly challenged by what the Spiritual Teachers call, "the scramblers."

Scramblers thrive on and identify with disturbance, disruption, and overall troublemaking. A scrambler may be a person or an entity, but often it is an aspect of our personality or ego.

Interestingly, in this lesson, the Masters' divulged their spiritual provenance, with origins from a star cluster in the constellation of Taurus – the Pleiades. The Pleiades are known in western mythology as the *Seven Sisters*, and sometimes are referred to as the *flock of doves*. In fact, some biblical scholars claim that the vision of Revelations (Rev. 1:16) is a reference to this celestial body, "…and he had in his right hand seven stars."

Saint Germain's guidance in the instruction encourages the spiritual cultivation of harmony, beauty, and personal balance to counter problematic *scramblers*.

Harmony and its counter, disharmony, are patterns of Co-creation. When we engage discordance and conflict, we psychologically hold either premise as an energetic pattern.

Now I can't help but wonder if the Spiritual Teachers were subtly asking us to tone down our own scrambling state of consciousness, to consider the benefits of harmony – the art of allowing and accepting another who disagrees with you!

All that has been set forth upon your planet and all those who step forth to sponsor the creation of a planet form an energetic pattern, a creative wave, that is duplicated or expanded upon on your particular planet. The process is one of duplication of the genetic code contained by the Creators.

Question: "I see. And the Creators were the Elohim?"

There were the mighty Elohim but also the Angelic Realm.

Response: "I see."

You see, Dear one, your Creators were also the Archangels.

Question: "Yes, because it was on each of their Rays that the Elohim worked?"

This is precise.

Question: "So, the subatomic particles that are now called quarks are indeed the Rays of the Archangels?"

They are, Dear one. They have been set forth in an energetic pattern. You will soon discover that the number fourteen is crucial.

Question: "You expressed concern. Was it about our project of the energy box being used incorrectly?"

This is precise, Dear one. What does it do, but alter the energetic pattern.

Question: "How do we protect it?"

It is important to not only secure a pattern that is cloaked in secrecy but that the location where you work upon such projects is well guarded. There are those among the universe who have come to watch this work. There are also those who step forth to scramble what you call the energetic pattern.

Question: "About the scramblers, is this of their own volition and will, or is this part of the design of the entire project?"

Dear one, how you understand adeptly. They serve indeed, both purposes.

Response: "I thought so. It is almost as though they are the spice in the dish."

There are always those who thrive on disturbance.

Response: "We have truly noted this."

Have you not seen this in your own organization?

Response: "Most assuredly, Beloved one."

There are those who have taken this identity as Cosmic Beings.

Question: "That is most interesting. And they continue to hold, in their own creative wave or flow, this pattern for themselves?"

It is so, Dear one, particularly in a planet of this nature. However, in the Pleiades, the planet from which we are from, Dear ones, harmony, beauty and balance are set forth as the creative, energetic wave. There is no place for disturbance.

Question: "And are we planting the seeds of this harmony and balance into this atmosphere and energy of this planet?"

This is our message as a family. That is what we have brought. That is what we sow. I AM of service and love of the Violet Flame. Eternally, Saint Germain.

3

Ascension is a work and service meant for everyone.

Work of Ascension
Saint Germain

Christmas was a few weeks away and the children were eager to pick out a Christmas tree. We found a beautiful pine tree, and I located my large box of holiday decorations in storage, which had, surprisingly, survived my last several moves. We opened the box and found our family treasures: blue-inked handprints carefully constructed into paper ornaments, reindeers, several Santa Clauses, and, of course, angels decorated with puffy cotton balls and pipe-cleaner halos.

We were a little short on cash that year, so I gave the children a list and asked them to mark a star on the gift they wanted most from Santa Claus. Thank God for my mom – she assured me she would help fill in the gaps that year, and asked what the children needed. I handed her a list filled with socks, pajamas, and, for each, their current size. We planned to spend the holiday at the ranch with my parents and grandmother. Our spirits were dampened a bit that year as my grandfather – the family patriarch – had recently been admitted to the nursing home. He was ninety-one years old and my grandmother could no longer care for him. And since my parents' home was filled with my younger sisters' family, Len and I planned to stay at my grandmother's home, next door.

My grandparents' home was my second home. That started when I was just eighteen-months old. My mother and four-year-old sister had boarded a train to Nevada to visit my maternal grandmother. My dad was occupied with autumn planting, so I was delivered to my grandmother Marie. I stayed at my grandparents' home for two weeks, and I was showered with love and attention so complete that when my mother came to pick me up, I ran and hid. I later found out that every night I would sleep between the two of them. After those two weeks, our bond was forged – they were essentially another set of parents to me.

My eyes gazed over the familiar bedroom as Len and I sat our overnight bags down. My grandmother's hands quickly straightened out the white, chenille bedspread commenting, "I hope you'll be warm enough in here." "No worries, Grandma," and my arm reached around her small frame to hug her. Her face was deeply worn and tired from the eight-mile drive made several times a day to visit her husband in the nursing home.

As I hugged her fragile body, I recalled the strong, yet petite, aproned woman who had held dozens of family Christmases, with, often, over sixty attending – sons, daughters, in-laws, and dozens of grandchildren. Leading up to the big day, my sister and I would sit at her dining room table after school. We learned how to perfectly tape wrapping paper with straight corners, tie bright bows on presents or, carefully, unwrap nearly a hundred delicate Christmas ornaments – some family heirlooms and many handmade – to glitter the branches of an enormous, lighted tree in the corner of her living room. Often, I would sit at her round, oak, kitchen table to recite, by memory, my lines for the church Christmas program. She'd correct me and would later reward me with a fresh baked sandbakkelse, a Norwegian sweet tart baked especially for the holidays – her mother's recipe.

This would be the first Christmas, in many years, that she would not awaken with Grandpa at her side, her partner for over sixty years. As Grandma poured Len and me a cup of hot tea, I sat, again, at her kitchen table and wondered how I could make this Christmas happy for her in some small way.

"I haven't made any cookies this year . . . I'd hoped to." she said. There was a tone of lament in her voice, and my grandmother continued, "I always loved baking at this time of year." I pointed to her kitchen countertop where I had left a plate of holiday cookies, "The kids and I baked and decorated cookies, and I brought you some." A faint smile erupted, "Do you remember when we baked cookies together when you were little?" "Of course Grandma," I replied. I reached across the table to touch her arm, and then I remembered that before we had left the river valley, Len had tucked a package of the shelled walnuts from our autumn's harvest into one of our bags. I got up from my chair, quickly retrieved and handed it to her, and said, "These are from our yard – maybe we can bake a coffee cake for Christmas morning?" Her eyes sparkled as she replied, "Yes, and we will save a piece for Grandpa."

The children arrived on Christmas day, after a morning celebration with their father and his family. After a long day of opening gifts, holiday foods and fare, and of course family, I noticed Len sitting alone in a corner, unusually quiet. "Everything okay?" I gently asked, as I sat down by him. "Everything's fine," he quickly responded. But I knew he was thinking about Christmas back in Pennsylvania, his family and, of course, his children, who were with his ex-wife.

That night we drove back home in the dark to our little bungalow in Asotin, with the children all buckled-up the back seat, and Christmas music faintly playing on the radio. Len seemed somewhat engaged in his own thoughts, when he suddenly turned the radio off and asked, "Does the Lutheran tradition embrace the Holy Family?" I had to think for a minute, "Well . . . to some degree – but the entire focus of its faith rests solely on Jesus – no saints and certainly no Mother Mary." "Catholicism is somewhat based upon the holy family – Jesus, Joseph, and Mary. I find it interesting that these are the same personages that have evolved in Ascended Master Teachings," he responded. I could tell Len was thinking carefully and introspectively.

This fact is perceptively true. Sananda is considered the ascended version of Jesus, who embodied the Christ Consciousness; however, before he took on physical form, Jesus was claimed to be the Angel of Unity – Micah. Saint Germain is said to have incarnated as Joseph, the Earthly father figure for Jesus, and husband to Mary. Mother Mary – the western archetype of Divine Mother – achieved her Ascension after her lifetime as Jesus' mother. However, prior to that, she was an initiate in the ethereal Temples of Nature, overshadowed by the Angelic Kingdom. No doubt, Ascended Master teachings contain unique parallels to Christianity.

"Have you ever discussed your beliefs about the Masters' with your parents or grandparents?" Len further probed. "No – not at all," I quietly answered, and then added, "As you can see, I am from a typical, conventional background, and I think to share my thoughts on this would be too much of a stretch."

We traveled for a mile or two when Len finally responded. He reached over and gently touched my knee, "But please consider that you have more than just belief." And then his voice became measured and somewhat deliberate, "You have *experiences* with the Masters." I turned the radio volume back up and didn't respond at all, but silently I thought to myself, "Yes I do – I most *certainly* do."

After a week of board games, leftover holiday cookies and candy, coloring books, extra laundry, and numerous movie and popcorn nights, the children reluctantly returned to the farm inhabited by their father and resumed school. Len and I enthusiastically dove back into our spiritual work at the I AM America office and into our weekly channeling sessions. Our insights on the Twelve Jurisdictions evolved into new insights, and I transcribed "Clarity – the Law of Non-Judgment," "Love – the Law of Allowing," and a lesson from Saint Germain that shared personal insights into Ascension.

Ascension is a deliberate and conscious process of mastering thoughts, feelings, and actions, which balances negative karmas. The progression of this spiritual evolution allows entry to higher states of consciousness, which inevitably frees a person from the need to reincarnate on the lower Earthly planes, or lokas, of experience. According to some Ascended Masters, it is possible to attain the Ascension in one lifetime, but that is a bit of an evolutionary reach for most souls, and is usually reserved for advanced or developed souls. For most, Ascension is a practice and activity engaged in throughout a number of lifetimes.

Saint Germain admitted to this fact and said that he purposely sought certain Ascension experiences and education that could only be given to him as a Tibetan monk. In that lifetime, Saint Germain claimed he was known by the name *Kajaeshra*, which translates to, "God's helper of life and wisdom." Ascension is also recognized as the process of spiritual liberation, which is defined as "moksha" in Hindu culture. Liberation of the soul is widely known and accepted in many eastern religious traditions, and the Spiritual Teachers acknowledge that Ascension is also a western religious practice and belief, founded on the essential premise of freedom.

~≋~

Greetings in the light of the most Radiant ONE. Dear Brothers, please enter into our light spectrum. You are most welcome. We invite you Brother Sananda, Saint Germain, Kuan Yin, Mary, Kuthumi, El Morya, Soltec, and any other members of the Spiritual Hierarchy of the Great White [Light] Brotherhood to come forth. We give you permission to enter into our energy fields. You have our light, love, and service always.

Welcome, Golden Beings! I have come forth to give you the information which you require. As you have already given your permission, we step forth to magnetize that which is known as the Human Aura. It is with greater ease that we step forth within your energy field, for you see, Dear ones, as you develop each energetic layer of light, it is easier for us to respond. I AM Saint Germain and I have with me my beloved Brother Sananda, beloved Brother Kuthumi, and beloved Brother El Morya, for we are all the Brothers who have stepped forward in this work of yours. We are the ones who have sponsored this work that you call the Map of Earth Changes for the North American Continents.

We realize that the work that you do, indeed moves much slower than we would, for you see, we have the ability to instantly impress. However, because of the Laws of Free Will, we understand you move much differently. And how well we forget being within your dimension, for you see, Dear ones, it has been long since I have been truly fully embodied in your dimension. Yes indeed, it was I who stepped forth in 1930 to bring forth the information of the I AM Activity. And it was indeed I who was present during the French Revolution and also the Revolution of the United States and stepped forth to bring Ascended Master Teachings and the Teachings of Freedom. However, I have not fully embodied since my full Ascension. May I answer questions, Dear ones?

Question: "Yes. In what embodiment were you ascended?"

Dear one, my last embodiment was that of a Tibetan Monk, his name Kajaeshra. For you see, Dear one, during that time of Earth history, the information that I sought and needed could only be obtained in what was then known as the Eastern cultures. However, it has been the work of the Spiritual Hierarchy of the Great White Brotherhood to move this work forward, move it into what is known as the Western culture, for it needs to be accepted by all races. The work of Ascension is to step forth to every Star seed. It is indeed founded on the premise of freedom, and the premise of choice. Do you understand?

Response: "Yes."

And so, Dear one, you have gathered, and we are here to give our assistance as usual. For you see, it is a work of service which we do for you.

Question: "I understand, but is it also a work of service that we do for you and mankind?"

Yes indeed, for you see, if you were to explore this in what you term "an energetic approach" or scientific approach, molecule for molecule, tit for tat, it is reciprocal in nature and comes forth on electromagnetic waves. It brings balance and harmony.

4

A Creator is both a Master of time and choice.

Time Theories
Saint Germain
Mary

Our finances were challenged. It may have been due to the Persian Gulf War, which was having an economic effect on almost everyone, or it may have been that we were not being realistic about our financial goals regarding our small publishing company. Either way, we needed to explore new ways to make and to save money. I went to Sherry, my psychic and assistant, for a reading. Before I could shuffle the tarot cards she blurted out, "It's time for Len to take over everything with the business." I knew how hard that statement was for her to make. The reorganization and mailing of the maps and newsletters had been like Sherry's baby; in fact, at one time, she had confided to me that it was one of her most favorite jobs. "Really," I said, "Are you sure?"

She replied, in a matter-of-fact tone, "Yes. You need to save the money right now. Plus, since I'm teaching art classes again, I will have extra income coming in to make up for it . . . and from what I can see Len will do a good job." She firmly added, "I wouldn't suggest this if I didn't think that this is best for you." I trusted Sherry inexorably. "Okay . . . well, I will talk to Len about it." I glanced down at the deck of cards and Sherry added, "And you don't need a reading to tell you what to do next. This is the right thing to do for your money."

I relayed the conversation to Len, and that day he rented a new storage unit where we could store the maps. It had ample space for wrapping and packing. Even though I encountered many new changes with the office and Sherry's departure, I was handling the transformation of I AM America just fine. I attributed this to daily meditation, decree work, and of course the semi-weekly channeling sessions.

The phone rang late one afternoon and it was a gentleman from San Francisco, the host of a small radio program that was broadcast on a public radio station. He asked to interview me. I decided to give it a try, even though I was a complete novice.

Not nervous at all, I actually found it a bit easier than lecturing in front of a group. I felt poised and calm as I answered his questions about the Ascended Masters, the Map, and how it came to be published. Then the telephone lines opened to anyone listening, and the second questioner ranted, "Why do you allow such crap on a public radio system . . . I fear for the children of this woman . . ." Because I couldn't listen to this questioner's harsh criticism and rants anymore, I promptly hung up. A few minutes later, our office phone began to ring and a listener from San Francisco was on the other end: "Just heard your interview on the air, good job . . . I would have hung up too!" Several more calls ensued, all with a similar message of support and interest in our spiritual work and message.

Then a call came from a woman named Sheryl, also from the San Francisco Bay area, who said. "Loved your message, and if I can help in anyway, please let me know." In the next two weeks, Len and Sheryl planned a day-long event in San Francisco for July – five months into the future. As controversial as our teachings were, it seemed that people resonated deeply with our inherent message of change.

I'd been asked to lecture at the Body, Mind, Spirit Expo in Spokane, WA, so this would give me a chance to practice before the July event. I would present the I AM America Map prophecies, but the promoters asked that I also include updated information. I wasn't certain that I'd fully absorbed the insights from the Twelve Jurisdictions, but I was anxious to share some of the Spiritual Teachers' latest teachings from our channeled sessions.

To thoroughly understand the next lesson, it is important to understand what the Master Teachers term *geometric language*. My hunch is that some of the material that they wished to provide was extremely unconventional and belief expanding, so they intentionally stretched the boundaries of words and their definitions to recalibrate our perceptions.

Here are some guideposts to delineate and understand geometric language:

Circle:	Expands energy.
Triangle:	Replicates and duplicates energy.
Rectangle:	Holds and duplicates energy.
Square:	Blocks and holds energy.

Because this lesson addressed the idea of time, and the many interpretations that we may hold of time, here are some additional definitions to help you navigate the Spiritual Teachers' insights.

Time Compaction: An anomaly produced as we enter into the prophesied Time of Change. Our perception of time compresses, and time seems to speed by. The unfolding of events accelerates, and situations are jammed into a short period of time. Saint Germain refers to this as, "they are grouped on top of one another." Sometimes events are seen only as possibility, or what are referred to as "sequential windows." From this viewpoint, events are not acted upon and viewed as they enfold or close up, but are possibilities, triggered into action through personal choice.

Time Warp: The process of Time Compaction that distorts our understanding or comprehension of time. The Spiritual Teachers claim that the time warp "bends" our familiar experience of time.

End Times: The ending of an epoch or era, and the simultaneous beginning of a new period of time. Because of the acceleration of Time Compaction, we experience both sequences of unfolded events and enfolded windows.

As an example, Saint Germain explained a potential enfolded event that apparently never occurred. According to him, a sequential window was opened for President Kennedy to become a contactee for the Pleiadians, to inform the public at large of their extraterrestrial presence. However, this possibility was blocked by the collective consciousness of that time.

It is interesting to note that choice, both personal and collective, seems to become the alchemic pivot for Co-creation of experience and events, as in the Kennedy potentiality. Saint Germain explained, "Your choices are indeed the steps . . . each presented as a choice you have faced before . . . they are duplicated, rhythmic patterns." Now I wonder if a future US President will get another opportunity, or *choice*, for this historic event?

This lesson is packed with nuance and subtly. To absorb it, please read it carefully. In fact, I suggest that you read it several times. Sananda prophesied a thousand-year-period of peace, which is brought about through the expansion of consciousness by the Divine Beings who reside at higher levels of consciousness. This will inevitably impact life for us on Earth. After all, Hermetic Law does state "As above, so below." Mother Mary ended this session with the assurance and blessing that beings of higher consciousness do exist and interact with humanity for our spiritual growth and evolution. "I AM with you," and she softly reassured, "Weave your streams of light and truth."

Greetings, my Beloved chelas, I AM Saint Germain.

Response: "Greetings, Saint Germain and good morning, Dear one."

I thank you for allowing me to come forth, Dear one, for it has been some time since we have spoken. But you see, there are still these lessons that I wish to give to you; discourses, as you and I both call them, in addition to the other works that you bring forth from other members of our family and hierarchy. There is still that which comes under my tutelage, for the true implantation for that which is the Seventh Ray.

Response: "I understand, please proceed."

I would like to instruct you this morning regarding time warp and Time Compaction Theories. Dear one, as usual, I must ask permission to come close to your energy bodies.

Response: "Please come close to our energy bodies."

May I be allowed to enter into such?

Response: "Yes, you may, you are welcome."

I AM here. I AM Saint Germain. Welcome, Beloved chelas. Today we will start discourse on time warp versus time compaction. There has been that which I have brought forth called Time Compaction Theories. What we are basically dealing with is the compaction of events. As you have learned, time as you perceive it is but a series of events. We have spoken of the sequential events and we have spoken of the timed, or singular events. The sequential events, when they are grouped on top of one another, is what we call time compaction.

Dear one, you know you are indeed in the End Times. This was the time that was long ordained from the creation of this universe. At the end of any creative pattern, there is a period of time before you reach what you would have known as the apex, or access. This is what you have perceived to be vortices or Portals of Entry. It is nothing unusual, Dear one, for when you reach the end of the duplication of one cycle, you have a chance, or a moment within that space, to make a choice: to continue the duplication process; or as a creative being, to go on to expand; or indeed, there are other times when this has come forth to store the event; or also, to block the event. Do you understand?

Question: "Block the event with the portal?"

Absolutely, Dear one, you are created beings and all that energy is at your command.

Question: "Would you give an example of a blocked event?"

For a blocked event, we can scan throughout your history. In the instance of John F. Kennedy, that was indeed a blocked event. This beam of light was brought forth to usher in a service to the hierarchy, a contact between the Pleiadian universe and the United States. The points of duplication had been reached. There was a time that the public could have become aware of such an event. As you understand, all this choice was in your realm of reality. It was indeed all of the parties' concern to block the event. There was neither duplication of the density upon their density; there was neither un-expansion of the program. In fact, we find it quite curious how so little of the events were even stored. Now do you understand?

Response: "At some point, when you deem it important, I would like you to tell me about all the events that he was to bring forth, but we'll save that for another lesson."

Dear one, I'll mention to you that he had been chosen to become a bridge; however, it was he who made the choice. Now, choice is the time that we speak of; it is the frame of reference in any duplicating process. This is a creative process, Dear one. Please understand this. Any duplicative process has this space in time we call the period of choice.

Question: "So, there are actually windows for choice?"

Indeed there are. They are on the triangular energy that we identify for you as the geometric language for you to understand duplication. This falls on what is the right-hand corner of the triangle.

Question: "As we would be looking at it?"

Precisely. It is the right-hand corner of a triangle that allows access to the center. Now, to the center, this is the point where the spins of this energy form will function, which is accessing what is known as the apex. Through the apex is the core energy which one may use to go to the realm of expansion.

Question: "So this was the function of the great pyramids of Cheops?"

Precisely, to change the rhythmic patterning within the cells. As we discussed last night, and as you were there to learn about the concept of allowance of the space within the cells, all shape and form have a space of choice.

Question: "Is the space between the cells the space of choice?"

This is precise.

Question: "As I look upon an energetic form, the space between the cells is where the enlightenment is?"

The enlightenment and also, as we discussed last night, the Theories of Allowing.

Response: "Please proceed."

We have spoken of the duplicating patterns. For our density and our planet, the triangle is probably the only one we need to deal with. It is the easiest for you to understand, Dear one. The circle has been misrepresented in your history.

Question: "Please explain?"

It has been used to represent Elemental Life Force in the Devic Kingdoms. While circles are indeed the basic building blocks of your universe, the circle is the geometric shape, or language, of Creatorship; the duplicating sign, the triangle, is the geometric language of Mastership. Do you understand that the two work hand in hand?

Response: "It is almost as though to duplicate in Mastership that which already exists in nature, one must Master that, become adept, if you will, then be able to move on to Creatorship."

This is the way that we all serve at function. While indeed, there is a small portion of Creatorship that comes along with the Mastership, there are different geometric and governing laws.

Response: "I see."

Dear one, now we get back to that of time compaction. Time compaction has been a series of sequential events, or sequential windows, as we have discussed. You experience many events. This is an End Time of Choice.

Response: "Ah! And there's a large window at the end of this!"

A very large window of choice. All the events that have been stored within your Third Density world are being brought to the forefront, for before one enters into Creatorship, one must Master choice. And as one comes through choice, we enter the series of time warp. Time warp is indeed as it would indicate, the bending of an experience. You have in front of you the experience. See it as a geometric circle. Toward the end, you have a bending of the experience.

Response: "Which changes the perception of the experience."

Correct! It is now your choice. You have spoken of a glass which is half full or half empty. There is a choice of perception, which is well understood in the human realm. Perception indeed is a key. We have long said, it is the feeling that will hold the shape. To understand, Dear one, there is a difference between time warp and time compaction.

Question: "The warp is the perception of the event?"

Perception of the event leaves you in that space of choice, to become that of Creator or Master. Master is indeed the one who has learned how to choose. You speak of discrimination; we speak not of discrimination; we speak of choice.

Response: "Discrimination is just another form of judgment."

It is indeed judgment, but there is that of choice. Certain vibrational frequencies resonate better with others. It is not the goal of the human to say that this vibration is more or less than that vibration. Vibration is vibration; resonance is resonance; blue is blue; green is green; pink is pink.

Response: "So, if we were to take this and use you as the example, for your particular Ascension from the Third Density to the alignment of the Fourth Density and then through Fifth, Sixth, to whichever density you're in at the moment, your choices were the steps that led you through this path."

Your choices are indeed the steps, the steps of the duplicated patterns, which lead you to time compaction. Each choice being presented to you has been a choice you have been faced with before. They are all duplicated, rhythmic patterns set up within your energetic life stream.

Question: "Otherwise, they would not occur, if they were not already incomplete patterns in the life or energy bodies that we carry?"

That is so, Dear one, those that would not align with the universal laws of your particular planet.

Question: "So, the tests that Lori and I go through, interacting together and in the expression of this work, are the incomplete energetic patterns that we have yet to choose to master?"

This is true, Dear one, and the key is again, perception, thought, and feeling. Now, I would like to explain to you, when you are dealing with the duplication of energy, you deal with eight energetic bodies. You are well aware of your seven energetic bodies and have just become aware of the eighth energetic body. Eighth, ninth, and tenth energetic bodies have the ability to deal with time compaction and time warp. In time warp, or thought and feeling worlds, you may successfully use up to fourteen energetic bodies. It is at the fifteenth level where one steps forth, out of the world of thought and feeling, as creation. This is explained as "state of being."

Response: "Sananda has just done this."

This is so, Dear one, and I am too at the fourteenth level.

Question: "You are about to do this?"

I will, Dear one, but not until after my thousand-year period of peace and prosperity. I was at this point before, Dear one, but I brought forth my energetic layers to be brought to this Earth Plane and Planet. Do you understand?

Response: "Yes, you mortgaged your accomplishment, out of your great love for all those who were continuing the incarnation process."

You flatter me, Dear one, but I did do this work, and I have offered myself in service to mankind.

Response: "So it is very important that we all succeed together."

You have spoken of agreement formation, of harmony and balance, abundance and prosperity, the flowing of creative love, and indeed, Dear one, that is a service. To create is to serve all. A lasting work comes through on vibration.

Response: "It is completed and sustained."

And how is this done, Dear one?

Response: "It is carried through by choice."

That is correct. I have given you much to think about, Dear one, and I am ready to close this small discourse this morning; however, in its smallness, you will review it for its largeness.

Response: "Well, there is an incomplete section." I am available.

Question: "About time compaction, do you mean by our choice of the experience, which is the time warp, time then becomes ordered in a sequence? I'm seeing a compaction and an expansion of time; it is almost as though it can be pulled apart by choice or pressed together by choice?"

Exactly. You have languaged this in such a way that pleases me. It is not so much that we refer to this as time, but as the "experience" or the "event."

Response: "And so, it is that choice that each life stream makes with regard to the experience or event that creates the perception."

It also allows for the duplication of the event again.

Question: "In the same lifetime or in another lifetime?"

Either one. It depends on the impact upon the life stream. Have you not seen many around you who repeat and repeat and repeat? And do you not see those who have had the exact same experience; however, the repetitious qualities have been expanded upon? Time compaction, plus choice, equals time warp.

Response: "Oh-h-h! They're actually numerical equivalents for each of these, and pitch equivalents for each of these?"

Dear one, all this theme and variation within your world.

Question: "Is it not the same in your world?"

It is simplified.

Question: "It is simplified because of the steps of the choices that you have made?"

It is true. It is refined, Dear one. I would take my leave at this moment. If you would like to continue discourse, beloved Mary has offered to come forth.

Response: "I would most happily accept her and I thank you for very much for your time and your patience with me."

I applaud your efforts, Dear one, and hold you in the continual Light of God that Never Fails.

Response: "Yes, my love is yours always. Thank you."

Welcome, my Beloved Children of the Golden Flame, I AM Mary and I come forth to give my blessing. May I have permission to come forth?

Response: "You have my permission to come forth."

Dear children, this message is simple: WE ARE INDEED HERE. There are those who do not believe that we are present. When you see the sun come up in the morning, are we not here? And that which goes down, are we not here? As you have known that we are here, there are those among you, Dear students, who question the presence of those who are committed to continue the outpouring of love as beloved beings of light.

There was a time when our purposes were crossed, and within each thread, I carefully selected a light for each misaligned vibration. The last twenty-five years of time were sequenced in simulated events, each thread carefully placed and woven to create a world of love, for Creatorship was founded upon this first principle. Dear one, send this law to the universe of your world.

Response: "I would be glad to do this. There are even the times when I find it difficult to find it in myself."

I understand what you're saying. Just as I have held the child close to my breast, I hold my family close to me, gathering it to me. How I long to protect you; how I long to draw you back to me, Dear one. Coming home is indeed a journey.

Response: "It is my desire to come home to you. It is my desire to always carry the great love of the universe within me; to be this expression always, and to never have hardness or coldness in any of my being."

There are many threads which make this cloth and weave this work. I hold a piece of this cloth and remember this work as a collective woven effort.

Response: "Yes, I do forget that. There are times when I feel very alone."

Remember, I AM with you, Dear one, as I hold this family next to me.

Response: "I am not alone. I am always with all of you."

Great Light of the Dove of Peace, come forth and stream your radiance to the Earth Plane and Planet. Weave your streams of light and truth in swaddling cloth. Hold and carry this swath of light, great fire of passion, I AM THAT I AM. Engrave this planet with the righteousness of love. I came into the conscious world and seek to heal the separation long felt. Dear children, I AM always close.

5

*It is our inner light that carries our
potential for enlightenment.*

Decree of Light

Sananda
Saint Germain

We finally finished the sessions for the Jurisdictions. Every insight and lesson was now recorded, and I was behind on the transcribing. In order to catch up, we hired a part-time student who was a whiz at transcribing, but I sometimes wondered if the material was a bit strange to her. Thus far, she seemed like an open, nonjudgmental type, and the work was moving ahead. This freed my time to work on my upcoming book.

Len and I started working on the world Earth Changes material. I carefully reviewed all of the information that I had previously received for Mexico, Central America, and South America. I decided that I needed a more efficient way to work. That material and the I AM America Map were received via clairaudient channeling, with Saint Germain relaying the information to the monitor during the question and answer sessions. Sometimes this work was inordinately tedious, and required several sessions to refine coastlines, correct mistakes, and then add additional details. During meditation, I asked Saint Germain if it would be okay if I used a trance state similar to automatic writing to receive the new Map information. My plan was to unroll printed Maps of each geophysical area, enter the trance state, and hopefully write in the applicable changes, as well as the information relayed and received by the Spiritual Teachers. This technique would save valuable time.

Saint Germain's response was that I could certainly give the method a try, but we would still need to follow up with voice-received trance sessions to double check the information. The subsequent sessions would also allow for important details, ancillary instruction, and questions surrounding the prophetic information. I immediately purchased several different map perspectives of Canada, Europe, Africa, Russia, Malaysia, and Australia. One of the more difficult areas to find detailed maps for was China, so I inevitably chose three different maps. I needed the locations of the Golden City Vortices to be as accurate as possible.

This entire process took about two weeks. Many of the outlines were completed with Maps strewn about on kitchen counters, our kitchen table (which was really too small), and our living room coffee table – which was inordinately awkward. I finally resorted to my portable dishwasher, which was the perfect height for sketching. Saint Germain was present at every session, and I observed his faint ethereal figure shifting about each map as he asked me to move my pencil several inches, or perhaps a minute quarter of an inch. He instructed me where to draw in new mountain ranges, and often described events that were far too detailed to easily write or remember. I asked him to please reserve those particular soliloquies for our recorded audio sessions.

On some days he appeared with El Morya or Mother Mary, who gracefully emerged at his side, and they, too, added comments regarding new shorelines or the geography of the New Times. Sometimes they materialized all at once, and this energy was extremely intense. In those instances, I could trance for only an hour, but surfaced back to waking consciousness with amazing detail that would normally take several arduous weeks of audio sessions. After this type of session, I would often take off on my bike and let the river's sentient energies restore me. Occasionally Len would arrive home after a session and sense the detectable remnants of ethereal energy, "Wow, it was crowded here!"

Soon the initial information was penciled in on about a dozen maps, yet Europe and Africa still needed refinement and details. Puzzled that this important material was still not entirely clear, a morning meditation simplified the process and Saint Germain reminded me, "Len can help."

As a small boy, Len saw ethereal visions of future Earth Changes literally morphing the Delaware River and the Atlantic shore. Later, while visiting Europe as a young adult, he had similar experiences, and in our first weeks together he readily shared his future visions of Europe and the Middle East with me.

I confidently offered him my pencils and markers, several fresh maps, and escaped for an afternoon at the office. I returned home to a neatly sketched map of Europe and Africa, "Does this look familiar?" he asked. Before I could respond, he added, "I had some trouble with the Golden Cities – I couldn't seem to locate them." I then clarified that Saint Germain had purposely left out the Golden Cities information – that would come after our completion of the first draft of the map outlines.

Excited, I unrolled my map of Europe and Africa and laid it beside Len's freshly drawn map. It matched by almost eighty percent! The only difference was that those areas, where I was uncertain, were now filled with glorious detail. Len was obviously pleased with his work, but he was energetically blown apart. While this type of session saved an enormous amount of time, the technique was a bit advanced for our energy systems. Later, we would learn that there are many reasons for this, which are explained in subsequent lessons in this book.

As the world Earth Changes information evolved, I now had to combine all of the smaller individual maps into one presentation. When this was complete, I unrolled the new map for Sherry. "Will you build another model?" she asked. "I don't know," I replied, a bit pensive. Dan, my previous channeling partner, still had the map model for the I AM America Map. I had asked him several times if he would please return it, but he refused. "I think I can paint the Maps – that would save you money for now," Sherry said quietly, as she simultaneously scrutinized the new topography. "Wow, look at the changes in Canada . . ."

Inevitably, we wanted to create another three-dimensional map, similar to that which was created for the I AM America Map. But in the meantime, I needed images to accompany the information for the new book. We decided that individual maps of Mexico, Central and South America, and Canada would best show the prophetic detail. Sherry painted a rendition of the South America Map and after reviewing it, I had no doubts that it would work. [Editor's Note: Full color copies of these maps were used in the first edition of *New World Atlas, Volume One*.]

Len and I jokingly referred to our little two-room office and map room as the "Ascended Master Sweatshop." There was an unpretentious satisfaction in our spiritual partnership and in running the fledgling business. Thankfully, we both enjoyed a modest lifestyle. And if we were driven by any goal, it was to see the work and message of I AM America move forward to its greatest potential.

Perhaps our second greatest and shared focus was that of personal spiritual growth and self-development. Surely, the Spiritual Teachers must have known and understood this, as their next lesson fueled that desire with insights on spiritual enlightenment and how to transmute karmic blocks.

In the provenance of Ascended Master Teachings, the Spiritual Teachers claim that, at one time, our Earth featured one continent, and that this landmass floated freely upon a singular ocean of waters, unattached to the Earth's core. This disk of land was purported to follow the spectrum of the Sun's Rays, never knowing or experiencing the dusk or the dawn of light.

According to that mythological metaphor, the continuous radiance of the Sun charged human energy fields, and humanity readily and easily evolved toward spiritual unity and enlightenment. Human suffering, through polarity or the separation from source, was rare. However, in the world that we experience today, this spiritual spectrum of Rays is allegedly blocked by our own DNA, and this anomaly induces a deterioration of the human body.

Thankfully, Saint Germain described a decree that we could use, three times a day, to transmute our inner darkness, which he describes as a "self-created veil." He prescribed the application of this decree for one sitting, to be chanted like a mantra forty-nine times, to treat each of the seven chakras and the seven energetic bodies. A decree is defined as a scientific series of carefully selected words, which are often spoken and asserted with the power of the I AM Presence. In this case, however, the decree is meant to be memorized and repeated silently, in the mind, much like a prayer, and recited with a rhythmic breath.

~

[Editor's Note: The introduction and opening remarks were not recorded and Sananda is speaking.]

You see, Dear one, time perception is a function of the human metabolic rate and the metabolic rate is a function of the imperfection of the genetic coding, the decaying of the energetic pulse of the I AM Presence anchored in the Heart Chakra. But radiating through the energetic bodies, it then precipitates through the DNA coding as a structured blueprint of the physical body.

Other creatures have altered perceptions of time, other than the human concept. A bee or other insect views time and functions in the same hour of the day, very differently than the human functions. Both the human and insect are sharing the same light radiance in the same moment, but the metabolic rate of each is quite different. Time for the insect is viewed as very slow and time for the humans is viewed as very fast, in the same moment of expression. The movements of the human are viewed by the insect as very slow and the movements of the insect are viewed as very fast by the human. Both views of the same moment of time expression are precise. So you see, time is a relative experience, relative to the metabolic rate of each and every life stream in expression.

At one time, the human expression was perfection, but the sustaining of perfection is a chosen loss and now unthinkable by your present standard of perception

However, the original DNA structure is of perfection and sustainable. The difference is, the human metabolic rate is slower now than in the time of the alignment to the sun of this solar system. Now that humankind has turned their face from the Light of God that Never Fails, the light energy is blocked in the DNA and the metabolism slows and the human body decays. (*See Editor's Note*) So time goes faster, as you say, and the inner light is the illusive enlightenment that you all seek in this present Time of Transition. So, as you think you are lighted, your light will resonate within and without. And now, I give the floor back to Beloved Saint Germain.

[Editor's Note: This is due to the influence of the dwarf sun and the Age of Kali Yuga. For more information see *The Ever Present Now*.]

As you now see, Dear ones, the light is inside all of you and is brought through your energy bodies and into your physical. But your ability to absorb and use the Light of God that Never Fails is blocked by your own self thought of being less than you are. Lifetime after lifetime, each of you has created a pattern of forgetting and separation. It is in all, as the focus of your lives. This has taken much practice on the part of humankind.

The Violet Flame Dispensation is the gift to you all, to change and transmute the darkness you create. Now, LIFT THE SELF-CREATED VEIL, and allow all of you to flow in your own light. Choose to decree the Violet Flame every day. The continuous use of the Violet Flame looses the Karmic blocks of the life experiences you create and fearfully hold fast in your energy bodies and in your physical. Do this decree three times per day; in the dawn when the stillness of God announces the light; at the midday, when the light is at the fulfilled radiance; and at the sunset, when the stillness promises the return. Do this seven times seven, equaling forty-nine times, each of the three times per day. That would be seven times for each of the seven chakras of each of your seven energetic bodies.

This will increase the rate of spin at increments of .063 revolutions per millisecond of the chakras of each energy body and the Eight-sided Cell Structure of Fourth Dimension. This brings the cellular awakening to your divinity and your I AM Presence, anchored within your Heart Chakra at the center of your body. The Violet Flame Decree will increase your rate of metabolism and allow your inner light to resonate and your enlightenment to unfold.

The decree is a continuous breath of inhale and exhale, nonstop, and is silent in the solitude of your heart. On the inhale, decree:

I AM THE VIOLET FLAME CONSUMING MY KARMAS.

And then, for the exhale:

I AM THE RELEASE OF MY KARMAS.

Do this seven times, then on to the next seven times, until all forty-nine are complete. This breath must be continuous to raise your metabolic rate and release the Karmic blocks, for the Breath of God Never Fails.

This is a lesson in perfection, for as consistent as the Earth spins on her axis and as consistent as the Sun is radiating to this planet, so must you choose this perfecting practice of realigning yourselves in the Light of God that Never Fails. I AM yours, Saint Germain.

6

Each breath we take contains the Divine Plan.
The inhale is Prophecy and creative possibility;
the exhale is self-determined free-will and probability.

Serving the Divine Plan

Sananda
Apollo

It was obvious to me that the Spiritual Teachers were sharing teachings on the principles of creation. This valuable instruction prepares consciousness for Creatorship; yet another important aspect of Mastery.

The first viewpoint presented by Sananda was that we must work to hone our perceptions to accept what we choose to see. Again, an emphasis was placed on "choice." We choose to experience situations and circumstances from a variety of viewpoints. His teachings encourage us to focus our perceptions beyond illusions, which include the limited position of disruption or interruption. His antidote for adjusting our lens of perception is the through the activity of love, which heals us by removing judgment and recognizing innate divinity.

The second viewpoint had to do with the simple metaphor of breath. According to the Spiritual Teacher Apollo – who is one of Sananda's spiritual teachers, the inhale is akin to our conscious level of receptivity, or how we accept, gather, and accumulate valuable spiritual experience. The exhale, or outbreath, is literally our action, engendered through our freewill after our exposure and familiarity with spiritual knowledge.

Yes, this is a bit lofty. However, it is helpful to understand the metaphysical tenants of this Ascended Master philosophy. Veiled within the words of this teaching is an interesting phrase regarding the possible timing of the prophetic *Time of Change*. After our first introduction to Earth Changes prophecies, we literally thought that geophysical change was imminent, and likely to be experienced swiftly, or in the near upcoming decades. As our insight and knowledge grew, further instruction from the Spiritual Teachers shifted our cataclysmic viewpoint. We realized that the *Time of Change* was currently upon us, and that each thought, feeling, and action could literally shapeshift prophesied events. In this teaching, Sananda's outlook on geophysical changes was that *the "Time of Change" is an expansive time period that could be experienced for a thousand years* – literally an entire millennium.

The Spiritual Teachers consider the Time of Change and geophysical changes as susceptible to *creative possibility*. Their potential manifestation is hypothetical probability, and it is detected as energy in the Earth's own aura. From this viewpoint, energy can certainly change as it moves through different layers of expression. To a seasoned metaphysician, this transformation could signal a healing process. Earth's Aura is viewed similarly to the Human Aura; however, there are a few differences, and each of Earth's first five light bodies is metaphysically connected to the five physical layers of Earth's atmosphere. The light bodies of Earth's Aura are:

Earth's First Light Body: Earth's First Light Body correlates to the Earth's physical Troposphere, where the weather occurs. This light body is metaphysically associated with the human Etheric Body (a light blue color), the human Emotional or Feeling Body (pink or magenta), and the human Mental Body (yellow). The Spiritual Teachers refer to this light body as the *Prahanic Light Body*, which is known as the life-giving force.

Earth's Second Light Body: Earth's Second Light Body is associated with the physical Stratosphere of the Earth where airplanes fly. Its higher elevation contains Earth's ozone layer, known as the Ozonesphere. This light body houses the metaphysical Astral Plane and its many levels of consciousness. It is claimed that we move into our astral body after the death of the physical body, and this plane of consciousness contains the many mansions of the afterlife. Earth's second light body is affiliated with the collective heart chakra of humanity. This light body is also referred to as *Everno*, which means "to know eternity." The Spiritual Teachers claim that Everno causes essential motion for spiritual growth for both the Earth and those souls incarnated on Earth.

Earth's Third Light Body: Earth's Third Light Body correlates to the Mesosphere. It is associated with the collective consciousness of humanity. It is also the middle layer of atmosphere surrounding the Earth, and this companion energetic light body holds the collective etheric template or pattern for life on Earth. This light body is constantly changing to meet evolutionary needs. Because this ethereal light body holds the Master plan for life on Earth, it is affiliated with divine intelligence and reflects the collective Mental Body of humanity. The Spiritual Teachers refer to this light body as *Eshano,* which means "to have knowledge of Creation and what gives shape to Creation, or knowledge of that which comes from Created forms." Eshano is also known as an etheric hall of wisdom and light.

Earth's Fourth Light Body: In the human, the Fourth Light Body is affiliated with our ability to process information, telepathically, beyond the Third Dimension and into the Fourth Dimension. This light body of Earth correlates to Earth's Thermosphere, the altitude where satellites orbit. The Thermosphere's higher elevations contain the Ionosphere, with an outer layer known as the Magnetosphere. Solar radiation, solar winds, and the Van Allen belt are attributed, respectively, to these layers of the Earth's atmosphere.

Metaphysically, the Fourth Light Body of Earth holds the "collective subconscious" of every form of life on Earth. This light body is affiliated with the spiritual qualities of devotion, and cultivation of the Christ Consciousness. It is often referred to as the *Celestial Body.* The Spiritual Teachers state that the Earth's Fourth Light Body is also known as *Buitsha* (pronounced Boo it' sah), which literally means "the exchange of energy."

[Editor's Note: Thoughts are controlled by the conscious mind; the subconscious mind controls our feelings and stores our memories and beliefs.]

Earth's Fifth Light Body: The Fifth Light Body of Earth links to Earth's Exosphere; that is, the uppermost layer of Earth's atmosphere, which combines with interstellar space. Metaphysically, this light body relates to Earth's Causal Body and holds the Golden Grid on Earth. Saint Germain claims that this light body has nine layers and dimensions that help to form a blanket of Vortices on Mother Earth. This light body of Earth, also known as the *Golden Grid,* is associated with the *Galactic Web,* the sacred city of Shamballa, and the Golden City Network. This light body provides contact with the I AM Presence and serves as a spiritual membrane that keeps the five light bodies of Earth intact. The lower planes of this light body regulate energies of both the Mother Principle and the Father Principle. The upper regions are associated with unity consciousness – what the Spiritual Teachers refer to as "Unana."

[Editor's Note: When referring to the aura, the terms *light body, layer, planes,* and *light-field* are often used. A *layer* is often an energetic portion of a light body, defined through perceptible differences in both light and sound. A *plane* is a level within a light body, often associated with vibration and the development of consciousness. Layers and planes exist simultaneously within a light body. A *light-field* is yet another term for a portion of a light body and is sometimes an energy layer.]

≈

I AM Sananda, your comrade and Brother, he who hath stepped forth to be of service to you, Dear one, and it is in service that I come forth to give this to you.

We are briefly interrupted by a telephone call.

Response: "Greetings, Sananda, my apologies for the interruption."

Dear one, an interruption is just that. It is that which has caused a lapse, which you perceive as time. You have had many lapses in your world of this work that you do. We have observed this and we have offered ourselves to be of service to you. You see, Dear one, it is the continual rhythm which you have seen as the setting of the Sun and the rising of the Sun, that assures that the lapse shall be overcome. There is no interruption in our world as we know it. However, in the world of thought and feeling, interruption is that which occurs most of your time. Interruption is a word that you see and associate as a disruption. It is a perception, Dear one, in how you see this. There is also that which is placed in front of you, Dear one, that serves what is known as the Divine Will.

Events are not to be seen as interruption or disruption. The events throughout your day are timed and brought to you as a choice to act with the Divine Plan. Each day, we ask of you and remind you to turn your life and your will over to your mighty I AM Presence in accordance to the Divine Plan! This is a simple act, Dear one, and all that shall proceed throughout that day shall never serve as a disruption or an interruption, but shall serve that mighty force working within you, your beloved, mighty I AM Presence. Should you have an event in your day that would appear to disrupt you, take a minute. In that moment, say to yourself, beloved mighty I AM Presence, allow the Divine Plan to come forth in full manifestation right now, this instant, and forever! At that moment, the Divine Plan is revealed and step by step you participate. Do you understand, Dear one?

Response: "I understand your request; I only accept that it occurs because you taught it. I do not completely understand its function."

I'm going to explain to you how I see him. He's standing in front of me, with a soft breeze blowing through his hair. He is wrapped in a white robe and on his shoulder sits a white Dove. He is also holding a staff. He leans a little bit from one side to the next as he talks. He gestures a bit too as he talks.

Dear one, the work that I bring to the Earth Plane is to understand the expansion of human relations. You have worked long and hard understanding the expansion of the Earth's field itself. We have discussed the energetic bodies and layers of the Earth and you have begun to understand that there is a relationship that exists between the human's and the Earth's energetic fields. Dear ones, you have yet to even understand the dynamics that exist in the human field itself. So few of you remain focused. This is only our observation and not a judgment, Dear one, for the human has this problem at times. It takes so little to choose interruption and then this focus is disrupted; we ask for this focus to be developed and to be understood only through that which is the Divine Plan.

When one understands the beauty of the Divine Plan working in their life and the lives of others, there is no interruption. There is an orderly timelessness and Divine Beauty and Form cooperatively coming forth. Divine Cooperation joins the Divine Plan. For this is what a plan is! A plan is the end result of the unique timing of events. There have been those who have asked for the timing of events, regarding Earth geophysical changes. Dear one, it is important that you understand that we are not in charge of such events; humankind is not in charge of such events; the Earth, itself, is not in charge of such events; but it is the Divine Plan.

We assure you, Dear one, geophysical changes will occur through the millennium. This is no mystery or secret. We have given you the information of how this shall be. However, there is theme and variation that is carried out throughout your world of thought and feeling. There are indeed the twelve Star seeds that walk upon your planet and each has been given a theme and variation of Earth Change events. There are also those who do the collective readings from each energetic layer (light body). However, Dear one, the work that we do is known as the middle way, for we have learned through tried-and-true practice and principles, that it is not through walking on the edge that one obtains Mastery. It is for the one who will walk with the balanced, steadfast footsteps of the middle way! Yes indeed, Dear one, it is through the middle way that you shall learn to be. Do you have questions?

Question: "The middle way is not an extreme. Is the middle way the focus of allowance?"

It is the focus of allowance and the synthesis of cooperation. The middle way is always that which harmonizes and balances. We have given you the Jurisdiction regarding Harmony; the middle way is that, which is indeed not extreme, Dear one. The Earth Changes, which we have spoken of, are indeed a form of Prophecy. Prophecy is that which is set forth to awaken one. Prophecy is an event not yet set into the Divine Plan.

Question: "If it is not set in the Divine Plan yet, then where does the Prophecy come from?"

Prophecy is that portion of the Divine Plan that is yet to unfold. Prophecy and that which is free will combine to form the Divine Will, for Prophecy contains within it several steps of manifestation. Do you understand?

Response: "Please explain."

Prophecy is indeed a form of creative flow. As a man thinketh, so he becomes; as a man decrees, so he is. Dear one, do you understand?

Question: "So, it is that focus of choice?"

There is the creative focus and there is the free will. These combine to form the Divine Plan. And then there is the pivot point of the Divine Plan, the point that the Creator then chooses that this shall be. For it is the choice of the Creator of your universe, on the mighty laws that have been set forth, that all is and all shall be. Yes indeed, Dear ones, you have your free will, but at any moment, the Creator may decide otherwise. It is his right and it is your birthright.

Question: "May I back up a moment? You referred to this as your universe."

Dear one, it is our universe.

Question: "I was just wondering if there was a differentiation?"

Dear one, this is where we have been brought to share in our Creatorship. However, there are those who are here who have yet to obtain levels of Mastery that would allow them to understand the principles of creation. It is a step-by-step process, Dear one, and there are those upon the Earth Plane and Planet who have yet to come to the levels of acceptance of responsibility. It is not our purpose to sit and to judge and to say who shall be and who shall not, for all contain within them the Divine Thought and the Unfed Flame of Love, Wisdom, Power, and Desire of perfection. All contain this within themselves, every man, woman, and child who walks upon this planet. However, there are those who have, through this cell, the Perfect Cell of desire, who are willing to understand Mastery. Mastery leads one to understand the principles of creation. To understand the principles of creation, one then accepts responsibility for that which he has or she has created.

You were speaking of manageability. Manageability and responsibility, Dear one, go hand in hand. Manageability deals with the responsible order and timing of that which is in your world of thought and feeling. Do you understand?

Question: "Yes, this I understand. Do you have thought and feeling?"

Dear one, this has only expanded. It is a choice that we shall use to serve what we shall serve. We are no different from you, Dear one. Would we come to you in such a manner to set ourselves up as gods? Would we come to you in such a manner for you to judge us or us to judge you? This is not our work, Dear one. We are your Brothers, simple and true. This is all we are. I would like to sit for a moment. May I?

Response: "Yes, you may."

The chair appears and he sits; a Dove hops down to his finger. He's holding the Dove out. A waterfall is behind him.

This little creature that I hold pleases me much. Do you understand, Dear one, that I too have desire?

Response: "Yes, I do. I do understand this."

Trumpets are sounding in the background.

Do you hear the music, Dear one?

It sounds like the Angelic Realm. There's a pink light off to his right-hand side and through the clouds, an opening is streaming light and a circle of angels are coming.

Dear one, this that I sit on is indeed the Throne, the Throne of the Holy of Holies. It has been placed before you so you would not be impressed, but that you would understand that you too sit upon this Throne with me. Every man, woman, and child upon this planet is an Inheritor of this Throne. They are an Inheritor of this Kingdom. They are an Inheritor of this mighty Realm and Legion of Angels. This music that plays, plays for all. This universe is not selective in who it shall love. This Creator is a mighty Creator Love. He has not judged his creation, saying that one shall be less or one shall be more, but all shall be loved for what they are.

I AM Sananda, Lord of the Green Ray. I AM the minister of health, the minister of healing, the minister of service. Dear one, the service that I bring to mankind is that you shall all see yourself in the radiance of the Light of the Creator as you truly are. I AM an Ascended Master and I AM Sananda. You, Dear ones, are initiates, chelas on the path of Mastery. You carry divinity the same as I carry divinity. Even where I am at this moment, you are as well. Are you not with me, Dear one?

Response: "I am always with you."

I am with you as well. Those who are your students are they not always carried within your heart?

Response: "Yes."

And you, Dear one, are always carried within mine.

Response: "Thank you."

This is my request, that you see who you are and keep your focus. Dear one, the illusion of disruption and interruption is just that. Carry forth the Divine Plan in all that you do and all that you do, do with love. There is no mistake that you are here at this time on this planet, and it is no mistake that I am speaking to you at this moment regarding this subject, for I am here. Two or more are gathered in the name of I AM and what happens? An Ascended Master, the great radiance of such, is present. This presence is an eternal Law of Creation, that which was determined at the creative flow, at the moment that this planet burst forth. When two or more are gathered in the name of I AM THAT I AM, an Ascended Master shall be there. It is then, the choice of those two that are gathered, if they shall listen or not, be guided or not. It is so, and to question this law is to question the authority of the Creator.

He's standing up now.

Hail, mighty Apollo! He, great Creator of this universe and He, who hath served this family so well.

Welcome, Beloved Brother Sananda, I AM Apollo and I must ask permission to enter your energy field, Dear one.

Response: "You have this, Dear one."

And I must ask permission of your student to enter into his energy field.

Response: "Please come forward, Dear one."

Beloved Children of the Golden Flame, I AM Apollo. I come forth from the Heart of the Central Sun. I am indeed blessed with or endowed with the responsibility of Creation. You have referred to me as a Creator. I am indeed such. I stream forth on that which is known as the Golden Ray, which has been brought forth in balance for the Earth during the Time of Grace and Prosperity. For you see, Dear one, that which is Creation is that which shall be allowed to perpetuate in what you've known as the expanse of inhale and exhale. To inhale in creation, one must go inside. The breath goes inside and circulates throughout the system. Do you not see, as you understand this work, how you have breathed this in? You have taken it to the very core of yourself. You take it inside and internalize it. And as you are willing to accept what it is, then you must exhale. It is this expansive exhale that you release in service or you simply release and discard. There is much upon your planet that you may inhale. Do you understand?

Response: "Inhaling is a process of life."

It is more than the process of life. It is the process and the first step for Creation. I AM Apollo, and I come to serve as Creator. This is a simple lesson I give to you, Dear one, that all that you breathe in, you do not necessarily need to exhale in service. There is some that you may simply release for what it has given you. Creatorship, Dear one, again contains within it the elements of timing and choice. You have a right to choose, for this is your free will. As I stand and as a Creator of this planet, I serve too through my free will, which has a line to a Divine Plan. All laws stream forth from the heart of the mighty Logos. All have theme and variation throughout the entire universe. However, they are all based on the same premise and those are the premises that have been laid forth in the Twelve Jurisdictions. Do you understand?

Response: "Yes."

It is time for me to take my leave, Dear one. I shall come forth from time to time.
Response: "Thank you Apollo, mighty I AM."

Dear one, it is time for me too, to take my leave. It is my request that you love one another. I AM Sananda.

Question: "I thank you Sananda. Will you accept my visit this evening?"

Dear one, you are always welcome at my side.

Response: "Thank you."

He's throwing the Dove up into the ring of angels. It's flying up. He's holding his arm up as he ascends with the Dove.

*The power of sound can move us beyond
our present limitations.*

HUE
Saint Germain

Since Len's arrival into my life, we had produced over fifty channeled sessions, most of them monitored by Len. However, only one-third of them had been transcribed to date. At this time, we were focused on material to be included in a book that would feature Earth Change prophecies and the Twelve Jurisdictions. However, the copious details and nuances, in the remaining two-thirds of the teachings, were significant to the entire work as well. We were concerned that, if we did not publish this information, it would be lost.

We asked the Spiritual Teachers about this in a private session, and they encouraged us to share the teachings with others. Since Len's talk at the spiritual center the previous winter, several people had called to inquire about possible classes. We decided that we would devote an evening a week to teach the material.

In an earlier lesson, Saint Germain and Kuan Yin presented a special prayer, now known as "The Invocation of the Violet Flame for Sunrise and Sunset." Len and I honed our skills with this prayer, reciting it many times; sometimes in the early morning, or at sunset, when the sky was adorned with a tinge of pink and light blue. Often, we'd leave the office just before sunset, and drive out to a small field located on a dirt lane, close to the river's edge. We'd sit in the little white Pontiac, fondly dubbed the "Grand I AM," and watch the sun fade beneath the brown, weathered hills that surrounded the mill town. Shades of pastel colors adorned the sky, and Violet Flame angels trumpeted the arrival of the transmuting fire while we decreed, "I invoke the Violet Flame to come forth in the name of I AM that I AM. To the Creative Force of all the realms of all the Universes, the Alpha, the Omega, the Beginning, and the End . . ." Often we'd read the words from a crumpled piece of note paper that Len kept folded in his wallet, scribed in pencil from the day the words were received.

I later typeset the prayer, and handed it out to over twenty students who would attend our weekly classes. Our voices formed a celestial choir as we invoke the sacred, karma transmuting fires of the Violet Flame.

We both found teaching immeasurably rewarding; however, Len found the Lewis-Clark Valley, our home at that time, a bit too isolated and rural. Ever since our beginning days together he'd often prophesy, "Our work together will be in Gobean."

The thought of moving to the southwest intrigued me; in fact, when I had visited Phoenix, AZ, several years earlier I had felt that someday I would return, perhaps to live. But I was not yet ready to leave the feminine Pacific Northwest, the sacredness of the bike trail along the soothing yet unfathomable river, and the comfort of living in a small town. Plus, my roots were entwined with this region that had produced fields of golden wheat and barley, fields that had supported my family for five generations.

Our office phone rang late one afternoon, and Len answered. "It's your friend Miriam." The last time we had spoken, I was still living in Coeur d'Alene, ID, and now that seemed light-years ago. We had sat in a local cafe over mugs of hot spiced tea, and she had revealed her dream to live in Montana and build a spiritual center, focused on the teachings of the Ascended Masters. She had been one of my few friends while living there, and I was grateful to hear her voice again. Remarkably, she had realized her vision, and had recently purchased a small home in Hamilton, MT – just south of Missoula, located at the eastern door of the Shalahah Vortex.

I updated her on the current events of my life – my move to a little cabin near the river in Asotin, and, of course, my newfound partnership with Len. "Are you still receiving messages?" she asked. "Of course," I responded. "In fact I am channeling about two to three times a week, still mailing maps, and working on my first book." Before we hung up she added, "Please come and visit me when you can – I think you'd enjoy the energies here."

Driving home from the office that evening, I shared the conversation with Len. However, it wasn't until the next morning, after meditation, that he said, "We should go and visit Miriam for a few days." I was a bit surprised. "Are you sure?" He responded, "Yes, I have guidance to go, and it should be a nice drive, now that the snow is gone." "Well don't be too certain that winter is over!" I replied half-jokingly. From Idaho to Montana it can snow on the Fourth of July, so there were no certainties for Montana in regard to the weather. So far, the spring was showing signs of a welcomed arrival. Lilacs and dogwoods bloomed along the river, and the smell of fresh-cut grass perfumed the air.

"We can load your bike up too." Len added. I sensed a bribe. "Is there more to your meditation that you haven't told me?" I asked. He paused for a moment, and then thoughtfully spoke, "We need a larger place to live, especially with the kids coming back for the summer, and . . ." He hesitated for yet another moment, "I'm not certain that we are living in the right place. There are times I don't feel comfortable here, and I think the children need more. . . We've looked for a larger home [here], but haven't found anything that will work," he added, and then he gently touched my hand, "Maybe it's time for a change."

I was defensive for a moment. Although our little cabin in Asotin was indeed humble, I preferred living a simple life. Perhaps it was too modest for Len, as sometimes he laughingly called our home, "The Ascended Master hovel." But I liked the fact that it was affordable, and our business had yet to prove itself financially.

It was true that we had casually looked for something a bit larger, but our searches through the classifieds had yielded next to nothing. And it was also true that the extra bedrooms were really the size of small closets, but I had never considered moving *away* from Asotin. I loved my front porch, and the garden space in the back with the walnut tree and the tree house. I liked that I only had to walk a few blocks and there was my bank, the post office, and a small grocery store. I had friends and family here, plus Steve and Sherry, our friends, lived just a few blocks away. I cherished the sandy beaches, the short winter and hot summer weather, nearby tennis courts and parks, the bike path – *my bike path*, and the glorious, beautiful river. More importantly, even though my lifestyle was simple, it was graced with ease and innocence. It seemed as though every significant moment in my life had finally led me to this place . . . and unquestionably it had taken *so much* in personal sacrifice and healing to finally arrive. Why would I leave?

I sat at the kitchen table the next morning, and I poured a second cup of coffee when Len walked in from morning meditation, "I know how much Asotin means to you . . . but would you consider the trip to Montana just to look? And no pressure, if you really don't want to go, I'd understand. And it's been several months since just the two of us went anywhere alone together. It will be an adventure."

Strangely, I had slept peacefully through the night. Now the morning light streamed into the large window and its rays cast a golden hue throughout the room. It felt like something had lifted, and today was a beautiful spring day – the Spiritual

Teachers often refer to this shift in consciousness as, "a new day." Len's face erupted into a large grin as I nodded, "Yes, I'll go and look."

We packed a suitcase, and called Miriam to let her know that we would arrive in the late afternoon. Soon our little white car curved along the meandering ribbon of Highway 12, lined with magnificent cedars, spruce, and fir trees. The highway follows the course of the Lochsa River through the Bitterroot Mountains. Undeniably, that day was a perfect day for travel, a new day for adventure, a new day for possibilities, and perhaps a new day to find a new home.

Soon after we arrived, Miriam was on the phone calling realtors and identified a four-bedroom home, with a large garage. We arrived at the rental, located on a country road near Stevensville, MT. The home was beautiful, with a large kitchen and dining room, two and a half bathrooms, and a large two-car garage. The rent was reasonable, and if we were to combine both of the rents of our office and home in Asotin, this home would be affordable for our budget. We filled out an application at the real estate office, left a check for a deposit, and waited for an answer, which would come in about a week. I still felt a bit apprehensive about a move, but Len was assuring, "Don't worry . . . if this is meant to be, it will happen." I admired his unworried faith.

After a night at Miriam's home, we decide to spend a few extra days to explore. We check into a small hotel, and I unloaded my bike for a ride. I discovered a paved bike trail, and as I glided by freshly bloomed wildflowers, cradled by magnificent views of the Selway-Bitterroot Range, I checked in with the I AM Presence. The message I received was short and simple, "You will move – soon."

Early the next morning it was clear that Saint Germain had a message for us. Fortunately, Len had packed the handheld recorder. Caressed by the sublime energies of the eastern door of the Shalahah Vortex, and the purity of the nearby mountains, I easily entered into trance. The teaching that followed was Saint Germain's insights on the one-syllable mantra, HU or HUE.

In Tibetan dialects, the word *HU* or *HUE* means "breath." However, the HU is also a sacred sound. When chanted or meditated upon, it carries the power of the Pink and Green Rays, and mirrors the energy of the Divine Heart. As one works with the vital energies of the HU, this mantra evolves to invoke the energies of all of the Seven Rays. This was its alleged purpose in the ancient Temples of Atlantis, and in the ethereal Temples of Venus.

The HU vibration opens the human Kundalini system so it can evolve, and chanting this mantra can instantly invoke the presence of the Violet Flame. This flame, in turn, evokes the Violet Ray that is engendered with the ability to transform and transmute energies to the next octave. Perhaps this is why the "HU" is so beloved and treasured by Saint Germain. The HU is also considered an ancient name for God, and it is sung for spiritual enlightenment.

This lesson holds valuable insight into our innate divinity, which for various karmic reasons, we cannot see or perceive. Saint Germain encourages us to remove this veil, or blindfold of illusion, and to see ourselves in light and unity as "God in continual motion . . . God continually sustained . . . and God continually maintained." Our god-self, which expresses beyond the limitations of corporeal man, is considered the divine HU-man, who holds the divine blueprint of Creatorship and Mastery.

Welcome, my Beloved chela, I AM Saint Germain and I come forth on the Violet Transmuting Ray of Mercy and Forgiveness, for this is indeed the most uplifting work that can be brought forth for humanity and mankind upon the Earth Plane and Planet at this time. Dear ones, we must stress to you that there is the difference between humanity and mankind. Humanity is that which carries the collective consciousness; that which carries the collective awakening; that which is from the very beginning and the very end, the Alpha and the Omega. Mankind is the expression of human thought and feeling in your world of thought and feeling. It is only the expression. It carries no memory; however, it carries what you call the forgetting. Dear one, humanity has been brought forth so that one may understand that the creative force, that which you call creativity or what we call the God Force, works through all and in everything that is. It is the beloved mighty I AM Presence that holds the continual form, or the continual shape, for all to express through.

When you say these mighty words, "I AM," are you not holding that as a continual thought and form in the world of thought and feeling? Are you not feeling and thinking that on a continuous basis? You are holding that form, perfected and carrying it continually. It is sustained and maintained in eternal form. Dear ones, when you use the words, "I AM THAT I AM," or the words "I AM," you are carrying that which is your Divine Blueprint. You, as Divine Inheritors and Co-creators, express through the collective thought form of humanity. You are carrying this force for all to be and all to become. Dear one, see that it is the Violet Flame too, that comes forth to lift you from the stance of mankind to that of becoming a member of the human race.

HUE is the sound vibration which carries within it the Pink and the Green Rays. This is what is needed at this time. HUE carries within it the heart form, and we have spoken of that of the Heart's Desire. We move to the foundation blocks of love, wisdom, and power and their application through the HUE upon the Earth Plane and Planet. HUE is indeed the sound vibration that you may access, Dear ones, for this period and Time of Grace. It was indeed the sound that stepped forth to cradle you, Dear ones. And now it is the HUE that comes forth to carry and to hold this which is your Creatorship.

I AM Saint Germain and I am most pleased and happy to serve humanity! Mankind has long expressed upon this world, this world of thought and feeling, and it is time for humankind or humanity to step forth. Dear ones, you are the expression of God in all that you do. You are the expression of the Creator in all that you do. Can you not see that you are to remove this Veil from your eyes? Take the blindfold away from your eyes, Dear one, take it and see who you clearly are!

And now Saint Germain has stepped forward and he has removed the blindfold from his eyes.

Look into my eyes. Do you not see that they are violet wells? Violet wells that carry within them the Blue Ray and the Pink Ray. Look, that I see truly that which is humanity, expressed as a creative wave upon this plane and planet to extend Mercy and Forgiveness and to walk hand in hand, Brother to Brother, Sister to Sister, in the act of service. Dear ones, it is through Divine Service that you step forth from mankind to humanity; for then, you are able to see your Brother and your Sister as yourself.

Dear ones, I AM Saint Germain and Chohan of the Seventh Ray and I call to you, every Brother and Sister upon this planet, to serve mankind! Serve mankind, so he recognizes that he is a member of this human race. Dear ones, it is through the beauty of this, it is through the expression of this—the joy of this service—that all upon this planet can then, and only then, form ONE body of light. This ONE body is united in service to the mighty I AM Presence and held in continual and sustained form.

He's standing in front of me and he holds a candle.

This light in front of you is the mighty Light of God that Never Fails! You see it in this form as a candle. I light this candle in honor of the Light of God that Never

Fails, for I know that it is truly this light that will bring each man, woman, and child upon this planet home to their Source, the Source that they all share.

He has taken his candle now and held it up.

HOLY, HOLY, HOLY!
HUE, HUE, HUE!
Almighty I AM, Almighty I AM, Almighty I AM.

This is the ritual and the symbol that represents that which we speak to you. These mighty rituals and symbols have come not only from the ancient temples of Atlantis, but they come from the beloved Temples of Venus and that which is served by Beloved Sanat Kumara. Dear ones, these rituals are rituals; however, they are also symbols of that which we represent. They are rituals of service and I share with you: HUE, HUE, HUE!

See yourself as God in continual motion; see yourself as God continually sustained; see yourself as God continuously maintained. And now that you see yourself as this Divine Form, what would serve in the sustaining and maintenance of this? That which is your mighty I AM Presence; that which has held the continual form and Creatorship; that which can no longer deny that you are of the mighty of mighties.

Dear one, I now call upon you to remember that it is the Violet Flame that comes forth in Mercy and Forgiveness. It is this Violet Flame of Compassion that we beg of you to use, for only through this can we remove any feeling that you are only man. Come forth in the beauty of human form and in doing so, recognize, that in this beauty, you truly are I AM THAT I AM! I AM continually yours for the service, HUE, and upliftment of humanity forever, Saint Germain

8

We are held in a blueprint of Divine Perfection.

Conception of Perfection

Mary

We drove home through the magical woods of Shalahah, and returned in the late afternoon to our little cabin on the Snake River. The next morning I was sitting again at Sherry's kitchen table and she was flipping over tarot cards. Even though we had paid a deposit on the new home and everything had easily fallen into place for a move to Montana, there was an uneasy feeling that haunted me.

Sherry turned over the High Priestess, a card of intuition, spiritual inspiration and dreams. "Have you been channeling lately?" she asked, quickly turning over several more cards. "Well . . . yes, in fact it has been prolific." I responded. She continued, "Hmmm . . . well, there is more to this . . ."

I could tell that Sherry was dipping within her vast resource of psychic knowledge. She went on, "It is time to do some work alone again. Remember when I suggested that?" I had experimented with trance work, perhaps once or twice, without a monitor. Without a monitor to ask questions, these types of sessions usually contained intense, focused messages. "Okay," I said. "Is that what is asked?"

"Oh yes, and . . ." Her voice trailed as she intently studied the next card, and she held the eight of pentacles card toward me and I could clearly see seven coins printed on the card, the eighth coin held intently and polished by a craftsman. "You have quite a bit of work ahead of you. You will have enough money, but there is still a lot for you to accomplish . . . I see you working in the public more, traveling, and speaking."

"Well" I said, "I've had a few interviews and we have a workshop in San Francisco in several months." "No," said Sherry, and her voice became strong and forceful as her psychic insight congealed into reality, "You will travel east, and that trip will be life-changing."

The next card – the Wheel of Fortune, was reversed, "This is destiny or fate. This change in your life is *meant* to happen but . . ." And her voice paused again, as she searched for the exact words to mirror the ethereal images flashing in front of her, "You will revisit a lesson, something you thought had concluded. But this time, the lesson will be finished." "Oh great," I thought to myself, "Can't the lessons stop for awhile?" Sherry's voice snapped me back to the reading, "But the end result is success and happiness – it looks like you'll be tested again, but you will persevere."

She collected the cards into a deck and placed them down between us. "Look," she said, and I could tell from the expression on her face that I would get the honest advice I was seeking, "Don't become too dependent on Len. I know that the last couple of months have been fun . . . but don't lose yourself."

"What about the move – did you see anything about that?" I asked? That was the real reason I had called her for the reading. She replied, "Nothing that is immediate is shown in the cards . . . but, remember, change is coming. So there could be a move, but it may not be where you think." Sherry looked at her watch, "Well, I've got to go . . . I have another reading in a few minutes." The phone rang and before I could say another word, Sherry grinned and silently waved good-bye. I nodded back to her, and let myself out her front door.

I sat still for a moment in my car and centered myself. The new home in Montana was truly wonderful, actually a dream come true. Yet a nagging worry kept creeping into my thoughts, creating a tension that rarely accompanied certainty. I decided that a ten-mile ride along the river would surely clear my head.

I breezed down the ribboned pathway, burrowed along jagged boulders, and passed the cliff of organ pipe basalt crystals. The river's glassy waters illusively mirrored the sky and I could barely tell where the water ended and the sky began. I rode past Swallow's Nest and into a green meadow sprinkled with dandelions, and then onward into the park's entry. Several months ago I had found a hidden, secluded spot along the water, nestled near a tree just feet off of the bike-path. I quickly braked, walked my bike, and leaned it against the tree trunk.

I caught my breath, and sat in silence alone with my thoughts. A perfectly curved rock served as my seat, as I tucked my legs up to my chin. This little rock had become my "thinking rock," and it softly grounded me to the Earth's energies. After fifteen quiet minutes, I decided that I could not move to Montana – not yet. That decision alone immediately settled the inner, gnawing turbulence. I wasn't sure how Len would receive my decision, but at least now my mind was settled. And if

Sherry's reading was an indication of possible future events, I was certain that my next move would not include Stevensville.

As I pedaled toward the final feet of the ride, my muscles groaned for rest and soon the site of the little blue bungalow came into view. Once inside, I drew a bath, stripped off my sweaty clothes, and when my feet entered the warm, bubbly water I literally felt myself slip into another dimension. A small, bright light moved toward me, and I realized that it was growing in size and luminosity. I could faintly see the outline of Mother Mary. "Oh, this is what Sherry saw . . ." and my thoughts stirred back to full consciousness. I stood up and draped myself with a white terry bathrobe, stumbled into my home office to retrieve the hand-held recorder, and stuffed in a new tape.

The lesson that follows is a transcript of the session with Mary. She presented her teachings and knowledge regarding the Eight-sided Cell of Perfection. This human cell of perfection has been introduced in previous teachings as a spiritual focus within our light bodies that can cleanse and restore spiritual light. It is best described as an atomic cell located in the human heart. It is associated with all aspects of perfection, and contains and maintains a visceral connection with the Godhead. Knowledge about this cell and the cultivation of its growth and evolution are the crux of Cellular Awakening.

Mother Mary claimed that this unique heart cell holds the "purity of thought and intent" surrounding human thoughts, our desires, and ultimately the blueprint of our physical bodies. These philosophical and metaphysical viewpoints can be crystallized into the Beloved Mother's immaculate conception of perfection, allegedly held within all of us.

What amazed me about this lesson was that while human experience can often be imperfect – including those plans that we sometimes agree upon, then question, and inevitably change – the Spiritual Teachers view it as *perfect*. Second thoughts, changes, mistakes, mishaps, accidents, and even calamities can contain a distinctive perfection that is yet to be revealed. Life's perfection is innate and individually sealed within our DNA. Mother Mary said that this perfection is "always, and always shall be."

I am going to explain to you where I am. There are Rays of light and all of them are crossing in front of me and another Ray of light is coming in closer to me. Now it's starting to densify and I can see a form taking place. I'm seeing the head and shoulders

and there's a blue light around the throat area. I'm conscious and I'm not channeling. There are other Rays of light. I see another Ray of light and it's like a cord and it's coming down to the heart area of this being. And now I'm going to invoke sacred space: Beloved mighty I AM Presence, come forth. Beloved mighty I AM Presence come forth. Beloved mighty I AM Presence come forth in perfection. Beloved mighty I AM Presence, great Host of Ascended Masters, to all the Beloved Archangels, I ask for you to come forth and that which is only for this work that I do, this work in the service of the release of love. Come forth, Dear ones, and I invite you into my energy field.

And now I'm going to explain to you what the light is doing. It is revving up. I can see an actual spirit and its golden thread access looks green. It's coming up closer to me and it's getting within three feet of me. And now, there is a message and I'm going to go ahead and introduce who this is.

Welcome, my Beloved chelas, I AM Mary and I come forth on that which is the Green Ray, brought forth for the ministry of service upon the planet. Dear one, that which is the service of the heart has long been seen as the Heart's Desire. There are those upon the Earth Plane and Planet who see desire as passion or desire as the whim of the ego. However, Dear one, it is I who would like to clarify that which is desire. Desire is that within the genetic coding, held within the heart's self, which strives the being, or the body of light, to obtain ONE with perfection for the removal of the separation. Dear one, you have known and you have felt separation and we have explained to you simply that it is not so. This is not a new concept to you; however, it becomes a perpetual and continuous choice that you make in your Third Density world.

Dear one, desire is that which comes from the Perfected Cell. It is indeed the cell that duplicates throughout the system and allows one to perceive or even have the conception of perfection. Dear one, it was I who individualized the conception of a Perfected Cell, even within a human body, itself. It was this conception of this Perfect Cell that allowed me to bring forth the individualization of the Immaculate Conception. Immaculate Conception is exactly as it states: "immaculate" means purity of thought and intent. There is indeed a focus that is held for that which is the Perfect Cell. The Perfect Cell is founded on that which is the space or frequency known as desire.

All of you hold desire within this Perfect Cell. For you see, Dear one, it cannot come forth without the desire of perfection. For any of you who have achieved anything in your Third Density world, anything that is held of great value to you - having assisted you in your growth and your world or work - was something that you desired. It was something that you held long, not only within your thinking world, but in your heart, longing for. This is known as desire, Dear one, this heart's longing. Desire is indeed a function of the Cellular Awakening. It is an important concept or perception that you must hold.

Dear one, it has been said that a man cannot win a race unless he sees himself as the winner. You indeed cannot become perfected until you have the desire to be perfect. This desire is built upon the Eight-sided matrix of the Perfect Cell. We ask for you, Dear one, to judge not the form, but to honor the function. Beloved Lady Master Venus has talked much about Divine Form and now I shall speak to you about Divine Function. The function of the Perfect Cell allows the body to accept the new energetic pattern of perfection. This is indeed a new concept to you; however, it is the concept that was held long in your own Immaculate Conception. Dear one, you carry the blueprint of perfection. This is always and always shall be. Dear one, I AM Mary and I step forth on the blueprint of perfection. I AM that which is held, the Immaculate Concept of perfection and that indeed is the work of a heart, individualized upon the Earth's Plane and Planet. Step forth, Dear one, immaculately conceived in perfection, for you are only that. Dear one, it is through your desire and the balance of love, wisdom, and power that build the foundation for the intent and motivation of desire. Dear one, I come to you, I come to you through that which I AM - Love.

She has just left my field and stepped back from my heart. She's standing now and I see her form. My eyes are open and I'm not looking at her through my Third Eye, I'm seeing her with my own eyes. She carries, over the top of her head, a brilliant gold color. She is de-densifying and leaving. I don't hear much sound but I see a dance of light. It goes and forms a triangle. This is her energy as she leaves.

*Energy creates light bodies, and within each body
are numerous layers and Rays of Light.*

The Fifth Ray

Saint Germain

When I first met Len, I became acquainted with energy work. I had some exposure to those techniques before, but it was limited. Having been born with the gift of auric vision, Len had always seen the light or energy that surrounds life – especially the human energy field. This light is known as the aura. This is both a gift and a curse. While attending Catholic Mass, he observed a gold light surrounding the host, or communion bread that he often saw after the Priest said a blessing. Apparently, one time when the Priest was having a bad day, the light failed to appear. Little Len, not knowing the reason, refused to walk up to the altar, and reported to a nearby nun, "It's not Jesus yet!" Incensed, the nun pulled his ear and sent him to detention.

In this environment, and after Len entered his adult years, he learned to censor those observations from others. However, he personally noted that some people had vibrant auras that were filled with life and health, while others were covered with dark spots and displayed grungy, dull colors, the signs of disease. When he finally enrolled in the Barbara Brennan School of Healing, for the first time in his life he did not feel alone.

After our first weeks together, Len offered to "work" on me. His massage table had just arrived, so I agreed. I felt his hands moving into my energy fields, swirling and reshaping various "layers" of my aura. Psychically, I could see golden light infusing my light bodies, and Rays of pure light reinvigorating me: violet, green, pink, and blue. I fought the impulse to sleep as this type of treatment is very relaxing.

Afterwards, as I sat on the edge of the table, I felt lighter, yet energized, more assured and self-aware, "What did you do?"

Len replied assuredly, "Oh, I rebuilt and charged your heart and relationship chakras . . . plus, I did a general balancing." I was immediately hooked. And now our conversations about Ascended Masters also included the nuance of the energy of everything from flowers to rocks, babies, children, and the elderly – Len even showed me the chakras on my dad's beloved hunting dog, Mica.

We began a sort of exchange. I shared information from my last two years of channeling, including my experiences and the many nuances and details about Ascended Master Teachings. Len taught me the locations of chakras and identified layers of the field of the Human Aura. I found that my auric vision was not as developed as his. But if I focused and relaxed, I could see the golden halo that surrounded each person. Later, I developed a psychic touch, could feel the viscosity of each layer of energy, and began to see their unique colors. Len further integrated his healing ability and would call in Archangels, Angels, Masters, and spirit guides to assist his energy work.

As our work together evolved, I experienced the subtleties of specific types of grids, energy meridians, and sub-chakras on the physical body and in the Human Aura. When we worked together, which was frequently, we perfected masculine/feminine energy balancing. The sublime energies of Saint Germain, Kuan Yin, or Sananda would often surround us. Sometimes, the Spiritual Teachers whispered suggestions and patiently demonstrated new techniques. Typically, they stood by, like watchful guardians of our process, streaming heavenly energy into the room and into our light bodies. By the time we began our weekly classes, word was also spreading, within the metaphysical community, about our healing sessions. Our downtown office began to serve double-duty for both business operations – I AM America and our energy work sessions.

We had been teaching for over two months, and it was time to take a break. Plus, we were still certain that we would move, but had yet to identify just where that would be. Len's meditations constantly advised eastern Shalahah (Montana), or Gobean (the southwest United States). However, this information was too generalized and we needed exact instruction. And there were many other considerations. We needed a larger home, and also a community that would be right for the children, especially if they were to stay throughout the school year. Plus, we needed to be located in or near a larger city, where we could teach and continue our energy-work practice.

We found that asking the Spiritual Teachers our own personal questions led to interesting discoveries. We discovered that an Ascended Master will never tell you exactly what to do. Instead, they will guide and instruct you in universal laws, and help you to uniquely forge your own individual and essential rapport with the I AM

Presence. They once said, "We will not tell you the way to do it; however, we will be there to serve you, to assist you, to help you. We are here to help you to attain." Yet, as we discovered, sometimes it is nice to get advice, and subtle hints often become invaluable.

On a bright May morning, Saint Germain appeared to me in meditation. He gently reminded me that everything in life's journey is indeed *choice*, and that he would never impose upon my "free will." However, there were certain choices that had recently been presented to us regarding a possible move, and we had options. First, we could stay exactly where we were; in fact, Saint Germain predicted that a suitable home would be revealed in the coming days. Second, we could move to the eastern door of Shalahah, and this option had already presented itself. Third, Gobean was a good choice, and there were two locations with suitable energies.

The first location was Taos, New Mexico, and the second location was Socorro, New Mexico. Taos is not located in the Gobean Vortex, but receives vital Gobean Vortex energies that would acclimate our energies to the Vortex for a future move. The second location was in the eastern door of Gobean, in New Mexico. That would also prepare us for a future move, elsewhere, within the Gobean Vortex.

I excitedly shared this information with Len, and we spent the next couple of days pouring over maps, and checking the locations in relationship to the Golden City Vortices. In the meantime, I perused the local classified ads, and, indeed, located a possible rental that was large enough for all of us, once the children arrived for the summer. Len and I drove over to Lewiston, ID, to view the home, located in a nice subdivision near the river, with easy access to the bike path. We knocked on the door and the owner greeted us. This home was a little smaller than our option in Stevensville, but it also had an ample two-car garage to house our office. We decided that our best option was to leave a small deposit, and fill out an application. The owner called later to let us know that we were approved. Now, we clearly have *two* options, and needed to make a decision.

Len was not certain that he wanted to stay in the Lewis-Clark Valley, and was inclined toward Montana or the southwest. I was leaning toward the home in Lewiston, and definitely ruled out a move to Montana. Was it possible that Gobean was our alternative destiny?

A year earlier, my friend Andrew had given me a beautiful lapis pendulum, instructing me in its use. He frequently used a pendulum to assist in making important decisions. I pulled it from its small velvet bag and handed it to Len.

Closing his eyes, he held the pendulum over the Map, and it spun over the Pacific Northwest, then suddenly moved toward the Southwest, centering over Socorro. I could hardly believe it. Len handed the pendant to me, "You give it a try." I murmured a quiet prayer to Saint Germain, Archangel Michael, and the I AM Presence, and closed my eyes. When I opened my eyes, I, too, saw the pendulum swirling in a small circle around Socorro, New Mexico.

"Well Socorro it is!" Len's voice was filled with excitement. Unlike Len, I was not as eager. At this point, I needed more proof that this was the right choice for us, and more importantly, I needed certainty that this move was in alignment to my life's path and spiritual growth. Montana was starting to look a bit better to me: it was only 240 miles away while Socorro, New Mexico, was over twelve hundred miles! "Here's what I suggest" said Len, his voice shifting, calm and centered. "We *do* have a choice, and if this move is meant to be, the *right* home will appear. Why don't you make a few calls and see what you can find?" "And if you don't," he continued assuredly, "We'll take the home in Lewiston . . . it will be okay."

After Len left for the office, I phoned the Socorro Chamber of Commerce. The chamber secretary recommended several real estate offices that handled rentals. I immediately called her first suggestion, and spoke with an extremely friendly woman who said she had the perfect rental for us . . . it had just been listed that morning. This home had three bedrooms, an attached sun room, a mother-in-law apartment, an office space, and a two-car garage, plus the home was *less* money than the rentals in Lewiston and in Montana. I asked her to fax over all the information and, again, another rental application. In less than a week we were approved. Now, with three different options available, we decided that Gobean would be our new home. I needed to break this news to my parents.

Our students were thrilled, although many of them expressed their regrets that we were leaving the area. Some of them had friends and acquaintances in the southwest and eagerly shared their contact information and phone numbers with us. Several volunteered to help us move and pack the truck.

From the start of our class offerings, many students asked if they could sit in on a channeled session. Initially, Len and I were reluctant to allow this. We had a heavy workload with our commitment to receive both the Twelve Jurisdictions and the world Earth Change Map information.

However, as this vital material was recorded and partially transcribed, we concluded that a student session would be helpful. In fact, all of the students were avid practitioners of the Violet Flame, and many of them, if not all of them, had received energy sessions. Plus, I wanted to leave them with the experience of a trance session, not only due to the information they would likely receive, but due to the sublime, ethereal energy they would experience, which was often present. We made arrangements for our final class and trance session at a student's home.

What emerged was the following lesson, "The Fifth Ray." This is a lesson about the Earth's varying energy bodies, and the Rays that draw vital energy from each subsequent light body. The best way to understand this is as follows: as the Ray streams through an energy body, it gains momentum and energy, and this important force births the Ray's definition and focus. The following definitions help to clarify the topic:

Earth Ray: This Ray draws energy from the *Prahanic Body* of Earth. It is a denser Ray Force, and gives life to all created forms on Earth. The lighter pastel colors of the Blue Ray, the Pink Ray, and the Yellow Ray also correspond to Earth's First Light Body.

Blue Ray: The Dark Blue Ray and Cobalt Blue Ray draw energy and force from Earth's Second Light Body, known as *Everno*.

Pink Ray: The Magenta-Pink Ray draws energy and force from Earth's Third Light Body *Eshano*. Eshano is affiliated with the ever-changing evolutionary needs of life on Earth.

Yellow Ray: The Yellow Ray draws energy and force from the Earth's Fourth Light Body *Buitsha*. This light body is associated with the "collective subconscious" of humanity.

White Ray: The White Ray draws energy and force from Earth's Fifth Light Body. Earth's Fifth Light Body is also known as the *Golden Grid* that empowers the fifty-one Golden Cities.

Green Ray: The Green Ray draws energy and force from Earth's Sixth Light Body – a *Cosmic Celestial Body*. Earth's Sixth Light body is affiliated with Avatars not only from Earth, but from nearby Galaxies. It is said to hold vast amounts of information: spiritual, prophetic, scientific, and Akashic. As a note, this is the energetic level that was accessed to download many of the I AM America prophecies and accompanying spiritual information.

Ruby-Gold Ray: The Ruby-Gold Ray draws energy and force from the Earth's Seventh Light Body, also known as the *Cosmic Causal Body*. The Cosmic Causal Body of Earth is associated with the Great Central Sun – the Galactic Center.

Violet Ray: The Violet Ray draws energy and force from the *Connectosphere*, also known as Earth's Eighth Light Body. The Connectosphere holds all of the lower Seven Bodies of the Earth together, and is associated with interstellar Unity Consciousness.

Overall, Saint Germain claims that Earth holds twenty-two energetic bodies, total, and each light body empowers a specific Ray. However, twenty-three Rays of light and sound stream onto Earth – the final Ray is likely that which manifests Earth, symbolized by a cross within a circle. This information is a bit esoteric, and perhaps is best for those who have studied the Human Aura, who wish to make correlations. The Spiritual Teachers call this, "the energetic reasoning."

[Editor's Note: To understand the Earth's first five light bodies, re-read the chapter "Serving the Divine Plan," and "The Web of Creation," in *Sisters of the Flame*. For complete information on the Rays, see *Light of Awakening*.]

≈

Greetings, Beloved children and chelas of the Golden Sun. It is I, Saint Germain who has stepped forth to give you discourse and it is I who come in love of service.

Response: "Greetings, Saint Germain. Please step forth into our energy field and welcome, Beloved one."

I AM Saint Germain, Cohan of the Seventh Ray. It is I who come forth for the service of humanity. Dear ones, once you see that it is the service of mankind to humanity that uplifts this planet into the Golden Age of Grace, Grace will bestow upon Prahna (Earth). We are speaking of Grace restored to Prahna, for this is the continuous cycle, the cycle of creativity. Do you understand?

Response: "Yes, this is clear."

And so, I come forth, Dear ones, to give you discourse for the dispensation of this work, given to you for the completion of the Fifth Ray upon the planet Prahna. There have been many studies that have been brought to your Earth Plane and

Planet and there is much material now about the changing face of your planet. Dear ones, we too gather information and look at facts and figures, the same as you should. You must understand that the information we give to you is what we call the middle way, that which is not only the quickest, but also, in a sense, the most conservative approach. Dear one, that which stands upon the edge always risks the crumbling earth beneath them. Do you understand this?

Response: "Yes, this is clear."

And so, this that has been brought forth, the Earth Change material, is from the Ascended Masters of the Spiritual Hierarchy of the Great White Brotherhood. You must understand, as Ascended Masters, we have walked and lived and breathed upon the Earth Planet itself. We contain within our energetic bodies that which allows us to access the genetic code of the Earth's Plane herself and Earth's Planet herself. You see, Dear one, we carry within us a resonance, or a vibration of frequency, which enables us to readily access and read clearly to the inner core.

There are those who also give their prophecies and who also do their research from other energetic bodies. This work that is brought forth now continues to go to what we call the Fifth energetic body. However, most of the information that has been given to you has come first from what we call the Sixth energetic body. You see, Dear ones, the work of the Fifth Ray draws its energetic work from that of the Sixth body. The work of the Seventh Ray draws its work from that of the Eighth energetic body. Now do you understand this Divine Plan in order and sequence?

Response: "Yes."

This work of the Fifth Ray that I bridge to you, I bridge to you from the beloved beings of light who have stepped forth to give their continuous radiance to that of the Fifth Ray work upon the Earth Plane and Planet. Dear one, they have within themselves, ready access to the energetic readings of the Earth's Light Bodies. Do you understand?

Response: "I see, so each of these beings brings a portion of the creative flow."

This is true, Dear one. And so you have those who work upon the First Ray. What would they bring to you, but the work of the Elemental Kingdom, that of the planet itself. You have those which do the work of the Second Ray. What do they bring to you, but the work of the energetic ring of the Third body. You have that which is the Third Ray. What do they bring to you, the work of the Fourth energetic body.

What do you have that is contained within the Fifth Ray, but the work of the Sixth energetic body of the planet. And so on and so forth. Have I made myself clear?

Question: "It is very much the same when I perceive the auric energy. The disease of the physical body occurs in the outer layers before it precipitates down to the physical body. Is it the same principle?"

It is so, Dear one, but you must understand that those who have individualized, have individualized that which is the Earth Ray. Do you understand?

Question: "Please explain the Earth Ray."

The Earth Ray, or the Earth harmonic, as you would call it, individualizes itself in these energetic bodies of the Earth Plane and Planet. You have, containing within the Earth Plane and Planet, twenty-two energetic bodies. And so, could you see that there would be twenty-three Rays to represent them?

Response: "Yes, following your discourse prior to this, I understand."

So, Dear one, that which individualizes, then takes its Home, Divine House, or House of the Father, as you would call it, into that which is the expression of "Sol" [the fifth tone of a diatonic scale] in light and sound.

Response: "Explain, please."

The expression of light and sound corresponds to the expression of thought and feeling. The expression of light is the expression of thought. The expression of feeling is the expression of sound.

Response: "This would make sense because much music in this density moves one emotionally. Please continue."

Dear one, the work of Earth Changes upon the planet, which has been dispensed to you through the Spiritual Hierarchy of the Great White Brotherhood of the Fifth Ray, contains within it all of the energetic greetings that come from the Sixth Body of the field. Those who step forth to give the information from the Spiritual Hierarchy of the Great White Brotherhood of the Fourth Ray give information that comes from the Fifth Level or energetic body of the Earth. That which comes from the Spiritual Hierarchy of the Great White Brotherhood of the Third Ray gives the information of the Fourth energetic body of the Earth. This is the code, Dear one, so that you will understand those who shall give timing of events, those who shall give detail upon detail. Do you understand now, Dear one?

Question: "So each one who steps forth for these timing of events and detail upon detail, is working in accordance with a certain Ray and a certain energetic reading?"

And a vibration, Dear one. And you must remember, there are indeed those who come forth through the other Brotherhoods to give their interpretation of this information.

Response: "However, we have within us a hierarchy."

You have within you a hierarchical structure. The energetic reasoning comes from that which is determined through the Spiritual Hierarchy of the Great White Brotherhood. We have a system that we too work with. However, remember, as we have said, it is the middle way that we always shall tread.

Question: "Does each Brotherhood fulfill this?"

Each Brotherhood serves from their own realm or dimension of expression, as we would call it. They are different expressions, primarily of the separation of light and sound. Dear one, the lists identify this work and the position where you sit. In your own governments, that you have enacted upon your Earth Plane and Planet, do you not see this same form of information as it filters through the different resources of the structures, such as the executive and legislative branches? Do they not address this same issue and interpret it differently? Yes, they certainly do. This is what we do, indeed, Dear one, for it was determined that humankind would have free will and therefore be individualized.

Question: "Was this also the same determination for mankind?"

Mankind has come forth, as I have said before, as the expression for humanity to learn service. If humankind is to learn free will, they shall learn to become responsible Co-creators. Only this lesson is available: responsibility comes through that which is known as service. It would seem to be a very hard lesson indeed; however, it is one that we take great joy in sharing.

This work that you do, let us identify it further. You, who come forth on this Fifth Ray, minister to mankind; you have come forth on the Fifth Ray to give service to the health and welfare of mankind; you, who come forth on the Fifth Ray, are to serve abundantly. You also represent the material Third Density expression of abundance. And remember what we said that abundance truly is: choice; your abundance in choice. And so you have this work that has been dispensed to you. All of your energetic reasoning for this planet comes from the Sixth Body of the field.

Question: "Now, each layer of the Human Aura and each layer of the planet correspond to a density or dimension. So, the reasoning, the correspondence of what is a core energy of understanding in the Human Aura, also is the same for the planet?"

Reasoning is thought and what is thought but light. The completeness of light is enlightenment.

Question: "It is in the thought that we have developed the desire of enlightenment?"

This is so, Dear one.

Question: "It seems as though the energy is dissipating. Do you have anything further to bring to us?"

Dear one, I am here as usual for your service and it is I, Saint Germain, who steps forth as Cohan of the Seventh Ray. Do you understand?

Question: "Yes. Who is the sponsor of the Eighth Ray?"

Dear one, you must understand, those who shall step forth to serve this Beloved Eighth Ray are now still embodied and incarnate upon the Earth Plane and Planet, gathering within them the completeness of energetic reasoning and energetic motion. I was incarnate upon the Earth Plane and Planet not that long ago, remember, Dear one?

Response: "I remember when we walked in paths along the sand."

And so you must see the completeness of this work, the thoroughness of this work also hinges upon the individualized focus of light and sound.

There are those who shall be placed strategically within your path to assist you, Dear one. It is important that these works are protected and sustained. I have sent three beloved angels, who shall come forth into this valley to protect and hold your work.

Question: "May I have their names?"

Ariel, Archais, and Zachio.

Response: "Oh yes, Archais.

Dear one, if you have no further question, I must take my leave.

Response: "I do understand and I thank you for lowering your vibration and for being with us."

I AM Saint Germain, Cohan and in service.

10

*We can intentionally assist the Earth's healing,
and she mirrors our divine, HU-man energy.*

Energy Lessons

Saint Germain
Mary
Soltec

The twenty-four-foot Penske moving truck was packed so tight, I didn't think it would hold another thing! And we still needed to stop at our storage unit and fit in the Maps, and several desks from our office. The kids were over-the-moon excited, and repeatedly ask, "Where is New Mexico," or "How far is 1200 miles?" And in those last few days, in the serenity of this sweet, little river village, packing, *yet again*, every worldly possession I owned, I'd often find myself asking the question, "*Why* 1200 miles?"

I'd never lived away from the feminine beauty of the Pacific Northwest, and while I was excited about moving to a new home and exploring the energies of the Gobean Vortex, I knew there would be many people I would miss. I escaped for a few minutes from the chaotic uproar in the little home and found myself at Sherry's kitchen table for one last cup of coffee.

"I have something for you," Sherry said, and handed me a black velvet bag. I pulled its string adorned with pink hearts and found a new packet of tarot cards. She continued, "These are for you . . . and when you come back, I will teach you how to read." Tears welled up in my eyes, and I stood up to give her a good-bye hug. While it seemed like only yesterday, it had been a year since Sherry rescued me from the cold snow of Coeur d'Alene, and helped me to reshape my life in the sanctity of Asotin.

Sherry stepped out to her front porch: "I know it is hard for you to leave. But really, this is the best thing you've ever done . . . and I have no doubt you are in for an adventure!" We hugged for one final time, and soon I was driving the Grand I AM, following the big yellow moving truck driven by Len, with my son, Carson, by his side. A few miles out of Asotin, I realized I had one final stop to make. I quickly pulled into Swallow's Nest Park and asked the girls to wait just a few minutes. I walked for several feet on the bike path and found the tree where I would often make a stop, rest my bike, contemplate my life, or receive guidance from the Masters or the I AM Presence.

There, on the bank was my "thinking rock," where I had sat for the last year. If this rock had been telepathic (and I think it was), it had seen and heard a lot from me through the last months. It had heard the Violet Flame decree repeating over and over again in my mind, as I worked to transform and change my life. It had sensed my frustrations and fears as I worried over starting a new business and entering a new partnership. And it had witnessed both tears and joy over swiftly changing relationships, uniquely filled with one compacted event after another. In essence, this rock had become my confident and intimate friend – I just couldn't leave it! The small granite chunk, with edges worn by time through pressure, likely smoothed by hundreds of years of rushing water, had sat so patiently next to me hearing my mental confessions, hopes, dreams, despairs, and desires. Her voice seemed to speak to me, "Don't leave me!" So I carefully picked her up and nestled her in my arms. I carried her back to my car, and placed her on the floor of the driver's side, next to me. She would be my traveling companion to the gates of Gobean.

We spent two nights at the ranch with my parents before our departure. My mother marveled over my almost military-style organization. As usual, money was tight, and I jammed several coolers with cold sodas and water, pickles, sandwich bread, chips, cheese, and fruit. My plan was to stop for picnics along the highway to economize. After paying the first and last month's rent, and a deposit on the new rental in Socorro, I cashed out my bank account. We had a little over four-hundred dollars left; four hundred dollars to see us through nearly a week's journey to the southwest, which would include gas, rooms, dinners at night for five days on the road, and extra expenses once we arrived – four hundred dollars total.

I'm certain my parents thought we were a bit crazy; after all, what could possibly await us in Socorro, New Mexico? It's not like we were transferred there for a job, and we had no family there, and most of all, we didn't know anyone. Len and I chuckled about this, "Do you realize that we are moving everything we own over three states for a bunch of guys only *we* can see and hear?" he said, with a smirk. A week prior to this chaos, we had sat quietly in our living room and had received the following energy lesson from the Spiritual Teachers. Oddly, there was no advice, and not a word about our move and what would soon occur. Instead, the information flowed like any other successive lesson, without fuss or drama. It was now clear to me that when you offer to "be of service" to this type of spiritual mission, your agreement is calmly accepted, and you innocently edge ahead into the known and the unknown. It's a bit like the proverbial saying, "Chop wood – get enlightened. Chop wood – get enlightened."

The following selection is an energy lesson from that session. The term "energy" refers to energetic bodies, our literal "fields of light," and how we can use our auric energy to assist and help Mother Earth calm her emotional body during frantic thunderstorms and extreme weather events. This can be achieved through grounding and breathing techniques.

Grounding to our planet is one of the first techniques in any type of energy work. This requires a fairly developed root chakra, also known as the *muladhara* in Sanskrit. This chakra is located at the base of the spine, the perineum. The energy of this chakra flows between the legs, downward, and connects to Mother Earth. When properly connected, energy practitioners will not use their own energy; instead, through the open channel of the base or root chakra, they direct the energy of Earth, through their chakras and energy systems, into streams of healing light energy. Most grounding methods focus on visualization, but use of the breath to physically and psychically connect to the core of the Earth is also an effective link to Earth's vital energies.

To do this, you close your eyes and visualize your root chakra – it is a ruby red light with a tinge of gold. Then you take a deep breath and on the exhale, see this root-chakra light literally drill into the Earth. Then you continue to intentionally breathe, as this auric laser light cuts through every layer of earth. When you encounter the golden ball of light in the center of the Earth, you connect, yet again, to this light as you did in your beginning breath. Now, you use your breath to channel this golden light back to your base chakra.

Envision the light as it moves through all seven chakra centers. Once you reach the crown chakra, channel the light, onward, to the Sun. This may take several breaths to achieve, in conjunction with your visualization. Once the light of the Earth's core is connected to the light of the Sun via your physical body, chakras, and energy system, you will notice a unique anomaly. A continuous, circular current develops between the two sources of unceasing light, and it pulses with your breath. Avid energy practitioners can expand or contract the amount of vital light energy, either faintly or strongly – and all degrees in-between – through their controlled breath. And the more you practice this technique, the better you get at controlling the light energy. "Practice makes permanent."

The current between the inner Sun of Earth and the Sun of our solar system is also similar to the current in the physical body, and this is known as the *Microcosmic Orbit*. This current, too, was described in that lesson.

Two other Spiritual Teachers joined Saint Germain in this lesson: Mother Mary and Soltec. Soltec shared teachings on the Eight-sided Cell of Perfection. This is the microscopic cell located in the human heart, which forms the nexus of the metaphysical heart-brain. Its sacred geometry is affiliated with the *Flower of Life*, the Chinese *bagua* or *pa'kua*, and the Kabbalistic *Tree of Life*.

I found the teachings of Mother Mary perhaps the most insightful for our current circumstances. The beloved Mother reminded us that we are created and held in perfection. I assumed we needed this lesson at this juncture, with the apparent life-changing decisions we were effectuating. Her words suggested that, "It is a perfect child which longs to come out . . . and play in this garden of creation."

"Oh Lord," I pray, "I hope Socorro, New Mexico *is* a garden."

✍

Welcome, my Beloved chelas, I AM Saint Germain and request permission to come forth into your energy field.

Response: "Please come forth, Beloved."

I come forth in service to mankind, and I individualize that which is the service of Mercy, Compassion, and Forgiveness. This has been individualized by the transmuting flame, known as the Flame of Transformation, and I give forth planetary service as that Cohan of the Seventh Violet Ray.

Dear one, we have discussed the energetics of the ninth energetic body, which you are to anchor and to hold to attain your eternal freedom. Dear one, we have explained to you the activation of the Perfected Cell. You have a spin ratio (vibration), as you have understood, from .285 to .317. Dear one, the spin ratio at the activation of the ninth energetic field, also contained within the Eighth-Sided Cell, grows from .485 to .617. Dear one, you shall be able to resonate this in a circular motion to obtain the spin ratio to access the tenth energetic field. We have given you the illustrations of the dimensions, so that you would understand the shape. You have understood the shape of the tenth energetic field; however, let's stay focused at this present moment on the ninth, from .485 to .617. Do you understand?

Question: "Yes. Is there a breathing technique to activate this?"

Dear one, beyond the breath, which you take into your own physical body, there is the breath of the planet itself. We ask for you to come forth into the service of the planet. There are many upon the Earth Plane and Planet at this time who understand that service to the planet itself is indeed of the highest integrity. For you must understand, Dear one, the one who enters into planetary service understands that the Earth itself is indeed a Cosmic Being, who has offered herself to be of service to you. So what do we do with the energetic remuneration of service? Dear one, there are small acts which you may do indeed for this Cosmic Being. You may work to breathe into herself, or you may work to breathe with her.

Response: "In this moment, I offer myself of service and I am committed to this completion."

Dear one, you may notice that there are times upon the Earth itself, in the second energetic field that she carries, that there are rainstorms and electrical storms. These are the times that she is suggesting the emotional field of her body. We would ask for you, at this time, to offer yourself in service and breathe with her during this time.

You have learned grounding techniques, through which you go into the inner core of this planet and then draw this energy up into yourself and extend it outward, in what you call energetic healing; however, Dear one, if you were to work with Beloved Terra, or Prahna, as I refer to her, I would ask that you would come forth during the time that she would need adjustment. This has been explained as Earth healing. Do you understand?

[Editor's Note: The second energetic field is part of the Earth's First Light Body.]

Response: "Yes. I accept this."

There are many forms that this takes. There are also the actions. There are those upon the planet who have decided that they will no longer toxify that which is her actual system. There are many acts of service here. You have this right to choose.

Response: "It is my choice to ask for your immediate recommendation."

A few have stood forth and individualized as a healer upon the Earth Plane and Planet in this expression. Would you not find it most compatible for you to do this work this way?

Response: "Yes, I agree."

I am always for your assistance, Dear one. Do you have further questions?

Question: "Just a further explanation. During the time of the storm or a change in the electromagnetic field of the emotional level, I am to ground to the planet, bring forth the core energy, and disperse this through the love that I AM into the atmosphere?"

Through what you know is the Heart Chakra.

Question: "And through the palms of my hands? Or just the chakra?"

At this present moment, Dear one, through the chakra; however, it is important that you are careful not to drain your own electromagnetic field.

Question: "It is understood. Is there a certain number of breath repetitions to do this?"

We would ask that you do approximately eighteen.

Question: "It is understood. Should this be done in conjunction with the Microcosmic Orbit?"

It is best if you do so, Dear one. This allows you then to revitalize and rejuvenate your own electromagnetic field. [This is a technique of directing the breath, inhaling from the perineum, to the Root Chakra, up the back of the spine, cresting over the top of the head to the Third Eye, and exhaling down the front of the body, back to the perineum. This is best done with the tongue turned up to the roof of the mouth, to complete the circuit.]

Question: "Is there a decree to do along with this?"

If you choose, Dear one. It is the intent of your heart though, to speak for the purification.

Question: "I understand. Will the Violet Fire suffice for this?"

Dear one, I shall take my leave at this present moment; however, Beloved Mary would like to come forth and speak.

Response: "As you wish. And I thank you very much."

Remember, Dear one, that I am always available for your questions and I will be glad to give you further discourse on the ninth energetic body; however, it is my belief at this time that you should review all materials and put together these illustrations so that you may understand them. And then bring your questions to me, Dear one, and we shall get this information down in the most knowledgeable and pragmatic way.

Response: "This is understood and my only request is that at the time of the illustrations, you stand by our hand and guide us."

I AM the Violet Flame and I come forth to that which is of service to mankind. [Editor's Note: These illustrations are published in *Light of Awakening*.]

Response: "I thank you very much for your service, and my service is yours also. Dear Beloved Mary, please come forth."

Welcome, my Beloved children. I AM Mary and I request permission to come forth into your field.

Response: "Please come forth, Beloved Mother."

I AM Mary, who has conceptualized that which is perfection. And it is I too who have fashioned within your heart the Unfed Flame, which is ready to receive the cradle that will hold the perfection of that which you truly are, Dear one: Divine Beings who have brought yourselves forth in service. This which streams forth from your heart, is it not the balance of love, wisdom, power which seeks itself into that which you know as desire? For desire is that which brings one to the point to even want to acquire perfection.

Dear one, this cradle which you hold within your heart, keep it such. Remember, Dear one, this is indeed a child that you nurture, that would bring you this Perfect Cell. Indeed, it is a perfect child which longs to come out; which longs to express itself in perfection; which is ONE in I AM THAT I AM, the Child of Creation. Kiss the child that longs to come to play in this garden of creation, and it is this child that shall come forth too, Dear one, to bless this Earth Plane and Planet. Dear one, this Perfect Cell which you hold within your heart, I ask for you to awaken to it, and hold it and cradle it, as you would a newborn.

Response: "Yes, as you wish."

I AM Mary and I come forward to fashion for you perfection. I shall hope it is immaculately conceived at all times, for it is Immaculate Conception, that pure thought of intent to perfection, that is able to be. Do you have questions?

Question: "You said something is activating in our hearts?"

Dear one, this perfection has been held within you. For you see, Dear one, you are immaculately conceived. You must understand, Dear one, that the activation comes forth and you make the choice to be as such. It cannot be denied that this universe shall respond. For you are a child of my own heart, Dear one. I am here for your service, Dear one, and I come forth on that which you see as the Immaculate Conception of desire. For you see, Dear one, it was desire which was held within the heart. That is what you know as coding, that this creation would be recognized.

Do you not see, Dear one, as the newborns come forth, each holds within them their cry. And when that child cries in the nursery, the mother recognizes which is her babe. You hold within yourselves this energetic we call desire; we recognize you, Dear one, and are of service to that. For I AM the Immaculate Conception of Desire and I stream forth from that which has been offered of the mighty Logos.

Response: "Yes. And I thank you for your service. And I AM of service to you also, if you have a request."

Dear one, it is my request to complete the Earth Change material, for this cradle which has been built must be filled with the child. The child must be nurtured and allowed to play upon the playground. The child steps forth in full manifestation in the image and likeness of I AM THAT I AM. Dear one, I AM Mary and I stream forth in love of the mighty Logos.

Response: "Thank you, Dear one."

Welcome, Beloved students, I AM Soltec and I am here to give you further refinement on the ninth energetic body. Sit at this table with me.

Response: "As you wish."

Look at these diagrams, Dear one.

He brings out five diagrams.

We have discussed geometric language. You have understood the language of the circle, the language of the triangle, that of the rectangle, and that of the square. Dear one, we shall discuss the language of the octagon. Eight sides contain within them the energetic for the perfection of desire that the Beloved Mary has brought forth. Do you see how this shape at all times is malleable?

[Editor's Note: To learn more about the Eight-sided Cell of Perfection, see *Points of Perception* and *Divine Destiny*.]

He is showing how the triangles can come out and take different forms. It can expand and contract.

Do you see this diagram?

Now he is drawing the triangle and at each point of the triangle, he adds a circle. He is taking the point and he is showing how you can pull the center point up and the circles can all expand into one.

You see how this Eight-sided Cell is a living and breathing organism? Do you see that it is not only the spin ratio, Dear one, but it is also that ability to expand and contract?

For it is in the expansion that this location of perfection has been allowed. It is the spin that allows the sustaining and the maintenance of perfection; however, that which comes forth, the duplication, only comes forth to what is called expansion. Now, for the understanding of the Earth energetic, you are quite correct, Dear one, in the assumption of the core energy; however, I would like to explain to you that within the core itself is not only the triangular shape of the energy from Beloved Helios and Vesta, but again the Eight-sided Cell of Perfection. The core energy of this planet continuously contracts and expands. Have you not experienced, upon your many embodiments upon this Earth Plane and Planet, times of expansion and times of contraction? This is determined by the inner core energy, or the Eight-sided Cell of Perfection within the planet itself. The ability of this cell to duplicate, or replicate, also depends on the ability for you to expand and contract your energetic consciousness.

All that we give to you at this moment is the energetic reasoning. You must understand that consciousness is also that; consciousness is only an energetic. It is indeed the Heart of Desire, though, that makes the choice to use this as a tool. I AM here for refinement and details, Dear one, and I shall take my leave and shall be available for further discourse if there are no questions.

Response: "When we actually do draw these into this density, I request your guidance."

I AM for your service and the upliftment of humanity.

Response: "I AM for yours also."

Welcome my, Beloved chelas, I AM Saint Germain. This has been great joy that we have come forth for this discourse. Remember at all times to use the Violet transmuting Ray of Mercy and Forgiveness, no less than three times per day.

Response: Thank you, Dear one. Blessings and greetings to you always.

11

Our spiritual growth is engendered in both physical and spiritual passage. Each passage activates the transcending process of Ascension.

Cloak of Divinity
Saint Germain
Mary

It was a beautiful Idaho morning, and I sat at the breakfast table with Mom and Dad, almost lingering, as that day we would depart to New Mexico. I was uncertain when I would return, and my mother, who was normally self-contained and assured, looked a bit worried. "You know honey, Dad and I don't feel good about you leaving," and she looked me directly in the eye with a look that only a mother can give a child, "Would you consider staying? You're moving so far away." It felt like my heart skipped a beat, and I saw tears in my Dad's eyes. I gathered what little courage I could find, and held back tears as I spoke, "Well, we'll see how this goes for now." I paused for a minute and added, "I can always come back if it doesn't work . . ."

Fortunately, Len walked in and interrupted. "Just checked the truck, and everything looks good. Ready to go?" he asked. His positive, upbeat attitude altered the tone of the room. "Yes," I answered and my eyes shifted toward my watch. "We need to pick up the kids," I added. The children's father lived about five miles away across the prairie. Since it would be several months before he would see them, they had spent the last two days with him at his farm.

Mom and Dad walked out with us, past the red barn, and into the parking lot. They stood still for several minutes and watched while Len and I arranged our suitcases and checked the coolers. I reached out for my Mom and hugged her, "I will be home for Christmas, Mom." She wiped away a tear and responded, "Oh, I hope so." Dad kissed me on the cheek and reminded me, "Punk . . . (that's *punk* for pumpkin, his nickname for his girls), when you get down there, you need new tires." And he quickly reached over to shake Len's hand and said, "You take care of my kids." I wasn't certain if he said that affectionately or not.

As I drove out of the graveled parking lot and onto the country road, my parents stood there with an arm around each other. It didn't occur to me until many years later that they were literally holding each other up as they waved goodbye.

For the next small section of the ride, I drove in front of Len. I easily navigated the back roads to the farm where I once lived. The prairie grass was tall and moved like the ocean in a gentle breeze. In a few days haying season would begin. As I drove through this small patch of the Camas Prairie, seemingly insignificant landmarks kindled unique memories. I passed the fence post where hawks often perched in any season, sitting still and calm – almost statuesque, yet fiercely prepared to claim their territory if challenged. I traveled onward past the field where I had learned to drive a grain truck and "load on the go," while bushels of wheat tumbled out and into the truck bed. At the bottom of Rocky Canyon, two gray rocks cast shadows where deer often hid after a cool drink of water in the snow-melted stream. About a half of a mile further I saw Tolo Lake, which shimmered in the morning sunlight. It was a beloved haunt of my high-school years. Perhaps my best memory of the lake was of my uncle's small boat circling around it, and we kids strapped in orange life jackets, each awaiting our turn for a ride.

I turned onto the roller-coaster road of hills several miles before the farm. The spring crops were losing their bright green color and before long would mature into fields of golden harvest. Five years earlier, I had traveled on the same road, perhaps even on this exact day. It was hard to believe that only a short time ago I was a farm wife with three preschool children, and my greatest worry was how we four would navigate the grocery store. My present juxtaposition seemed almost surreal. Today I would leave these bountiful fields of hay, wheat, and barley, and move onward to Gobean, and hopefully its fields of unending light. This thought almost caused a brief panic, and I reached down to touch my river rock, to feel its cool, calm presence.

"Mom, will we see mesas?" Kaitlin asked, as she bounced into the back seat of the car. She had recently studied the geography of the southwest in anticipation of our trip. "Will we see cactus?" "I think we will, but not for a few days," I answered, and I reached over and buckled her in. Bryn, just two years older, was much more reserved. She quietly handed me her carefully packed suitcase, and gently placed her Barbie dolls and coloring books in the space between herself and Kait. She sweetly asked, "Mom, after we stop in Boise, can I ride in the truck with Len?"

We pulled out of the driveway and made our way across the remainder of the prairie and onward to Highway 95. About five miles before Riggins, ID, I notice that the fuel tank was low. Len was driving about a mile ahead of me, and there was no way to signal or stop him so I decided to stop in the little canyon town. Inside the gas station Kait begged, "Mom, can we get a treat?" I opened my wallet and glance at the cash — exactly four hundred and thirty dollars. I hesitated for a moment; how do you tell a seven-year old that you're broke? I thumbed through the bills and found a one-dollar bill and handed it to Bryn. "You two can share." I thought to myself, "Now, four-hundred and twenty-nine dollars."

I helped the girls back into their seatbelts, and we were back on the highway, heading south to McCall. We were several miles out of Riggins along the Little Salmon River when it occurred to me, "Where is my wallet?" I couldn't remember placing it back in my purse. And it wasn't on the passenger seat either. Maybe I placed it on the floor? I glanced down — not there either. I started to get a sick feeling; did I leave it at the gas station?

I found a place to pull over and rummaged through the car. No wallet. I started to panic, and the thought that I had lost what little money we had began to sink in. First, I needed to tell Len as soon as I could and then decide what to do.

My foot hit the gas pedal, and even though I was traveling as fast as I could, within reason, the yellow truck was still not in sight. My throat began to choke, and I could feel a cool sweat over my brow. I remembered my mother's plea earlier that morning, "Dad and I don't feel good about you leaving." A thousand thoughts entered and left my mind as I swerved through one winding corner after another. My mind was swerving too — maybe I wasn't *supposed* to leave?

The little white Pontiac Grand I AM entered the alpine town of New Meadows when Kait pointed out, "There's the truck, Mom!" I sped up and waved Len over. I must have looked like a mad woman because when Len walked up to the car his first words were, "Are you okay?"

"No — I'm not," and I burst into tears. Trying to contain myself, I told him what had just happened. "I have no idea where my wallet is." I was literally desperate. Len remained silent for about a full minute, and then calmly stated, "Follow me into New Meadows. We'll park the truck there and drive back to Riggins together and see if you left it there." Len was a voice of reason.

As we rode back to the gas station, I retraced every movement in my mind. Fueling the car . . . helping the girls in the bathroom . . . paying for the fuel . . . giving the girls a dollar . . . helping them with their seatbelts. And then it dawned on me . . . I had placed my wallet on the car roof as I helped them with their seatbelts! And even worse – I had driven off! When I realize this, I told Len, "There is no way we are going to find my wallet. And even if we do, it's a snowball's chance in hell the money will be there." Len continued to assure me, "It will be okay…it will work out." I feared it would not. My discouragement quickly morphed into hopelessness. And, again, my mother's prophetic plea from this morning echoed in my mind.

We pulled into the gas station and I ran up to the counter. "By any chance, did anyone find a wallet here this morning?" The heavy-set woman looked at me suspiciously, "What is your name?" I was so rattled I wasn't even sure who I was. "Ummm . . . Lori Wilkins?" I said. "Yes," she tersely replied, "Your wallet's been found. But it isn't here . . . it has been turned in to the sheriff's office at New Meadows."

In our car and traveling back, yet again, to New Meadows, I had some relief that my wallet had been located. I was thankful that I would retrieve my driver's license, but I was certain our cash was gone. "I'm sorry," I repeated to Len about six times until he said, "Stop . . . it *will* work out."

When I inquired about my lost wallet, the clerk unlocked her desk drawer, and compared me with the picture on my license. I signed several forms and she handed it to me. Yes, it was my wallet – a black and brown checkbook style wallet, a gift from my grandmother the previous Christmas. I pensively opened it, and nearly shrieked with joy to discover that every dollar – all four hundred and twenty nine – was there! A small note was slid in with the money, and it read:

> "Dear Lori Wilkins,
> I don't know who you are, or what you do, but I want you to know
> that today the good Lord made sure that we would find your wallet.
> We were traveling on Highway 95 and took a wrong turn and
> found ourselves in Riggins. We were stopped for road repairs and
> I glanced down at the roadside and I discovered your wallet. I've
> counted your money and there is exactly $429.36. God bless you."

I can now say without hesitation or any doubt whatsoever that angels exist and interact in our lives in mysterious ways. Or, perhaps, a skeptic might say that I orchestrated this cosmic fire drill subconsciously so I would *know*, without disbelief and with complete certainty that, indeed, our move was the correct and right choice at this important juncture in our lives. And one more thing . . . *miracles do happen.*

We journeyed past Boise to spend the night in Twin Falls, ID. Bryn took her turn riding with Len in the moving truck, and Carson joined me in the car. He sat quietly, and carefully studied a small map from my Super 8 Hotel locations booklet, peering over the highways and the states we would soon travel.

The truck could not move as fast as my car, but we traveled on to Utah, caught up in Salt Lake City, and found a hotel for the next night. We woke up early so the children could see the Great Salt Lake with the beautiful Wasatch Mountains to the east. Our plan was to continue to drive south through the center of Utah, and take Interstate 70 to Grand Junction, CO. We arrived at Grand Junction just before sunset.

Fuel for the large truck was quickly eating away at our budget, so Len urged me to forgo an additional night in Colorado and push south to New Mexico. It would be a long day of traveling, but if we got up early and were on the road by 5 AM, we could stop for a picnic lunch in Colorado Springs, and then continue to Socorro.

We made good time and arrived in Colorado Springs a bit too early for lunch, but everyone needed a break. Plus *Poobah*, our tiger-striped cat who is usually mellow, was terrified of traveling and was wailing in his pet carrier. It was too hot to place him in the back of the truck, so we had no option but to keep him in the truck cab. Because of his ruckus, the children jumped ship and opted to ride with me. I also sensed Len's patience was growing thin with Poobah's constant serenade of meows and occasional howl.

Carson, with my road atlas, had become my official navigator. He located a park in Trinidad, CO, where we'd stop for lunch – the Kit Carson Park. By the time we arrived, we were a bit road weary, and my cooler of lunch goodies was becoming unappetizing. The kids asked, "Can we go to MacDonald's?" I promised that when we arrived in Socorro it would be our first stop. Len was quiet. I was thinking that the stress of the move, the drive, and fatigue were catching up with him. I took a look at the roadmap and said, "From what I can tell – we have about six more hours of driving. Do you think we can make it?" Len didn't respond; he just nodded his head "yes."

The sun was setting by the time we left the chaos of Albuquerque, NM, traffic. Brilliant stripes of pink and orange adorned the sky, and I began to notice an unusual frequency. Even though I was driving, my fourth-dimensional senses were suddenly alive – I knew I had entered Gobean. Through the whine of the tires I heard a high-pitched ring, and off in the distance, through the colorful shadows of the sun, I saw it – a mesa. "Kaitlin – look!" I pointed off to the southeast horizon. "Oh Mom, it is beautiful . . ." After driving over eleven hundred miles, we had arrived in the southwest.

It was dark when we pulled into the hotel parking lot. The kids ran up to the room, quickly adorned their swimsuits, and scampered off to the pool. I unpacked the cooler, added ice, retrieved several bags from our car, but couldn't seem to locate Len. I walked out to the truck and he was sitting there, a bit in a daze. "You look whipped," I said, as I hopped into the cab and sat next to him. "I know . . . I just need a minute" he said.

No doubt, we were fried. In four days we had traveled from one end of the United States to the middle, with three kids and a complaining cat; had hauled all of our worldly possessions; had lost all of our cash, and then miraculously found it. And now we were here, in Gobean – the Vortex of transformation, harmony, and peace. On the horizon, I saw a sudden explosion of light – fireworks. "Len, look . . . I guess they knew we were coming," I joked. We both smiled. We had almost forgotten; we had arrived on the Fourth of July, "Independence Day."

At nine o'clock the following morning we met a brash but bouncy redhead, Cindy, the real estate agent for our new rental. The house was large, and compared to our little cabin in Asotin, it was a dream home. The girls giggled as they picked out their new rooms, and Carson seemed relieved that he would have a room all to himself. I was excited to find that the sun room would make a perfect workspace for me, and the garage was a perfect location to store the Maps. Adjoining the garage was a work space that would soon become our new office.

After several days of unloading and emptying boxes, we finally spent our first quiet night in our new Socorro home. The next morning I counted our remaining cash, ran to the supermarket, and purchased fresh eggs and tortillas, cheese, pinto beans, potatoes, and salsa. I noticed a pay phone as I walked out of the grocery store, and remembered that I should call my mother and let her know that we had arrived safe and sound.

The phone rang almost five times before she picked up. "We're here . . . and our home is really just great . . ." But before I could share another word, Mom interrupted, "I have some sad news." I caught my breath for a second and asked, "What?" She continued, "We lost Grandpa a few days ago, and I know you can't come home for his service . . ."

"Oh . . ." I replied. I was a bit shaken. Even though he was ninety-one, and had been admitted to the nursing home several months before, the last time I visited him he seemed relatively healthy, and was happy to see me. "What happened, Mom?" She replied, "Oh, I guess he decided that he didn't want to be here anymore, and he refused to eat. After that he grew weak and slipped away." I then realized that during our entire trip, while we were moving from Idaho to New Mexico, my beloved grandfather was dying.

I must have been in shock because it wasn't until much later that night that I finally told Len. That larger than life man, the patriarch of my family who had built a local farming dynasty out of a small 160-acre homestead and who was a second father to me, was gone. Len consoled me as I sobbed in his arms. At that moment Idaho seemed far, far away.

That night I traveled to a state of consciousness beyond dreams and visions. I stood on the bank of a flowing river. But this was not a river of rushing water; it was filled with a stream of flowing, conscious light. It glittered and sparkled as its waters trickled and surged, and the sound of its movement emitted a soothing energy. I felt comfort and peace. In the center of its current stood my grandfather and he was feebly navigating the stream with difficulty. I saw his trepidation and sensed his fear. I stood on the shore watching, beside my two sisters and brother, and we all felt a bit helpless. I found a wooden branch lying next to me, and I picked it up and waded into the rolling river of light within several feet of him. My body seemed to stretch as far as it could as I pushed the tree branch, which had now morphed into a walking stick, toward him. He reached for it and grasped it, stabilized his footing, and slowly but surely traversed the waters to the other side. Wading back, I stood on the opposite shore with my siblings.

The minute his feet touched the bank, his body restored itself! He appeared like a 28-year old young man, not the grandfather I had known in life since his late fifties. A German shepherd rushed up to greet him, wagging his tail. He was undoubtedly an old friend. Grandpa stood there, waving to us as we remained on the other side of the ethereal river. He grinned at all of us, simultaneously waving to us and petting the dog, and telepathically conveyed to the four us as we waved back, "Goodbye . . . goodbye!"

When I woke up I knew that I had traveled far away from this Earthly reality. I knew that I had been given a rare glimpse of heaven and that my grandfather had safely and joyously arrived.

In the next two weeks, we completely unpacked, organized ourselves, and started to explore Socorro. "Why not begin to fit in?" I thought. I joined a bike riding group, and we met every morning at dawn to bike the country roads around the community. I admit that it was not as beautiful as biking along the feminine Snake River, but there was an earthiness to this seemingly masculine area that I had never seen before, with its many colorful wildflowers and deep arroyos, through which we would often find a rocky trail. Inevitably, our ride would be accompanied by the sweet serenade of melodic songbirds.

I signed up the children for swimming lessons at the college pool and an afternoon reading program at the library. In the meantime, Len completely organized our small office, which included a wrap and pack area for the Maps.

Amidst all of this reorganization of our lives, I'd had little time to channel, but was completely absorbed in transcribing and organizing my first book. Before leaving Idaho, I was able to convert an old IBM file, with all of my early work from several years before, into a 400-page printout. I was carefully selecting excerpts from this material, and transcribing the new work that Len and I had completed in Asotin. In the meantime, I needed to find a photographer to convert the Earth Change Maps that Sherry had drawn of Canada, Mexico, Central and South America.

Before long, we found ourselves on the road yet again, heading to San Francisco for one of our first workshops together. Sheryl, the event organizer, was extremely thoughtful, and along with hosting the event in her home, she arranged nearby accommodations, along with a babysitter for the children. They were now at an age where babysitters were a bit annoying, but they were patient with our schedule. I had promised the kids a full day at Disneyland after completing the two-day workshop, so they eagerly awaited our trip to southern California.

The set of slides, which I had prepared months earlier, helped my presentation immensely. I shared the Earth Change prophecies alongside the lessons on the auric layers of the Earth's field. I also prepared about an hour's lecture on geometric language and the sacred geometry of the Golden Cities. Len complemented this lecture with his presentation on the human energy field, including how our personal thoughts, feelings, and individual actions play a much larger role in shaping collective consciousness. He offered a sign-up sheet for private energy sessions, and after our first day of the workshop, every session was filled. So it looked like we would stay for a few extra days.

About a handful of attendees asked if I would participate in a channeling session. Because I had free time when Len was busy with sessions, I agreed – why not? I had packed my hand-held recorder, so I could certainly record the information. Plus, it would be interesting to work with a different group and see what type of material the Spiritual Teachers were willing to share with beginners.

If you've read *A Teacher Appears*, or *Sisters of the Flame*, you'll note that I write about the importance of the session monitor in trance-channeling sessions. As I've mentioned before, the monitor plays a vital role in sculpting the material, primarily through the type of questions that the monitor asks at that time and then, again, following the Spiritual Teacher's response, through further dialogue and questions. In addition, the *sitters* – those who participate in this type of session—also play a significant role.

Along with the session monitor, the sitters' auric energy is literally channeled and redirected in the session so that the Spiritual Teachers can leverage their energy to move from the Fifth Dimension, and downward, into the Fourth Dimension, for communication purposes. This important nuance is often referred to as "energy-for-energy" by the Master Teachers. According to the teachers' tradition, for the teachers to successfully lower their consciousness to our plane for "discourse," those attending must make every effort to raise their energy to meet them. In channeling sessions with beginners, I've found that meditation and decrees work quite well to heighten the energy of the room before the Spiritual Teachers enter.

I explained this thoroughly to the potential participants, and they were all eager to attend.

The following excerpt is from the trance material that was received in San Francisco. It features a beautiful lesson from Mother Mary on topics that included the Unfed Flame and our innate divinity, which she described as an *immaculate conception.* Saint Germain also provided insights and teachings on Ascension, which continued to evolve as he introduced the difference between physical immortality and our spiritual immortality. He reminded us, "It is no secret that you are spiritually immortal," and suggested that the physical Ascension is a transcending passage that perfectly reflects our inner light. This teaching, he claimed, is mirrored in Hermetic Law, "As above, so below."

If this were true, then my experiences through the previous months of continuous, time-compacted, transcending passages of fear, rebirth, doubt, hope, loss, and letting go should have had my light-fields calibrated for lift-off. My only question was, *was I ready?*

Dear one, you see, this is the foundation on which we bridge to you, for this is what we call "agreement," that we are able to come forth and you come forth into what we would call the planetary service of the Cosmos. Dear one, I AM Saint Germain, and I serve as an energetic bridge. This bridge comes forth to awaken mankind to his true purpose, which is the spark of divinity that is within each of the hearts of all of you. For you see, Dear one, this is the spark of perfection, or that which Beloved Mother Mary has called immaculately conceived. For you, Dear one, are indeed divine, and is it not divinity which comes forth to Co-create upon this planet?

Dear one, we are delighted to be here and we offer ourselves of service to you, for we understand there is much that you do not understand about this work which we do upon the Earth Plane and Planet. But, Dear one, it is of vast importance that you understand the focus of this work. Along with this focus, which is the Violet Flame of Mercy and Forgiveness, the transformation of the Violet Ray upon the Earth during the Time of Transition, there is also this focus which comes forth with the Golden Age of Ascension.

For you see, Dear one, your bodies of light are ready to transcend. This transcension, as we would call it, is indeed something that comes forth, not only a day at a time, but at this time - this epic in time - Ascension is possible. For you see, upon the Earth itself, is the geo-energetic, which is the twenty-first energetic body of Earth itself. This comes forth to give itself in service to you, Dear one, so you may have this Ascension. Do you want your eternal freedom?

Response: "Yes."

As I have stepped forth in planetary service, there are many here who would also like to come forth and discourse with you. And now I would like to introduce to you Beloved Mary.

Welcome, my Beloved hearts. I AM Mary and I ask permission to come forward into your energy fields. Dear one, I offer you the Cloak of Divinity.

She takes the shawl off of her shoulder and holds it up.

This that I have offered as the cloak, or the Swaddling Cloak, is that which comes forth to hold you and to carry you. For you see, Dear one, there are times that you may feel in this work that you are alone, that there is nothing that covers you, nothing that holds you. And I, as Mary, come forth to offer this, for I shall accord myself to you, heart of my heart, child of my child. So you see, Dear one, it is I who came forth to fashion the perfection of your heart; it is I who came forth before you came into embodiment upon this Earth Plane; it is I who came here to hold you, Dear one, as your Immaculate Conception, who stepped forward into this which you know as the Third Dimension.

This beloved cloak, hold it near your heart, close to the Unfed Flame of Love, Wisdom, and Power, for you see, Dear one, this work upon the Earth Plane and Planet is also a work that is in much peril. There are few who are willing to carry this light and there are few who are willing to carry this staff and rod, which is this work of carrying the message. But you see, Dear one, we are indeed a family of torch bearers, a family of those who step forth to carry this message. I offer you this cloak, this Swaddling Cloak, so you shall know that you are never alone.

Mary steps back.

Beloved chelas, I AM Saint Germain and I thank you, Beloved Mary, for the discourse of the cloak. For you see, Dear one, it is the cloak that you are to carry, the cloak of protection. In this work upon the Earth Plane and Planet, there are few among humanity who even wish to ascend. Do you understand, there are those who do not even wish to attempt the physical Ascension? For you see, Dear one, it is no secret that you are indeed spiritually immortal, but there is that which is the reflection of your inner light and that which is the outer shell. And while the emphasis should never be placed upon that which is the physical body, how could there be another law than such: As above, so below? You all know this to be true and just, and such is the energy which comes forth. You have learned about the space which it carries.

We learned about the space of stillness, or the space of silence. It has been said that silence is golden, but beyond this golden rule, there is the space that is carried or held within the square configuration. To hold space is also to carry space, as one would the cloak of protection and carry it around you. Carry it around you with Beloved El Morya, who serves on the First mighty Ray, which serves the will, the focus to always be carried forth. Dear one, this work that you must do is to carry work. It is not to be held so close to you that it is only yours, but carried, Dear one, so that it can be shared. It is a simple lesson, but there are many upon the Earth Plane and Planet who do not understand the need to carry this forward and to carry it onward.

There is also the work of Ascension. You must carry light within you. It's not a matter of taking this light and holding this light, but there is that which is carrying the light. There are also those upon this planet who understand that it is important to protect this which comes forth from the mighty Logos. But, Dear one, we invite you and ask you to carry.

There have been many directed—at this time upon the Earth Plane and Planet in transition—to return to areas of birth. I am not speaking of your birth in this embodiment, but we return to many areas where we have birthed many times. In this instance, you have carried these five birth times in this area and so you carry within you, what is known as the twenty-second energetic body, the memory of this, Dear one. You are returning to re-collect this experience. It has been explained that there is no time, but only a series of events; however, this time you are in we refer to as time compaction. You have a series of events that you must complete. You have two people to complete a series of events in this area, those which were cut short through the act of your own will. Do you understand?

Response: "I think so."

Dear one, it is a work of joy, this that is completion, for as you go to the top step of this work, are you not ready for the next flight?

Response: "Yes."

Step forward, Dear one, in the divinity of the perception; awaken, Dear one, to the call of Ascension and come forth as the glorious god that you are. Dear one, do you wish to attain your eternal freedom?

Response: "Yes."

To individualize upon this Earth Plane, particularly in Third Dimension, is a work beyond description, for I too know this, as I stepped forth and declared:

I AM THE FREEDOM OF THE ETERNAL GOD
MADE MANIFEST NOW.

It's been said, Dear one, that in order for new wine to be poured forth, new wineskins must be fashioned. And so you must come forth and fashion this new identity you wish to be. To individualize yourself is really the question: To be or not to be? Are you ready, Dear one, to step forth? Are you ready to be fashioned anew from the heart of the mighty Logos, streaming forth in the identity of eternal life, which is the wellspring of All That Is? Dear one, it is not up to me to grant you this identity; it is not up to me to determine whether you should have it. It is only up to me to remind you of what you shall be, as you are indeed conceived in Immaculate Conception. Dear one, it is I who come forth to remind you of such, but it is you who must choose. Do you understand?

Response: "Yes."

I realize that this may seem such a simple lesson, and yet, is it not so; it seems in Third Dimension, that the simplest lessons are the hardest to yet achieve. And so, we repeat them again and again, pattern after pattern. And let me remind you, Dear one, that it is only a pattern, and you may choose to change this pattern anyway that you wish to Co-create.

If you have understood the geometric languages that exist upon the planet, I invite you to take a look at that which is carrying. We have referred to that which holds or carries space as the perfect square; however, contained within the perfect square are the duplicated triangles, triangles which come forth to duplicate energy, or replicate energy. To replicate energy, a perfect duplication, or a perfect representation, is made of what this energy should be. To bring forth duplication of energy, you have a choice. Twins, for example, held within the mother's womb, are brought forth either as identical twins or fraternal twins. Here, you can have an absorption of the duplication of energy, like a twin withheld and carried within; this energy you wish to carry, or store, in a sense, for future use, can be identical individualized energy called fraternal or patterned energy. Do you understand?

Response: "Yes."

To carry or to hold energy is to bring light within this configuration. Hold the light there, draw it into each of the chakra centers. Look within and see within your own heart, these patterns that you hold and carry. Close your eyes, Dear one, and we shall travel within the heart itself. Go within the center of your heart. Do you not see the organ, pumping and beating, this that gives you life? See the vibrant pink, and the flame that is held within your heart. Go deep within and discover that which is the Perfected Cell. Within the Perfected Cell are the cells that are held about it. In all creation, each creation which comes forth upon this planet, in the center of each Vortex, or chakra, as it is known, is held a Perfect Cell for that particular life stream.

You each carry the Perfected Cell, identified by the Creator I AM. Through what is known as the DNA coding, you have been able to evolve upon this planet; however, close to the perimeter of this Cell, this mighty Perfected Cell, is what is known as the RNA coding. It is possible for you to go inside yourself and to discover this. As I may be able to point this out for you, it is best for you to see it yourself. Do you not see the double helix as it comes forth? All these shapes that are carried upon this helix of yours, Dear one, what do you choose for them to be? We have discoursed about that which is carrying energy, or in this case, carrying light. I ask for you to see, surrounded by this Perfect Cell, that each hold six of these helices to come forth. Count them, and what should come forth on these six helices but that which we have just discussed, the subatomic blocks of energy. Dear one, do you understand?

Response: "Yes."

You are here, Dear one, to make these choices; you are here, Dear one, to choose your Ascension; you are here to carry this light forth and to stream forth to bless humanity. You, Dear one, make the choice to serve or not to serve. In this moment, I ask for you to come forth as representatives of the Spiritual Hierarchy of the Great White Brotherhood. Do you agree?

Response: "Yes."

You are my blessed children. Come forth eternally free. Take this cloak and wrap it about your shoulders. Know that you are never alone and that we are always quartered in that which is your heart, for we shall always carry with you the perfection of divinity. I AM Saint Germain and I come forth on that which is the Violet Transmuting Ray of Mercy and Forgiveness.

I AM A BEING OF VIOLET FIRE;
I AM THE PERFECTION GOD DESIRES.

This is your decree, Dear one. Come forth into the Golden Age, I AM.

12

We are inextricably connected to the
Universal Forces of light and sound.

Cosmic Service

Saint Germain
Archangel Zadkiel
Amaryllis
Babajeran

While driving back from California, we traveled through Scottsdale, AZ. After perusing the road map, I mentioned to Len that we might want to take a shortcut through the small town of Payson, AZ, before returning to Socorro. "Why not," Len agreed.

Before long we were traveling North on Highway 87, also known as the Beeline Highway. About twenty miles before Payson, we both noted the intense energy of the Gobean Vortex, and later discovered that we had traveled near an Adjutant Point of the Vortex. An Adjutant Point is a point of convergence of two or more ley lines, a point which forms the sacred geometry of a Golden City Vortex. The Vortex energy in these locations is concentrated.

Golden City energies can wax and wane, but these convergent points are sometimes so strong that they literally create small portals or doorways into the Fourth and Fifth Dimensions. As a result, sensitive humans often report the phenomenon of time rifts (tears in time-space orientation), contact with the Nature Kingdoms of the Fourth Dimension, and psychic experiences.

Along with Gobean Vortex energies, Payson is filled with pine trees, red rocks, flowing streams, and a glorious view of the Mogollan Rim – whose dramatic cliffs and canyons follow the Grand Canyon, and then onward, to New Mexico. We decided to stay an extra day and explore Payson's charming landscapes, a feminine contrast to Socorro. The next day, on our drive home, I commented to Len, "I think we'll be back." "Yes," Len replied, "I like the energy . . . next time, we'll bring our bikes and explore."

The few days off had been our first vacation in many, many months, and I'm not sure that we were ready to go back to work! Len was planning a trip to the East Coast, his first in almost a year. I was pensive about his leaving, and my being alone with the children in Socorro where I hardly knew a soul.

"You'll be just fine," Len said, and he kissed me on the forehead as we saw him off at the Albuquerque airport. I admit that I had mixed feelings about his trip back to West Chester. He needed to connect with his children, both teenagers, and also check in on his elderly parents. From a practical viewpoint, his trip was long overdue. Yet, in the back of my mind, I feel like it might be a long time before I saw him again. And even though we were very close and committed to one another, I still had misgivings about his leaving.

"And don't forget to call Madge," Len reminded me, as we embraced one final time before he boarded the plane.

We had met Madge our first week in Socorro. After following through on a contact from a student, and then from one friend-of-a-friend to several more calls, we had found ourselves at a small metaphysical group gathering, at a home a few blocks from our new home. During the break, an engaging woman came up to Len and me and introduced herself. "Hi, I'm Madge – and welcome to Socorro. I want to mention that if you ever need any help with your sessions or transcribing, I was once a legal secretary, and I'm a good typist." Len immediately secured her phone number and assured her that we'd be in touch.

I called Madge and invited her to a local Mexican restaurant for lunch, a friendly get-together. The children sat quietly at a table next to us, happy that I allowed them to have a soda. "Oh this isn't hot at all!" said Madge, as she dipped another corn chip into the tongue-scorching salsa. I gulped water after the first bite, nearly choking.

"New Mexico is an interesting place to live, and it is filled with characters," Madge openly shared as she sipped her ice tea. She was a petite woman in her late fifties, with a few extra pounds, piercing blue eyes, and a husky voice. Likely, her apparent grit resulted from years of living in the desert. I immediately sensed her love of people and an interest in the nonconventional.

"So, how long have you been trancing?" she asked. She was interviewing me – not the other way around. I slowly responded, "For over two years now . . . it has been quite a journey." My mind drifted through my first memories with my channeling partner Dan, the colorful and wondrous summer with my friend and assistant

Sherry, and the sublime presence of the Spiritual Teachers at the Asotin cabin with Len. I continued, "I've worked with a number of Spiritual Teachers, and with several different monitors." Madge quickly responded, "Oh yeah . . . and whoever sits for this type of work plays a role in how good the material is." I was amazed that she knew something as nuanced as that. I asked, "Have you worked with a channel before?" Now, my interest was piqued.

"Yes, I've been into consciousness studies for many years. I had an opportunity to work with Dr. John Aiken and his research with LSD. I had some remarkable experiences then. I also had the opportunity to speak with the spirit guide Bartholomew – maybe you've heard of him?" I responded, "Just heard about his teachings, someone gave me the book, *I Come as a Brother.* I haven't had a chance yet to read it. I don't normally read others' channeled works, as I don't want [them] to influence the work that I'm receiving." Before I had left Idaho, a student had literally placed this book in my hands with the caveat, "You need to read this."

"Well," said Madge, "Dr. Aiken played a large role in Bartholomew's appearance," and she described how Dr. Aiken had worked with a hypnosis patient when the spirit guide and teacher appeared and began to share spiritual insight and wisdom. She continued, "One thing I remember, [from] when I sat in on one of his teaching sessions, is that 'there are no mistakes,' and I think there is no mistake that we are sitting here together in Socorro, New Mexico." She paused for an introspective minute, and completed her thought, "I have no doubt that I need to help you…And you should be careful. This type of work attracts the fringe element."

I was startled for a brief moment. I guess I had never considered this as I had always had someone working closely with me who screened telephone calls and personal invitations – Sherry and Len were both experts at this. I wrote my address on a paper napkin, and handed it to her, "Can you come over tomorrow?" She promptly replied, "Yes, I'll be done with work around four. I can transcribe for a couple of hours."

A feeling of comfort settled over me as I drove home from the restaurant. Len had been gone for about a week, and I purposely stayed as busy as possible and made a conscious effort to not be lonely. Thank god – I've finally met someone! Other than the three children, my cat Poobah, and Master El Morya, I now knew someone else, on a more than casual basis, in Gobean!

The doorbell rang and I excitedly opened the door to find Madge standing there. She asked, "Okay – are you ready for some help?" I invited her in. I gave her a quick tour of the home and escorted her to my office space with the transcribing equipment. After setting her up at my desk with several new tapes to transcribe, I asked, "What do you think . . . will this work okay?" Madge responded, "Oh, yes, it's just fine. And I'm anxious to hear your trance work."

In spite of the fact that Madge was dressed professionally, she carried an organic air of informality, and I could tell that she was definitely a nonconformist. She sat down at my desk, and immediately got to work. I glanced in the room a few times, to see if she was doing okay, and I could see her fingers flying across the keyboard. She was probably transcribing about eight times faster than I could.

After several hours, Madge entered the wrap and pack office where I was filling orders. She said, "I think I'm finished for the day." She looked directly at me, and continued, "You are definitely a trance channel, and I'd love to sit in on a session sometime." I glanced at my watch and said, "Do you have a minute for a quick cup of tea?" Madge agreed, "Yes, I'd like that." She sat down at my dining room table under the two beautiful oil paintings of Saint Germain and Lord Sananda. I said, "I'd like to continue with my trance work, but currently Len isn't here to monitor sessions. Would you like to give it a try?"

I could tell from Madge's resounding "yes" that she was sincere and whole-heartedly enthusiastic. We agree to meet in the evenings, after dinner, when the children could watch television and supervise themselves. The additional mother-in-law apartment was quite private, and would work perfectly for our channeling sessions.

Before the following session started, four bright lights entered the space. I got the impression that extra spiritual reinforcement was needed for our initiatory voyage into the spiritual realms. I recognized Saint Germain, along with the protective stance of Archangel Zadkiel, plus two new Spiritual Teachers. These light beings were definitely feminine: one was dressed in a beautiful white gown, in the inverted shape of a white lily, with a cascade of flowers flowing from her auburn hair. The second feminine energy constantly shape-shifted from an elegant ebony face to a druid Goddess, into an Egyptian princess, and into a stunning, beaded, Native American woman, then a serene Asian deity, and finally a loving caramel-brown Peruvian mother or exotic Persian princess. Each face was magnificent and exalted. Heavenly energies streamed from each transcendent presence. I realized that this sublime energy represented the feminine essence of our Earth Mother, also known as Babajeran. She embodied the Divine Mother of every culture and race on Earth. The name Babajeran translates to "Grandmother rejoicing." So, apparently, Babajeran is both Divine Mother and Divine Grandmother, equal archetypes and deities of the feminine ancestral lineage that sponsors our many lifetimes on Earth.

On the surface, the lesson that ensued may seem somewhat general. However, those who have "the eyes to see, and the ears to hear" might note interesting nuances and details in the teaching. First, the lesson gives a subtle clue to the connection between Madge and me. Apparently we had both experienced lifetimes in the Elemental Kingdoms, and had sought incarnation in human form to support and give voice to the Nature Kingdoms of Earth. I've pursued confirmation of this metaphysical incarnation with great success, through Life-Between-Life hypnotic regressions (LBL sessions), and through personal spiritual understanding that was provided to me years later by the Indian Avatar Mother Karunamayi. These lifetimes explain the instant connection Madge and I both felt upon meeting, and our immediate rapport.

Overall, the result of this channeling was a lesson on the Green Ray, also known as the Fifth Ray, characterized by discernment, science, education, healing, and spiritual awakening. A Ray is a force or type of energy that divides its efforts into two measurable and distinct spectrums: light and sound. Light and sound are the building blocks of our universe; therefore, the Rays permeate everything in our world of thought, feeling, and action. In Ascended Master teachings, there are Seven Rays of Light and Sound, and each Ray is defined through a unique system that ascribes attributes, color, sounds, gemstones, scents, spiritual energy and specific Spiritual Teachers. Earth Mother Babajeran shared a decree to further activate light within the Gobean Vortex. [Editor's Note: for more information on Rays and Ray Forces see *Light of Awakening*.]

According to this lesson, the Green Ray is connected to the fourth-dimensional Nature Kingdoms of Earth. It guides the evolution of Earth and incoming souls through its interaction with the Pink Ray; an energy of unconditional love and devotion. Evidently, Socorro is located in what is known as the "Achilles Heel" of this Vortex. Energetically, this heel represents a vulnerable location that needs reinforcement. The Spiritual Teachers described this energy anomaly as a point that if "touched, is felt throughout the entire system." I wondered, "Is this one of the reasons we had been guided to move to Socorro; to stabilize, reinforce, and send the Green Ray throughout the area?"

I glanced toward the barren hills just west of our home, and I couldn't help but miss the green I would normally have seen if I had still been living in the Pacific Northwest. Alternatively, if I looked beyond the physical and into the spiritual realms, I wondered if I would see the ethereal Blue Ray of Gobean, outlining the perimeter of this Vortex community. I reminded myself that I had traveled here to *be of service*, and chanted the Earth Mother's decree of activation, "Into the Golden Light that streams from Divine Creation . . . we dance in the joy of being ONE."

〜

Greetings in the light and sound of the most radiant ONE. Let me introduce myself to you, Dear one. I AM Saint Germain, Chohan of the Seventh Ray, that which is the Seventh Ray of Transformation and that which you also know as the Transformation Ray of Healing, Forgiveness, and Compassion. Dear one, before I proceed I would like permission to enter into your energy field.

Response: "Yes, you have permission."

Thank you, Beloved, for it is I who come forth as [like] Archangel Zadkiel, that which comes forth on the Ray of Mercy and Forgiveness. As you must understand Mercy and Forgiveness, does this not assure and sustain that love will bring forth to the Beloved Planet? And this is the discourse which I shall give you, not only the discourse of Mercy and Forgiveness, but that which we shall understand as the continual Forgiveness that this Beloved Planet has given to mankind.

Dear one, I form the function as the energetic bridge for this body of work. This comes forth from the Sixth collective body of the field of the planet itself. This Beloved Planet is indeed a Cosmic Being. This is no secret or mystery to you and it is we who come forth to remind you that this planet, from which you spring and are, is indeed an individualized Cosmic Being who has offered itself in Divine Cosmic Service. I bridge myself to you, Dear one, and bring forth a Beloved Sister.

She is stepping forward.

Welcome, Dear one, my name is Beloved Amaryllis and I come forth as one of the Cosmic Beings who sponsors this Beloved Planet into being itself. I have been the sponsor which has held the creative space for the Devas and the Elementals upon this planet, upon that which you know as the Green Ray. I individualized the Green Ray upon the planet during that time when her creation sprang forth. And when we speak of creation, we do not speak of that which you understand as the Big Bang Theory; for you see, creation only comes forth on expansion. All that comes forth in this universe comes forth on the Expansive Ray, or that which you know as the geometric language of the circle.

I, as Amaryllis, step forth to sponsor this Beloved Fifth Ray, and it individualized itself in the form of plant and animal life upon the planet. In the beginning, Dear one, this was brought forth to bring the coding of the Green Ray upon the planet. It individualized even further as it mixed with the Yellow Ray and also with the Blue Ray. My work has been known also through Lady Virgo. I AM indeed Lady Amaryllis and I have individualized myself and come forth upon the Earth Plane and Planet as that of Beloved Lady Virgo.

Dear one, it is important that you both have streamed forth on the Fifth, Green Ray, and have given your service as an Elohim. You have incarnated in human form to be the speaker, or the voice, which comes through the human form to speak of the Devas, the Elementals, and the mighty voice of the Elohim. Who are these mighty Elohim? The Elohim is indeed the wind, rain, fire, and the earth, that which has been known throughout many of your times in Earth histories as the four elements. However, this is embodied even further in refined focused consciousness. Occasionally, there are those Elohim who step forth in human embodiment to bring the message of the Cosmic Being forth.

This work that you bring forth is a balanced work, Dear one, for there are those who have individualized, who typified that which is known as the hierarchy. There are those who have individualized, who typified the Earth itself. This work, brought forth to this planet, streams forth to that which is the Fifth Ray, and is brought to the office of Archangel Raphael. He has served as Chohan of this Fifth Ray, individualized as an Elohim. This work that you bring forth, Dear one, has indeed also been touched by this Beloved Fifth Ray, as you have understood these Beloved Deva and Elementals that have danced at your feet.

Dear one, your service first originated on the Pink Ray. This was the Ray in the creation and formation of this world, as you know it, that offered itself so compassionately to the rest of the universe, to offer a home, or a creative, safe space, as you would call it, for the Slows, as we have known them. They have been referred to in other times in your history, as those of the laggards; however, we prefer to simply call them the Slows. As you have understood, this all is energy, the choice of how fast or how slow energy shall spin. Through this spinning, space is created through the cooperation of light and sound. It is the beloved will then that is breathed in through the mighty I AM Presence, and the Higher Self. And through this, choice occurs. You have the choice to fill the space creatively, through mixtures of light and sound Rays to the language of the geometric shape. Do you understand?

Response: "Only in a general way."

Specifically, there is a balance to be brought forth, Dear one. Rest assured that the message of the Beloved Planet is brought forth, not only from the Heavenly Host, but also from grounding - not Earthly grounding, for this is not the message - but to be grounded in the wisdom and in the nurturing and in the love of the Beloved Planet itself, whom we know as Babajeran. I AM Lady Amaryllis and I bridge to you now Babajeran, if you so choose.

Response: "Yes."

I AM Babajeran. I AM the heart of this that you know as the planet that you live on. I AM indeed a Cosmic Being who has offered myself of service and in this service, I have taken, what you would call, much abuse. However, it is important that you understand that I welcome this abuse, for these tears that stream from my eyes are welcomed indeed, for the alignment is soon to begin and in this alignment, you Beloved beings of light will harken yourself to the Heavenly Host and be held as a mother holds her child to her breast. Dear one, it is with great joy that I come forth as Babajeran.

Now you shall understand that I AM THAT I AM, for it is indeed so true that Beloved Sanat Kumara has released the breath of love and service. This that I release to you, is all for the embodiment of love. Is it not to be that which will sustain and maintain energy at all frequencies, at all weight? Dear one, I AM Babajeran and I have offered myself to give to you that which would preclude your body, but also that which would preclude your energetic rates. For you see, Dear one, you contain within you not only seven or eight energy bodies, but you contain within collective bodies that we indeed share. It is my hope that together, Dear one, we shall ascend. This Ascension that we speak of is not the end-all or the be-all. Again, it is the opportunity to create; creation, not as an implosion or explosion, but only as a peaceful, expansive wave. Do you understand?

Response: "Yes."

It is important in this geophysical location that you understand that this is the only Golden City Vortex for the Golden Age that is activated [Editor's Note: several more have been activated since.].

Question: "How long has it been activated?"

It was activated approximately 12.3 years ago; however, it has not been until the most recent eight years that it has spun in the proper clockwise positioning. The activity that occurs within this area is, at times, a bit of a discomfort to Beloved Saint Germain and that which you know as Sananda. You must understand that the energy of this geophysical area is coarse indeed. We ask for you to offer yourself, if you choose, in service to the healing and the entry of the Golden Age. Are you ready to receive the prayer?

Response: "Yes."

> Beloved being of light that I AM,
> Stream forth these Golden Rays into my being.
> I AM resonating with all my focus,
> All that I AM,
> Into the golden light that streams from Divine Creation.
> Together we dance in the joy of being ONE.

I would be most happy to give you a brief history of Babajeran. I was accompanied by one who offered himself in service to me. As you see, all energy is expanded, and what is known as service is that which is founded on the laws of seven times seven. I have held within me up to fourteen genetic codings and these codings have streamed forth and graced this that I AM. This has been held, not only within what you refer to as DNA, but within what we call the Divine Coding. You are indeed as I AM; as I have offered myself, you are part of me. Is not that which is part of itself the same? As you hold within yourself Divine Creation, I hold within myself as a Divine Inheritor of the cosmos. You may call to me, Dear one, for this is where you speak to me. This Golden City Vortex serves as a great capillary of thought. This is indeed the most perfect place to usher in this Golden Age and you, Dear one, have been selected to bring forth this material. This is to reach as many as possible, for the healing of our bodies, as I would refer to them, is indeed a collective momentum. Do you understand?

Response: "Yes."

Understand, Dear one, all thoughts in this area direct to Babajeran, which incidentally, is only the coding of sound. All that you need at any given moment, all that you are at any given moment, is what is known as the symphony of life and sound to the focused will. And so that which you wish to create, or in this instance, Co-create, streams far to this mighty Vortex and radiates as a great capillary of thought to every point upon the planet. In your body, you hold within yourself that which is known as an Achilles Heel. Everyone holds a point within them, that if it is touched, it is instantly felt throughout the system. This which is known as Gobean is known also, or referred to, as an Achilles Heel. All that is touched, all that is thought, all that is, can instantaneously be projected through what is known as my entire planetary system. Through this, it may travel back to you and a continuous breath is then assured. It is time for me to take my leave.

Response: "Thank you for coming."

Blessings from the Heart of the Logos. Greetings, Beloved chelas, I AM Saint Germain. Do you have questions, Dear one, regarding that which has been brought forth by our Beloved Mother Babajeran?

Response: "Not unless there could be more specificity involved."

Dear one, we will take our leave. Ponder what has been brought to you and I will be glad to be of assistance, for you see, Dear one, I have worked long with Babajeran and I would be most happy to assist in any way that I can.

Response: "Thank you very much."

13

*Life is filled with invisible forces and unseen patterns
that drive the development and growth of
human consciousness.*

History of the Rays
Saint Germain

Madge returned the next evening and we continued with the spiritual instruction of Rays and Ray Forces. In the introduction of this teaching, Saint Germain clarified certain terms:

Light: An emanation equal to thought.

Sound: A vibration equal or similar to feeling and emotion.

Third Dimension: A dimension composed of thought, feeling, and action.

Dispensation: A conscious thought activity that occurs when one is aware, especially when applied during the release of a Ray Force.

Lightworker: Those workers who consciously use the focus of thought to change, heal, or alter Earthly circumstances and situations.

The following lesson on Rays includes important prophecies concerning the Golden Age and the appearance of two worlds that exist simultaneously.

The Golden Age is cyclical, and comprises a period of approximately ten-thousand years. Vedic texts describe four ages of time in relation to energy received from the Galactic Center – which is similar to the Ascended Masters' Great Central Sun. This larger sun is alleged to emit the non-visible light spectrum of the Rays of Light and Sound. During a Golden Age, or Kreta Yuga, one-hundred percent of this light is available on Earth. In a Silver Age, also known as Treta Yuga, fifty percent of light is available; and in a Bronze Age, often called Dvapara Yuga, twenty-five percent of light is available.

Currently, and according to the classic Puranic timing of the Yugas, Earth is in a Kali-Yuga period that started around the year 3102 BCE – the year that Krishna allegedly left the Earth. During this time period, which according to this Puranic timing lasts a total of 432,000 years – the ten-thousand year Golden Age period, also known as the *Golden Age of Kali Yuga*, is not in full force. Instead, it is a sub-cycle of higher light frequencies within an overall larger phase of less light energy.

This Golden Age is prophesied to raise the energy of Earth as additional light from the Galactic Center streams to our planet. This type of light is a non-visible, quasar-type light that is said to expand life spans and memory function, and nourish human consciousness, especially spiritual development. There are many theories as to when this prescient light energy began to flow to our planet. Some say it started about a thousand years ago, and others claim it began at the end of the nineteenth century. No doubt its influence has changed life on Earth for the better, and according to the I AM America Teachings, its effect began to encourage and guide human spiritual evolution around the year 2000 AD.

The Spiritual Teachers say that living in Golden Cities can magnify Galactic Energies and at their height, the energies will light the Earth between 45 to 48 percent – nearly reaching the light energies of a full-spectrum Treta Yuga or Silver Age on Earth. The Spiritual Teachers state, "The Golden Age is the period of time where harmony and peace shall be sustained." [For more information, see *The Ever Present Now*.]

I also channeled the Prophecy of "two worlds." That information explained how evolving human consciousness drives polarity, a gap fed by the unique differences of fear-based thinking and "a world of love." That lesson further explained unique parallels of those who spiritually evolve to experience the anomalies of Fourth- and Fifth-Dimension consciousness and those who do not. They, instead, stay within the confines of the conventional, Third-Dimensional world.

Saint Germain explained that as we grow and develop through the New Times, we literally shape-shift through several worlds, and learn how to integrate a new reality based on a new experience of time and space. "Worlds shall exist simultaneously, and they shall be judged not."

It was apparent that Madge had yet to find her place with the information. In the past, Dan, Sherry, and Len had avidly engaged the Spiritual Teachers and their limitless knowledge, yet for some reason Madge was often like a bystander, a detached witness. The Spiritual Teachers must have sensed her reserve, yet continued to supply a fascinating stream of spiritual instruction, analogy, and engaging new content.

Perhaps some of the most enchanting storytelling in this lesson was the Ascended Master creation-myth of the Rays and their historical impact on humanity. The esoteric science of the Rays explains the appearance of the Lemurian (Blue Ray), the Brihaspatites (Yellow Ray), and the Atlantean (Pink Ray). From the masters' viewpoint, civilizations are currently moving forward into the energies of the Fourth Ray, said to be the White Ray of Ascension. They are affiliated with the divine HU-man, the realized God Man. [Editor's Note: For more on the provenance of the Rays and the civilizations they helped to shape and form, see *The Map of the Ancients, Divine Destiny.*]

Toward the end of this lesson, the teachers shifted to the topic of the *Star seed*; spiritual terminology akin to group soul, or the *oversoul*. Analogous to the I AM Presence, the teachings of the Star seed divulge that we likely have simultaneous lifetimes, streaming into different, unique physical bodies, each governed by an individualized Higher Self. Apparently the I AM Presence can oversee up to twenty-two simultaneous lifetimes! That describes the sense that many of us often experience; a knowing that we are concurrently living on several different levels. Undoubtedly, I was moving beyond the initial excitement that I had discovered in the soul invigorating Spiritual Awakening. I humbly realized that this seemingly singular lifetime was interconnected with many other souls on Earth. Our conscious awareness, perceptions, and experiences were driven by immensely large, yet subtle, forces designed to instigate spiritual change and growth.

≋

I AM Saint Germain and I must ask permission to come forth to bridge to you, Dear one.

Response: "Proceed."

Welcome from the realm of the Spiritual Hierarchy of the Great White Brotherhood. We have listened to your questions regarding this work on the Earth Plane and Planet and we would like to step forward to give you a brief description of that which we have asked to be brought forth, to be dispensed among the Earth Plane. This work that comes forth is bridged to you through the Seventh Ray, the Transmuting Ray of Mercy and Forgiveness. When we speak of a Ray, Dear one, we speak of light and what is light in your world, but the world of thought? And so, we ask for you to focus your thought along the Ray of Mercy and Forgiveness, and all that streams forth is brought to take away the sense that you would have of separation with your divinity. You are a Divine Inheritor of this mighty Kingdom, of which I AM and which we all share and participate in.

Dear one, this work that this beloved vehicle has brought forth upon the Earth Plane and Planet is the work of the Fifth Ray, or what we would know as the Ray of Science and Healing. This is also the Ray that Beloved Mother Mary and Beloved Jesus, now known as Sananda, served upon, and it is also the Ray that brings forth this abstract thinking, which would break down and show the structure of all that is among the planets and creation.

You see, Dear one, we have said that there is truly no such thing as "spiritual"; there is no such thing as "etheric"; there is really no such thing as the "physical." What there is, Dear one, is energy, and this energy rotates, or "accelerates in spin." This acceleration, or this spin, as you would see it, is what determines where it shall be placed. It is qualified, then, to what is called "light" or "thought," and to what is also called "sound" or "feeling." In your world, as you know it presently in your Third Dimensional world, your life is composed of three layers: your Elemental Life Force, your thought, and your feelings; also, Dear one, the breath, or the aligned wheel. Do you understand?

Response: "Yes."

We shall proceed, and at any time, Dear one, if you wish to ask questions, we are here for your assistance. Assisting me is Beloved Mother Mary and Beloved Kuan Yin, and later they shall come forth to give their discourse to you.

This information which has been brought forth, streams forth to what is called the Fifth Ray. This Fifth Ray serves as the dispensation. All dispensation works with what is called a consciousness, or a conscious thought. Have you not, Dear one, seen a time in your life where you consciously thought that you could achieve something and, because you could hold the space for your conscious thought, you achieved it.

Response: "Yes, indeed."

This is what we refer to as the conscious thought, or consciousness, that streams forth among mankind. This is what we refer to as "light." Upon the Earth Plane and Planet at this time, there are many people who refer to themselves as light workers, but few who understand what this concept truly is. You are dealing with the energy of thought and how you wish or choose to qualify your thought.

We enter into what is called the world of sound, or the thought of the feeling, or the intuitive world among the human. The world of sound is indeed, as we would call this work, the desire to lead one to achieve. You have many feelings within your world; you have known anger, lust, even at times, you have misidentified the feeling that you would call love, joy, extreme happiness. All of these that you recall feeling are actually associated with pitch, for what are they, Dear one, but only that which resonates a desire within the thought itself. Again, it gives the pattern for you to go forth and Co-create with your thought. So, this is your world of thought and feeling. Do you understand?

Response: "Yes."

Thought and feeling then proceed on to the world of the aligned will. We have explained, in short, a bit of the work of the Beloved El Morya and that which he serves, the focused will to stream forth for the First Ray. The work of the Golden Age is soon to come upon the planet and you shall be living and breathing it. This Golden Age has long been predicted and prophesied by many upon the Earth Plane and Planet, for over six centuries, and now you are at this turning point, or pivot point, as we call it. This pivot point is where you may choose to come forth into the Golden Age.

The Golden Age is the period of time where harmony and peace shall be sustained. As we have said before, this is yet to be achieved upon the Earth Plane and Planet, and the Earth, herself, or Beloved Babajeran, has offered herself as service to you. And she has offered herself to align with that of the human will. As you have offered yourself to align with the Divine Plan, she offers herself to align with the human plan. And so, what comes forth is the cooperative, collective effort and global Ascension. This work, if I may continue, Dear one, comes forth on the Fifth Ray, or that which speaks of Babajeran. This work that we have given of Earth Change material comes from what is known as the Sixth collective body in the world of human bioenergetics. Do you not see, Dear one, how light can change around what is known as the Human Aura through the thought?

Response: "Yes, I can intellectually understand. I've never seen an aura, however."

Have you been able to feel this field as it changes?

Response: "That I can do. I can feel it, but I've never seen it."

Beloved Babajeran, who has offered her energy, which is in the core of this planet itself, is no different. Are there not days, Dear one, when you awake and the energy actually feels different?

Response: "Oh, yes . . . every other day."

And so, she has offered herself to align with your energetics. As you offer yourself to the Divine Plan, she offers herself to the human will. These two Co-create together and an alignment occurs and the ascent to Fourth Dimension; the sustained period of time in Fourth Dimension of peace and harmony is then allowed to be. This is what we ask of you, Dear one, to accept your eternal freedom in the Ascension, for Ascension is the sustained energetic. As you have understood your world of thought and feeling, that all is continual movement and change; we ask for you to expand into a world of change and also a world that can sustain. For these two shall stand side by side, Brother to Sister.

It has long been prophesied that there would be, at this time, two worlds. There would be a choice for either a world of fear or a world of love. But there really is no choice. You know in your mind, that perhaps the easiest way to be is to discern, to make the choice, but I ask you to expand beyond this and to understand that there really is no choice, that it really just is. This is a Fourth or Fifth Dimensional concept that we ask you to expand to. You may ask of yourself, 'Well, how can this be, if I have no choice? Do I not have my free will to exercise?" In this world or density that we speak of, beyond the world of the Third Dimension, there exists the world where all is. For you see, Dear one, these two worlds shall exist simultaneously and they shall be judged not; for there to be a period of sustained harmony and peace, mankind must judge no longer. Do you have questions?

Response: "No, I'm following you completely. I realize that I have passed the point where there is no choice. In other words, the choice was made long ago and so now you are on the path of the choice. That's the way I see it, anyway."

And yet, Dear one, have you not been asked to individualize?

Response: "Well, yes, but that doesn't mean that you're not on the path of your choice, I don't think so, anyway."

What we have instructed our pupils is, "to be or not to be," to accept life or to not accept. One would see this as a path of choice; however, you are simply accepting the path. Life is an eternal creation. However, there must be the one who will step forth to the power of desire; to step forth to the desire to be as a created being, made in the image and likeness of I AM THAT I AM; to step forth as a Co-creator. We have given you many discourses, given you the many laws of the universe, to show you, Dear one, how energy reacts with other types of energy. It is only that we wish for you to be educated, Dear one. And while, in a sense, it has been your choice to accept or not to accept, are not these laws just as they are? I hope that this explains individualization, for you see, Dear one, to individualize is to focus your energy and focusing your energy allows you then to achieve - or, better yet, to express that Divine Spark within you. And while you have within you a reciprocal relationship with the mighty I AM Presence, remember, Dear one, you are indeed created, and you are indeed creative.

And now, I would like to give you further information. You had asked yesterday for more specific details regarding your work. There is one slight detail that we have overlooked; however, it is of vast importance. We would ask if you would like to be of service to the Spiritual Hierarchy of the Great White Brotherhood?

Response: "I'm sure I would. At this point, if I said 'Yes,' I wouldn't even know what I'd be saying 'Yes' to, so give me some time on that, if you would."

He's laughing.

Would one please pardon my expression of joy; for you see, the reason we would ask is that all energy is founded upon the bond of agreement.

Response: "Well, I'm sure you're exactly where I'm headed for. I just want to give you an intelligent answer is all. I'll probably go there - yes, I'm sure - otherwise, I wouldn't be here."

Well, this is so, Dear one, for are not all things timed and ordered in a way that we would say, not divine disorder, but Divine Order? I understand what you have imparted, Dear one. I would like to give you a brief history of the Rays and Races as they have come to this planet, so you will understand your part, if you so choose, in service to this work. May I proceed?

Response: "Oh, yes . . . do."

As I have discussed before, the first race to come to this planet was known as the Blues. This race of great beings lived in water, which covered the entire planet. At that time, there was no land whatsoever, but only a ball covered by a continuous body of water. You have seen remnants of this great race and civilization of beings. They are known as dolphins and whales. They carry within them a consciousness that even supersedes the human. They have offered themselves in service, to remain upon the planet to hold space for the restoration of Prahna.

The Second Ray to come forth was known as the Yellow Ray. You will remember the Yellow Ray as the great Golden Ray, for during this time, the consciousness was held in a like form. These beloved beings were known as the Golden Ray and during this time, a continuous body of land floated over the continuous body of water. It was during this time of this beloved Second-Ray Race, the Golden-Yellow Race, that the Light of God Never Failed, for their body and energetic structure was built upon staying within the Light of God that Never Failed. This is what many of you remember as Prahna. As life would go in, life would go out; the continuous cycle of sunlight into these bodies of light assured a continuous circulation into their system. The expression of divinity became complete and many expressed the great creation of this Golden-Yellow Ray upon the Earth Plane and Planet, then known as Prahna. And many ascended and continued their work as life streams upon other planets.

The great Creators decreed that the Third Ray should stream forth, this which is known as the Pink Ray. This beloved Pink Ray held within it, the continuous love of the heart, and recognized that it was indeed connected to a Source beyond their own Brother or Sister. And in realizing this connection, Divine Compassion streamed forth upon the face of this planet. And those life streams that were held in planets far away cried to the planet and said, "Take me, Dear one, take me to your planet. Give me your home; let me too learn compassion." And how could this race turn them away, this noble Red Race, which indeed was the first race ever to walk upon land. Again, the continuous disk still floated over the continuous body of water, and as the others came and incarnated, the genetic mixture evolved the physical body as you would recognize it. This was the beginning of civilization, as you know it, and this is where your epoch has begun. This beloved Pink-Ray Race, which accepted the others from the universe, had heard the cry through their heart of compassion and offered their intelligence and this beloved planet in service. And this, Dear one, specifically, is where we all are.

We have yet to perceive beyond the Third Ray. However, this opportunity is soon to be. The Fourth Race is ready to stream forth; the Fourth Ray of Resurrection and Purity; the Fourth Ray from Archangel Gabriel and Serapis Bey. In less than twenty years, Dear one, this Ray shall stream forth upon the planet, for the work of this Pink Ray is soon to be complete. Have you not heard all that has been said through other beings that are coming forth through what you call channeled material? Is it not time for you to enter into the agreement of your heart?

Response: "Oh, yes . . . I think I have."

This is the common thread, the commonality, as we would call it, that you see, for we are at the end of an epoch.

Response: "Yes, and I also feel that we're at the beginning of one. We're in the birth pangs."

You are correct, Dear one, and it is beloved Serapis Bey who shall come forth to sponsor this Ray and this great race of beings. They shall understand the purity of physical expression and also the resurrection of, not only the spiritual immortality, but physical immortality. As we have explained, life is only the movement of energy. Now, Dear one, do you have questions?

Question: "Just one little detail. It's going to get a little crowded around here, isn't it, if this physical body does not die? Or, are you saying that the energy will just take another level, another vibration?"

As you have understood soul groups or soul clusters, yes. There will be the collection of certain energetic life streams back into the ONE, original, Beloved I AM. In previous work, we have brought forth the illustration of the Star seed and I would ask for you to review this. Perhaps this will give you an insight into understanding.

Question: "Are you saying a Star seed is similar to the group soul?"

Very similar, Dear one. Beloved mighty I AM Presence, through that which is known as the Higher Self, is allowed, at any given time upon the Earth Plane and Planet, to embody up to twenty-two life streams.

Question: "Are the same number of souls in a group, or do they vary?"

To further explain, you have what is called the Higher Self. This beloved Higher Self has been misrepresented as the I AM Presence. The Higher Self is connected to the I AM Presence. The I AM Presence, as an ascended body, knows no limitation of time. All it understands is creation. The Higher Self descends from the I AM Presence. This Higher Self then streams forth from its energetic fields, a space to create your embodiment. It is through the I AM Presence that the expression of divinity is allowed and the energetic is anchored at the center of the Heart Chakra. Have you not come up to one that you felt the energy of their heart? Were you not drawn to them, as a child would be drawn to his own parent?

[Editor's Note: For more information on the I AM Presence and the Higher Self see *Divine Destiny.*]

Response: "Oh, yes."

This is an instant recognition of the intuitive feeling, or the sound or the pitch.

Question: "You have met a kindred soul from your group soul, is this correct?"

This is correct, Dear one. Your mighty I AM Presence has the right to dispense what is known as Dharma. You have understood the Law of Karma. That which we dispense as the Law of Dharma, is the abundance of the universe, to stream forth into the life stream at any given time. Perhaps, mighty I AM Presence is ready to reunite with its collective energy; it has set out into the Earth Plane and Planet to gather information to bring a wholeness to itself. Perhaps it has individualized the Ray of Divine Wisdom and shoots it out from six beings. Few have understood that there is truly no time, but only the timing of events. Have you not felt yourself living in two places at the same time?

Question: "I've felt myself living on two levels at the same time; is that what you mean?"

Have you ever had the experience that perhaps you were bi-located? In other words, living in two physical places at the same time?

Response: "I have experienced that, yes."

I would like to tell you, Dear one, that presently you have five embodiments expressing at this time.

Question: "Do you want to tell me where they are?"

Two are . . .

The phone rings, disturbing this taping, and the tape runs out.

14

Never forget your divine, immortal spiritual self!
Beauty shares both burden and joy – witness
and spiritual experience.

The Cup
Saint Germain
Mary
El Morya
Babajeran
Kuan Yin
Sananda

The phone rang early one morning; it was a call from a Long Island, NY, metaphysical bookstore. The owner, Marjean, invited me to speak for an afternoon in the bookstore's conference room and offered to pay a small speaker's fee, plus, my airfare. Excited, I mention this to my sister who lived in Oklahoma, and she suggested that if I could drive to her home in a day, she would watch the kids and I could fly out of the Tulsa, OK, airport the next day. I studied my road atlas and quickly figured it would be about a nine-hour drive from Albuquerque to Tulsa. Even though it would be a long day's drive, I could rendezvous with Len in New York and the two of us could teach together. After speaking again with Marjean, she scheduled me for a four-hour presentation.

The children were thrilled that they would, yet again, be able to go on another summer road trip. A week later we were up and on the road by 4 AM, and arrived in Albuquerque around six o'clock in the morning. I treated the kids to breakfast at Denny's Restaurant, fueled the car, and began our adventure across the panhandle of Texas and onward to Oklahoma. The drive was much longer than expected and by the time we arrived in Oklahoma City, I was exhausted. I found another Denny's Restaurant where I pulled over, and I located a phone booth to call my sister. "How much further is Bartlesville?" I think she sensed the desperation in my voice. "It is about another two hours and you will be here . . ."

I was so tired I could barely think, and my mind was floating on a cloud of fatigue when I heard Sherry's voice repeating a phrase from a reading about a year ago: *you will take a trip to the East Coast that will change your life.* These words jolted me back into reality, and I immediately realize that *this* was the prophetic trip from her vision. Excitement and caffeine fueled my next couple of hours as I drove the Grand I AM onto Bartlesville, OK.

After settling in at my sister's spacious home, the children happily played with their cousins. "Are you sure you're up to this?" I questioned my sister, one final time. My older sister, always self-assured, and perhaps one of the strongest people I've ever known smiled, "Of course – and I hope you'll stay a little extra longer, after your trip, so we can visit."

Like my grandmother, my sister Karyn is a petite, yet physically strong person. Early in married life she had been thrown a curve ball: her oldest child had been born with a rare form of congenital muscular dystrophy. I'd often asked her, "How do you do it?" And my question would always be followed by a gentle laugh, reinforced by an underlying breath of unshakeable faith and perseverance, as she'd say, "I just do it. This is *what* I do." I had no doubt that the children would be just fine while I was away for a week.

My slide presentation was safely tucked under my seat as the airplane flew above irrigation circles and a patchwork quilt of fields that covered the undulating landscape of the mid-west states. This was my first trip to the Northeast, and to date, the farthest east I'd ever traveled was to Oklahoma! It had been over a month since I'd last seen Len, and I yearned to see his face, with his generous smile, and feel his arms and his loving bear-hug embrace.

The plane landed smoothly into MacArthur Airport. While walking toward the luggage area, I notice a small statured woman, with long dark curls and dark eyes, holding a piece of paper with "Lori" written on it. I walked up and offered her my hand, "Hi, I'm Lori." She reached out to hug me, "I'm Athena, and I want to thank-you, again, for flying all the way out here. How was your flight?"

I instantly felt comfortable. There was a gentleness and kindness in her eyes, yet I noted an air of focused intensity. "My trip was amazing, and . . ." I lost my train of thought while my eyes were searching for Len. I couldn't seem to locate him. "Sorry, I'm looking to see if my partner Len has arrived . . ." As soon as the words were spoken, I saw his familiar face. He was tucked in a corner, with his massage table learning against the wall.

"Well this will be a challenge!" Athena said. She was a bit frustrated as we fit the large table, with the three of us, into her small sports car. It was a bit comical. Len's table and our suitcases were in the back, and the three of us were crammed into the front, with little space for Athena to drive, let along shift gears. "I guess this is a good way to get to know each other," Len joked, as we pulled into the driveway of her small two-bedroom home, about twenty minutes from the airport.

"Well, we've made it," Athena said. "Are you hungry?" I glanced at my watch, and it was now dark. It was five o'clock my time, 8 PM here on the East Coast. We unloaded ourselves from the crowded cab and gathered our luggage. Athena's home was located on the Long Island Sound, and in the background I could hear the tide of waves – coming from the Atlantic Ocean. Wow, the Atlantic Ocean, I'd never seen it before.

Athena continued, "Maybe I can make some pasta? I know an Italian recipe with broccolini and garlic – you're vegetarian, right?" She escorted us to her guest room, a small neat space with a vase of fresh flowers adorning the window sill. "That sounds great Athena. Can you give us a moment?" I answered, and quietly shut the door. Len leaned the large massage table against the wall and placed the extra suitcase on the floor. "Gosh, I've missed you so much, and I have so much to tell you!" he said. I fell into Len's arms, yet I noticed something was subtly different and a bit off. He seemed remote – distant.

"Everything okay?" I intuitively asked. "Just tired," Len answered. "It's been a long day." Again, this was an odd response as Len is rarely, *if ever*, tired. I was a bit nervous. Something *had* changed. But before we could speak another word to one another Athena's voice interrupted, "The pasta is almost ready!"

That night we lingered over a pot of French-pressed coffee and conversation about the Ascended Masters. Athena was connected and fervently devoted to the Spiritual Teacher El Morya, whom she referred to as the "Commander."

The next day our presentation went smoothly, and I marveled over how well Len and I presented and taught together. After Len shared the *Violet Flame for Sunrise and Sunset*, a gentleman approached both of us. He had a kind demeanor, yet was somewhat persistent in his questions: "Will you be back to teach again? Do you have any other connections here? If not, I can make arrangements . . . do you do private consultations?" Len stepped aside, and the two engaged in deep conversation that lasted for almost an hour as Athena and I tidied up the space and collected the slide projector and presentation materials.

Len had planned a day of sightseeing in New York City, and nervously held my hand as we traveled on the train toward Grand Central Station. "Is there any place special you want to go [to] or see?" he asked. "No, you're the tour guide," I responded. I felt a bit like the country mouse, even though I enjoyed the synergy of city. Most importantly, I was happy just to spend time alone with Len.

We walked everywhere; from Times Square to Rockefeller Center, and found ourselves at Macy's for a quick lunch. As a small girl, my sister and I would watch the Thanksgiving Day's Parade on TV, and I always wondered what it would be like to be in the city at Christmas, away from the blowing snow of the open prairie and among the tall skyscrapers glittered with storefronts. And now I was here, sipping an iced tea on Thirty-Fourth Street, in downtown Manhattan. "Remember the guy that we met yesterday? Len asked between bites of a grilled cheese. "Yes," I said. I assumed he meant the short guy with all the questions, who offered to help schedule classes.

Len continued, "Well, he is interested in energy work and I've scheduled a session with him. Would you like to travel to New Jersey tomorrow to meet with him?" Len was reflective for a moment. Before I could respond, he blurted out, "Also, I have something to tell you." He paused again, "I know you've noticed that something is different, and I don't know how to tell you this. I'm uncertain if I am coming back to Socorro, at least for a while . . ." His voice trailed off, and I sensed a note of confusion in his voice.

"What's going on?" I asked, trying to hold back my emotion and obvious disappointment. "A lot," Len replied, "You know I've been scheduling energy-work sessions in Philadelphia and I've been giving short living room talks – it seems to be working well and I've been able to earn some extra income. I think I should stay here a bit longer. It will help us out financially."

I didn't respond. For some reason, and perhaps because of my own denial, I couldn't deal with facing, yet again, Len's continued absence in my life, or better said, *our life*. We now had a home together and obligations, and the children missed him – *I missed him*. Yet, a part of me completely understood; we actually did need more money and he was apparently having success in manifesting that. In the back of my mind though, I still asked, "Is there another reason that he is staying away?"

We took the subway to the World Trade Center and stood in the cool shadow of the towering megaliths. Walking back to the train station, Len pulled me over to a brightly lit café, "You've never had a slice until you taste this," and he handed me perhaps the largest piece of pizza I'd ever seen. I noticed Len folding the large slice while he explained between bites, "You've never tasted anything like this in the west . . . huh?" For a moment I thought of the little pizza joint Len and I had often stopped at for a quick supper when we lived in Asotin, just a few blocks from the bike trail in Clarkston, ID. This was an extraordinary moment, and *no* – I'd never tasted pizza *this* good. But it was a bit unfair to compare the east to the west – they were two unique, and different experiences altogether – almost like trying to compare the color red to the color blue. They each had a distinct pace, flavor, and vibration.

At that moment I silently asked myself, "Maybe he is missing his culture? Is that why he doesn't want to come back to New Mexico?" Before I could deliberate another insecure thought, Len grabbed my hand and pointed to the clock, "We need to go or we'll miss our connection." We boarded an early evening train back to Long Island. I gazed out the train window at the busy concrete landscape and the setting sun, and noted the brilliance of the Violet Flame, with its glorious wisps of pinkish purple. In the center of the city, with its office buildings, warehouses, traffic and crowds of people rushing home, I noted the peaceful, calm, abiding silence of the flame.

The minute we arrived back at Athena's home, she handed me a note, "He's called several times, and I think you'd better call him back." I immediately noticed the phone number – it was from Oklahoma. I called my brother-in-law to discover that my niece had accidentally fallen and broken her hip. She was in surgery and I needed to return there as soon as possible. I made several calls and realized that the earliest I could return to Tulsa was in forty-eight hours. I changed my flight. I called my brother-in-law back and he was undoubtedly annoyed. My sister, who was watching the children, was now at the hospital with her daughter and had to hire a babysitter.

"Well, I won't be able to go with you to New Jersey tomorrow," I told Len. He responded, "That's okay, I think I can handle it." I got the feeling that he was actually relieved that I wouldn't be there. Suddenly, a swirl of repressed emotion erupted into righteous anger, "Are you still in this with me?" I asked, my voice obviously expressing annoyance. I didn't care that I was standing in the middle of someone's kitchen, someone whom I barely knew. I had completely rearranged my life to be with Len and the vision that we shared, and now it seemed like he was quietly slipping out an open back door. Not only was I angry, I was sincerely confused. "Please – enlighten me!" My voice was now a bit higher, almost terse, and

I stared directly in Len's eyes. Immediately Len walked toward me and held me, both to calm me down and reassure me. "I promise I will be home soon . . . I promise."

Len left early the next day to catch his train, and I had one day alone with Athena before my flight back to Oklahoma. Athena was a unique combination of spit-fire passion, with a deep loyalty to the Ascended Masters while, contrarily, she was also extremely feminine. She sensed the conflict between Len and me and responded with understanding and compassion. "Is there anything you'd like to do today?" Athena asked, always the flawless host.

I looked out her living room window onto the beautiful shore with the sun lightly dancing off the water, "How about a walk and staying put today?" I asked. I admit, I was feeling tired. After teaching, and the previous day in the city, my energy level was low. "Perfect," she responded, "That was just what I was going to suggest. And we'll go out for dinner tonight at one of my favorite cafes, my treat."

While we walked along the water's edge, Athena shared her background with me. She had worked in the real estate industry for many years. Yet several years earlier, she had begun to study Ascended Master Teachings, starting with the Bridge to Freedom material, then into the Ballard information, and onward into contemporary teaching. After that, she experienced a full-force Spiritual Awakening, and similar to what many people often report, she began a unique re-prioritization of her life. She meditated daily, worked vigorously with the Violet Flame, and noticed that alongside lifestyle changes, her overall energy shifted. She began to spend time at and volunteered for a local metaphysical-spiritual center.

There was a unique ease about our friendship. Even though we had just met, it felt like we had always known each other, and that our meeting at this exact time and exact place was indeed no mistake. Also, if there was ever a time when I needed a good friend, and in this case, *an enlightened friend,* it was *now.*

I revealed some of my personal experiences with her about the Masters, the channeling of the Map, and our recent move to Socorro – the eastern door of the Golden City of Gobean. "I've always wanted to live in the Southwest," she commented, after I shared my insights about the spiritual Vortex with its stunning orange and gold sunsets, and the indigo nights adorned with brilliant stars so close you can almost touch them.

"What projects are you working on now?" Athena inquired. Late evening was approaching, and I knew I should get to bed for my flight the next day. I sensed her sincere inquiry, and volumes of information suddenly streamed from my almost channeled, second wind of energy. I divulged how my first book was almost ready for press, and that it contained all of the prophetic information from the Spiritual Teachers regarding the I AM America Map and the Golden Cities. "Well this book needs to be published," she stated matter-of-factly. "How much money do you need?"

The last bid I had received for printing the book was over $8,000 for a minimum run of 2,000 units. Plus, I knew I would have extra expenses with photography, film costs, and cover design. "Well, I know I will have at least $8,000 in printing expenses alone," I replied. Athena interrupted me, and her dark eyes flashed with certainty, "I am writing you a check for $10,000 – will that be enough?"

I was literally speechless. With the exception of Len, I'd never had anyone help me financially with I AM America. My eyes watered and my voice filled with emotion as I said, "That is a lot of money – how do you want to be repaid?" Athena promptly responded, "I'm not too worried about that . . . I know that some way, somehow this will all work out." And with that, she handed me a check.

On my flight to Tulsa, my mind was a jumble of many thoughts; my current conflict with Len, my niece's surgery, Athena's generosity, the presentation and the possibility of further classes, and the most pressing question, "when would Len return?" I couldn't help but reflect again upon Sherry's prophetic words, and I felt the winds of change upon me. Yet, I was uncertain if I welcomed yet another transition into another of my life's numerous transformations. And more importantly, I needed to place my focus back on my children – summer would soon come to a close and our time together would be limited.

Back in Tulsa, and after checking in with the children and relieving the babysitter, we all piled into the car to visit my sister and niece at the hospital. Chelsea seemed to be recovering from her surgery. However, my sister was totally spent from the ordeal, and needed rest and the privacy of her home, without company. I decided it was best to head home in the morning.

Before I had left Long Island, Len had handed me an envelope stuffed with cash: "Be sure to pay the rent and the utility bill." As I drove away from the red hills of Oklahoma and headed west toward the high desert lands of New Mexico, I decided that I had enough money to stop for a night. I pulled off the interstate into a dusty little Texan town east of Amarillo, and found a roadside hotel with a large sparkling pool and a nearby Pizza Hut, for our dinner.

The children splashed in the pool and then, later, in our room, finished the last slices of pizza while they watched a movie on the TV. Even though I was a bit road weary and my day had been inordinately filled, I felt an unusual emptiness. I grabbed my personal notebook, and gave David, my ex-partner, a quick call. The phone rang twice, and immediately he picked up, "Well hello gorgeous, I'm so happy you called." It felt so good to hear his voice and before I could respond he asked, "Where are you?"

"I'm someplace in Texas, heading toward Amarillo. I've just left my sister's [home] in Oklahoma, and pulled over for the night," and then my conversation released a floodgate of words; words that retold the story of my flight to New York, words that enthusiastically described the presentation in Long Island, hopeful words that expressed my meeting with Athena and our friendship, and most of all, the words that disclosed Len's departure and revealed my deep concern that our relationship hung by a thread. And then I added, "David, I have moments that I think I may have made the wrong decision by ending our relationship . . ." My voice trailed off and for about a minute, I heard nothing but the static of the phone line.

Then I heard his eloquent voice, "Thanks for telling me . . . that means a lot to me." Another pause, and then the wise words of this friend I'd known and trusted for many years said, "Give it time. Be patient. He obviously has something unresolved," and he chuckled, "Remember I told you – you're a packaged deal." I smiled when he said this, and remembered the first time he said this phrase that described the four of us – a single mother with three children, and his desire to buy us a home.

I glanced about the small hotel room and I tightly hung onto the telephone receiver. Carson was lying on the bed quietly reading a book, and Bryn and Kait were sitting on the floor in their pajamas, immersed in television. At that moment I realized that all I really wanted was to go *home*. And even though Socorro did not feel like home, for the present moment it *was* my home. The next week Madge and I resumed our channeled sessions.

As I've mentioned in the past, that the Spiritual Teachers must know every detail of our lives, from the most pressing to the minute. I listened to the following lesson several times after it was received, and each time I gleaned new insight. Even though the Spiritual Teachers would not tell me exactly what to do regarding my present circumstances of living without Len, they astutely reminded me of the universal laws through their spiritual teachings of *The Cup*. The best advice that I could understand and apply to my situation was, "as you give out, is that not the measure in which you receive?" So, apparently, and especially now, I constantly reminded myself that the remarkable love that Len and I shared would survive time and distance.

In order to gain further understanding about *The Cup*, I offer these insights. The Cup is both literal and metaphoric. According to the Spiritual Teachers, the Cup is filled with an elixir, also known as an *amrita* – in Sanskrit terms. Amrita is a special, unique liquid formula that is often drunk by the Gods, and it grants immortality. This teaching is both myth and reality. To drink this special elixir is akin to accepting that we are, indeed, divine, and our divinity is innate and cannot be separated or taken from us through physical death. This form of spiritual immortality is carried with us through our many lifetimes upon Earth, and inevitably holds a blueprint for Ascension, unstained by karma or human imperfection. This elixir is offered to us so we will not forget our gift of spiritual freedom, and to engender a remembrance of our spiritual immortality. The Cup is also a symbol of neutrality and grace. In its purest state, it is held by the Angelic Host, who pours it upon humanity to restore harmony, abundance, and peace.

This lesson is also filled with many new insights on Ascension. Saint Germain described spiritual liberation as the "expansion of the soul." The spiritual teacher El Morya further developed this lesson to include a *personal expansion*, calibrated by a gentle, yet disciplined, will. Interestingly, he described a meditation that he asked to be performed at 1 PM, every afternoon, within the Golden City of Gobean. The meditation is simple and can be done anywhere: just close your eyes and visualize the color Blue surrounding your aura and energy fields. Use intention to manifest Transformation, Harmony, and Peace.

Intention is perhaps the most vital component of this meditation. If you focus on the Blue Ray for only one minute – fine. If, however, you are led into a twenty-minute visual meditation with the Blue Flame, that's even better. Of course, it is best to practice this spiritual technique within the Gobean Vortex. Apparently this Vortex's energies will help to magnify results. But if you are not in the actual Vortex, yet you feel an affinity for this Spiritual Vortex and its spiritual attributes of Transformation, Harmony, and Peace – you can still practice this meditation and become a *Step-Down Transformer* of this unique energy.

Look up Step-Down Transformer in the glossary, at the end of this book. I have added this information so you will understand how important this spiritual work can be on both personal and global levels. The technique is restorative to your will and it empowers personal choice. It is also remarkably healing for humanity, and is akin to the heavenly angels pouring the amrita of Transformation and Peace upon the Earth. Perhaps Sananda's words explain this best, "Live your life as ONE and live your life as one of many. I raise this Cup, as we shall never forget the divinity housed in the heart of service."

Undeniably, throughout the previous month, my beloved sister Karyn, my new friend Athena, and my old friend David poured the angelic, grace-filled Cup of the heavens upon my life. Now, with acceptance and love, I poured a Cup of patience upon my relationship with Len.

❧

I AM Saint Germain and I welcome you to our round table. Before me are four others who have joined us this evening. To my right is Beloved El Morya; to my left is Beloved Kuthumi; behind me is Beloved Mother Mary; and off to the side is Beloved Archangel Michael. Dear one, we all request your presence this moment, and your permission to enter into your energy field. Do we have this?

Response: "You certainly do."

I have come forth on the Transmuting Ray of Mercy and Forgiveness. I realize, Dear one, that you may be bored at times in hearing my introduction; however, according to Hierarchal Law, it is our duty, our responsibility, and also "agreement," to ask permission to enter into your field and also to identify who we are and the Ray that we work upon. For the work of Forgiveness upon the Earth Plane and Planet assures that love will stream forth into the hearts of men forever. Amen, Amen, Amen. The angels sing this choir to the Heavenly Host. Mercy and Forgiveness shall reign upon this planet, and peace, prosperity, harmony, and abundance will be restored to what you know now as Earth, to what we know as Prahna. Dear one, we gather now with our Cups to drink together; for as you know, it is the Cup that we drink from which we will never forget.

Response: "I'll drink to that!"

Dear one, life is to be enjoyed and it is to be a celebration. We judge not the actions of mankind, only that which is the motive, the pure heart. For you see, Dear one, life is motion and eternal and that is what we celebrate. So, take your life and use it to the fullest. Take your life in celebration and joy. Take your life in the fullness of All That Is. Dear one, is not this the Ascension? Using your life to its fullest expression of our moment? Is not this pure joy, that which you would extend at all times? Take your life and use it constructively. Create and enjoy. Do you understand?

Response: "I certainly do!"

This is the message that we bring forth to the Earth Plane and Planet. It is not a message that you would see to be dark, or that you would see to be burdensome. Do you not understand, Dear one, that when you release discrimination, or even decision, that would take you away from that position you would call blame? For you see, Dear one, for you to blame, you must also judge, and it seems as though humankind, particularly, blames mostly itself. Man must understand that he is not to blame, that he is the expression of full creation and that full creation is indeed divine.

Response: "I understand that."

And so, we raise the Cup that we might drink and never forget. This Cup, as Sananda has explained, is the Cup that we all touch, for once you touch the Cup, are you not responsible for its contents? When you lift this Cup to your lips and drink of its contents, are you not taking this into your being and into yourself? And so, you return the Cup to the table. Is not the Cup still your responsibility?

Response: "Absolutely!"

Dear one, we appreciate your understanding of this lesson. You see, there have been many who would take the Cup and its contents and discard the Cup and say: "This is no longer mine. I shall put this from me, and that which I have used, I shall not return." But you see, Dear one, it is an Eternal Law that for every intake, there is the outtake. With the continuation of the cycle in this particular universe, there is a balanced exchange between "in" and "out." It's that simple, Dear one: As above, so below. You could observe this in nature and in all things that occur in your worldly affairs. Do you not even see this in the friendships that you have upon this expression that you share? For it is indeed, "as above, so below," as you give out, is that not the measure in which you receive?

Response: "Yes, I agree with that, certainly."

And that is not to say, "An eye for an eye" or "A tooth for a tooth," for that's too limiting. For you see, Dear one, that which is given with a pure Heart's Desire will return sevenfold. It always does and it always shall. These are the eternal Laws of

Creation which your universe has been founded upon. This universe was created to have abundance; this universe was created to have harmony. This is the expression of God in Action: Harmony, Abundance, and Peace. This period shall be sustained for longer than a thousand years, and it is our hope that humankind is ready to rise. And so, I raise this Cup and toast you, humankind. Come forth, Dear one, as the glorious God-Free beings that you truly are! Accept your eternal freedom in the Light of God that Never Fails. Dear one, this is a banquet and a feast prepared for you, a celebration from the hosts of the heavens! Welcome, welcome to our banquet.

Now, I would like to explain to you the Elixir which we drink and that which I share with you. You see, Dear one, the civilization which was known as Atlantis, and even beyond that, from the solar system of the Pleiades, this substance came, Dear one, so that you would never forget. It is brought forth to grant you your longevity, to hold a continuous state, so you would accept, and enjoy, and create through your Ascension. Ascension is not only that which disciplines the body, but it is brought forth for joy; it is brought forth for the alignment; it is brought forth so that you may create as an eternal being of creativity. Dear one, Ascension was never brought to burden mankind; it was never brought so that you would say, "This is the way" or "that is the way"; "my way is better"; "that way is wrong and this way is right." Dear one, it was brought to glorify creation – *All That Is* – so that the greatest majesty of All That Is shines forth and expands into eternity. Accept this, Dear one: Ascension is expansion. It is nothing more, nothing less. It is as simple as that. It is only expansion.

Dear one, you are the Divine Inheritors of this Kingdom, and this shall not be denied to you. It is so, Dear one. You hold within your hearts what is known as the Eight-sided Cell of Perfection, that which streams forth in Divine Immaculate Conception. With your permission, Beloved Mother Mary would like to speak.

Response: "Granted."

Mary comes forward. I'll explain to you what she looks like. She is small in stature. She has a cloak about her and over her head. A brilliant green light is all around her. Her face is a milky-cream color, and her eyes have gold and green in them. The vibration is one of total warmth and acceptance.

Welcome, Dear heart, I AM Mary and I come forth on that which is the Fifth Ray. I have individualized upon the Earth Plane that which is the healing heart, where the healing heart takes within its hands the fashioning of the actions from which this work comes. Beloved Saint Germain has explained to you the concept of being held immaculate. Dear one, I hold you in my hands as immaculate beings. I see you never stained by what you would call karma; I see you never stained by what you would call imperfection, for I hold you immaculately and, as you know, it is the thought that determines the action.

Is this not the most beautiful thought that you could hold of yourself, that you are indeed immaculate? Dear one, how could I see you in any other way? It was I who fashioned this which streams forth now to your heart. I have held it close to my own heart and I extend it on to you. This is a simple lesson, Dear one, to see yourself as nothing but immaculate; fresh, clean, streaming forth into the universe.

You are only children, and I see your innocence. Would I weep to see you? Never, I say, for the tears I hold in my eyes are tears of joy. You are washed clean, Dear one; washed clean, not through that which you would call trial or tribulation, but you are washed clean because you are immaculate. I see your innocence; I feel your innocence; and I perceive your innocence. As you have understood that the thought will hold the space, continue to hold the space that you are immaculate, Dear one, fashioned from the heart of God, and streaming forth with divinity.

She steps back.

Earnest students, I AM El Morya, Cohan of the First Ray and I stream forth on that which is the mighty Will of God; that which is the focused Ray of Truth. I realize, Dear one, that this work that you have brought forth and are ready and willing now to extend to Earth Plane, is a work that is too gentle. At times I may appear to be stern, and at times I will appear to be gentle; for you see, this is the nature of the will. You have known those in your lifetime or this life expression where the will was totally broken. Is this so?

Response: "Oh, yes."

And could you see how it was so easily restored and built upon, and the life stream was brought forth with great earnestness and focus? Did they not then have the impetus to move forward with direction in their lives?

Response: "Absolutely."

This is what is known as the Will of God. And immediately on the flipside of the will is such gentleness, such ease. It is important, Dear one, you who come to teach and to heal in this Vortex, that you understand the delicate balance of the will. There are those who would push their will forth. And what would happen, but only the implosion of such. There are those who meekly use it and never acknowledge that it is even there. For those, it is never there. This will is the basis of what we know as breath, for breath determines the rate of spin.

The amount of will which you put forth with your thoughts and feelings will determine the amount of space that you are able to expand to. We are not indicating that you should push or expand this beyond your limits; however, as Beloved Mother Mary has stated, there is no limit to your Immaculate Concept. The Immaculate Concept that she speaks of is of course directly related to this will. For you see, it was indeed the light and the sound that came forth. But what would determine that it would spin? It was the will that focused direct creative force that we also refer to as the fiery breath. And so, you have been brought together in the Gobean Vortex to anchor in this First Ray of which I speak.

Response: "Am I then to be an anchor?"

You most certainly are, Dear one, if you so choose.

Response: "Oh, definitely. I would consider it an honor."

This work, Beloved Dear one, is not an easy work.

Response: "I know that."

Those who have been chosen to come here to do this work are those who will not be faint of heart; they are those who have known the trial and tribulation of the heart; they are those who know the fine tuning of emotion.

Response: "I've lived here, off and on, for twenty-five years, and not one year has ever been easy."

This is the earnest student and teacher which we seek: one who will give compassion and yet never let up; one who will love with all their heart, but never give herself away; one who will stand to hold her Brother's hand and walk that mile with him, but stop if it should hurt herself. You see, Dear one, where will is to be restored, one must take the step herself. She must have the desire to step forward. You cannot take the step for your Brother. But you may walk by his side and hold his hand. And yet, there even comes the moment when you may release the hand and say, "Walk!" This is the work of rebuilding the will. Upon the Earth Plane and

Planet, we see this as the greatest problem facing mankind. Throughout the society, there is no will; however, we have great hope and aspiration for humankind. Dear one, the restoration of the will is the first step in anchoring in this First Ray.

How should this be achieved? There are a number of measures. Dear one, I AM El Morya, and I AM here too as your student and teacher. Shall we walk together, Dear one, in this which is Gobean? Shall we verse with one another and be comrades and friends?

Response: "I would consider it an honor!"

Shall we not be the best of friends? Come one to one with our problems?

Response: "I hope so."

But when you say to me, "Walk on your own," I shall.

Response: "And, likewise, I'm sure."

Dear one, you and I have worked together before.

Response: "I knew that. I felt that from the beginning."

Do you have questions?

Question: "Isn't the birthrate throughout the world putting more and more stress upon the planet?"

Perhaps what we can say is that the quality of birth, the quality of parenthood is the problem, not the life stream that is coming forth. Dear one, it is the environment that the life stream comes into.

Question: "Is Babajeran here? I would really like to hear what she has to say about this."

I AM Babajeran. I AM the cosmic mother. Restore that which is mine. Return to man what is his.

El Morya steps forward.

Dear one, it is not so much birth control, but it is recognizing the movement of energy. When one begins to understand the Taoist practice, the breath and the eternal breath, this is not the problem. For you see, there will come a time upon the Earth Plane and Planet when a physical vehicle will not come forth in the manner that it does now.

Dear one, it is our hope that this work will extend beyond the lightworkers, for it has been our observation that it only stays within a group. This work is not to become elitist; it is not for the few; it is to stream forth to the heart of man, so that all may come into this mighty work of Ascension and realize that the expansion of energy is the choice to continue to live. It has been the request of this Council that a mass meditation shall be held in the Vortex of Gobean, to anchor in the First Ray. At one o'clock in the afternoon, every day.

Response: "Starting when, tomorrow? Why not!"

Dear one, how we enjoy the non-hesitant heart.

Saint Germain steps forward.

I am most happy that we have returned to discourse. For you see, Dear one, this banquet that has been spread in front of you is indeed a feast, a feast that all may come to share in. For this planet that you live on is a place where you have come to share in these experiences. And now, I would like to offer Beloved Kuan Yin, as she would like to give her discourse.

Welcome, Beloved, I AM Kuan Yin and I request your permission to come forth.

Response: "Absolutely, you have it!"

Dear one, the work of compassion is indeed the work of understanding, understanding your Brother as that which you have within yourself. When one will come to you and say, "I have this problem or that problem," say, "I understand, for I too have had that problem." When you see this planet that you live on and you see how she shakes and you see how she has had her many wounds, understand how you too have shaken at times and you too have had these wounds.

Compassion, Dear one, goes beyond what you would call the thought. Compassion is sound emotion. It is an emotion for you to carry it at all times. Thought is that which you can select to take action upon, but it is the emotion that you carry. Carry compassion at all times in your heart, Dear one. Carry it for your planet, Beloved Babajeran. Also, carry it for your Brother and your Sister. Remember, for the restoration of the will, one must have a compassionate heart to walk each step, to know when it is time to rest, and when you rest, to sit next to your Brother and your Sister. When they are rested and ready to stand and walk again, you continue the journey, for you understand and carry compassion. My message is simple, but my work is simple. Bless you, Dear one, and I send to you from my heart, Compassion.

She steps back.

Dear one, I AM Sananda, and I would like to come forth into your energy field.

Response: "You have my permission."

This work that we share on this planet is indeed a feast. It is a work in which we all have our part. It is a work that we tear apart, piece by piece, and distribute among all of you. You know, as well as I do, that to achieve a great task, we all must carry our share of this load; however, Dear one, remember the load is not the burden. This work is a feast. We are all collecting to contribute. We each carry within us our Divine Heritage. You carry no more than I carry. And I carry no more than you carry. What is the difference? The difference is experience, not that you don't realize your divinity. You know you are divine, for I have just reminded you. You have yet to have the experience that you are divine. In order to have the experience and to assure what the experience will contain, you must use the creative action of thought and carry your thought to your feelings and express this with your will, aligned to the Divine Will.

The Divine Plan is simply stated: YOU ARE THE DIVINE PLAN. This work is a work that we share. I invite you to sup with me, Dear one. I break this bread; I raise this Cup; together we share our troubles; together we share our joy. Beloved Saint Germain brings forth the information of what is known as the collective energy; however, I speak with simpler words. I AM Sananda and the work of Earth Changes and the transition of this plane is my responsibility. For you see, Dear one, this was the Cup I held to my lips and drank of it, and now I place the Cup down. Would I abandon it? Never! Never, for the Law of the Universe says, "Intake and outtake"; "As above, so below."

The beauty of this work that comes forth is a beauty beyond the birds that sing; the beauty is beyond the harmony of the music of angels; the beauty is in watching and having the experience. Create your experience. Understand that each day, as you proceed, it is yours and your choice for it to be commanded with your divinity. Live your life as ONE and live your life as one of many. I raise this Cup, as we shall never forget the divinity housed in the heart of service.

He steps back.

Dear chelas, I AM Saint Germain, and as I serve as that which is the energetic bridge, the Spiritual Hierarchy of the Great White Brotherhood has prepared this banquet, this feast for you, which is indeed a feast of light. Sup with us, Dear one, as we usher in the Golden Age and anchor in the First Ray into Beloved Gobean. I bless you and thank you and keep you in my heart for the Light of God Never Fails. It truly never fails. I AM

15

Release old patterns of toxic inertia,
apathy, confusion, and fear.

Discipline
Saint Germain

After my return to Socorro, I completed the first draft of my book, but still questioned just what it should be titled. The phone rang and it was my friend Andrew, now home in Sedona. Andrew is a full-fledged Lightworker and had recently returned from several months of business travel and lecturing. "What's new in your world?" he asked, after sharing a quick update.

I tried to explain, as quickly as possible, the vast array of rich experiences I'd encountered since we last saw each other on the trail at Mount Shasta, including my move from the Pacific Northwest. "I need a title for my new book," I mentioned. Andrew had an extensive background in copywriting and advertising and we tossed around several possibilities. "I like the last one . . . *New World at Last!*" he joked. "Really, *New World Atlas?*" I asked. It did describe the content quite clearly. Plus, the book would feature a color section, with small versions of the I AM America Maps: the United States, Canada, Mexico, Central and South America. I wrote the name down, and immediately visualized the topography on the book cover.

He went on, "How is your schedule this fall? I'm planning a trip to Santa Fe, and thought I'd stop by and spend a few days with you and Len." My summer schedule was maxed out until mid-September. I'd purposely marked off two weeks that exclusively belonged to me and the children. While we'd had an active summer with several road trips, we'd had little quality time together. Their father was flying down in less than a month, and then they would return to the farm to start a new school year.

"When do you think you'll be here?" I asked. I wanted to see Andrew again, but I didn't want to compromise my schedule with the children. "Should be the first week of October – will that work?" he said, as he quickly continued, "Looking forward to seeing the two of you!" I didn't say anything, but I wasn't sure if he'd see the two of us. In fact, I wasn't too sure if there even was still "the two of us."

The next couple of weeks flew by. I had just enough time to enroll the children in another swimming class, and that left our afternoons open. There was little or no shopping in the small high-desert town, so we decided to venture into Albuquerque, for a day at the mall, and purchased a few back-to-school outfits. The girls seemed to be okay with returning back to Idaho with their dad, but Carson was a little emotional about the topic, almost resistant. Clearly, he did not want to leave me. If I'd had my choice, none of them would ever leave my side, but this was not my unilateral decision. I tried to explain this to my ten-year-old son, and he covered his ears, pretending not to listen.

Mark, the children's father, flew in at the local airport and we were all there to greet him. Bryn skipped up to grab his hand and immediately reminded him, "Tomorrow is my birthday!" Her dad grinned, and began to tease her, "No . . . it's not *your* birthday!" Kaitlin grabbed hold of his other hand, and Carson stood back, almost hiding behind me.

That evening the five of us went out for dinner. We were all sitting in a booth, at a local diner. I'm certain that on the exterior we appeared like any normal, everyday family. Yet, there was an uncomfortable silence between all of us. I had learned some time ago to accept this uneasy silence.

Mark and I had come a long way from those first years of searing emotional pain, during our separation and divorce. Our healing balm was the sacred vow we made that the children would be our first and only priority. I glanced at his sandy blonde hair and his tanned face; the result of working in the fields. He looked a bit older, but still had a boyish quality about him. It was this boyish wildness that had attracted me to him when we first met and became high-school sweethearts. And we had married young; really, *too young*, when we were both just nineteen years old. He had grown into a good man: responsible and successful. In fact, he had piloted the private plane to Socorro. Yet, I had no attraction to him, anymore, whatsoever.

That night, after dinner, Mark remained for a few hours. We drank iced teas, and sat out on the backyard patio in the cool summer night air. While the children played, I whispered, "Carson doesn't want to go back." Not one to waste words, he calmly replied, "Oh?"

The next day Kaitlin scurried up the grocery isle and grabbed a boxed cake mix off the shelf, "This is the one Mom – cherry chip!" She tossed it into the grocery cart and impatiently asked, "Can we buy her [Bryn's] present now? I know what she wants . . . we already picked it out." The two girls were close. In fact, best friends.

I took comfort in knowing that they would have each other during the school year. It would be difficult not to see them on the weekends. I gave them preaddressed and stamped envelopes so they would write to me. They'd memorized my new phone number.

I was, however, concerned about Carson. He was sullen and quiet, and passively sat motionless when I asked him to pack his bags for Idaho.

Carson helped me place the candles on the cake, nine altogether. He had always helped me in the kitchen, but I noticed that he had stayed especially close to my side that particular evening. We all sang "Happy Birthday" to Bryn.

I couldn't help but tear up a bit, as I knew that this time tomorrow they would all be gone. Someway, somehow, I would face being alone here, in this big house, in a town where I literally only communicated with one person. It would be inordinately empty, and my heart was heavy. I almost wished I was going back with them . . . and why hadn't Len called? It'd been almost ten days since we had last spoken.

The next morning we were all up at dawn and by 8 AM the doorbell rang – it was Mark. "You all ready to catch a flight back home to Idaho?" he asked? I could tell from the tone in his voice that he was anxious to get started.

"I'm sorry," I said, "Carson is still not packed." I was a bit embarrassed at my parenting skills, but I could not find the inner strength to force him. Mark lightly touched my shoulder, and silently directed me to a quiet corner in the living room, "Just let him stay." My heart leaped for a moment, and then I noticed Mark's apparent disappointment – he would not return to the family farm with his son.

"Are you certain?" I said, as I pensively searched his face for a moment. Our eyes met, perhaps for the first time in many years. "It's okay . . . just let him stay," he gently repeated.

I helped the girls with their bags from the car trunk, and the five of us walked out to the airplane. I hugged my daughters for about a full minute, and then realized that their dad was standing near us, waiting patiently. I tore myself away from them, tears welling in my eyes and spilling out onto my cheeks. "Good-bye my darlings, I will see you at Christmas . . ." I wanted to blow them kisses, but I could not. The tears were flowing now, and I tried to compose myself while I sat in the Grand I AM with Carson by my side. Carson reached over and touched my knee, "It will be okay

Mom." I wiped my eyes and then faced my son, a little boy quickly learning how to be a man. I reached over, gave him a hug, and said, "I'm sure glad you stayed." School started in less than two weeks. Our home was located across the street from the middle school, and Carson and I walked over on registration day. After filling out the required paperwork, a gentleman escorted us to a private room, and asked Carson to wait outside. Apparently this was the procedure for new students.

"Okay, looks like we have everything in place. Carson's records from his previous school are here," the man with sympathetic, dark eyes and silver hair said. Then he paused for a moment while he checked off his list. "You know this is completely your choice, but if you earn under this amount per month...," and he circled in red a figure on a sheet and handed it to me, "you qualify for discounted lunches."

I was silent for a moment as I viewed the figure. I definitely qualified, but my pride left me speechless. Apparently, he had experienced this before. Socorro was not a wealthy community by any means, and there were likely many families with similar needs. He interrupted my apparent inner conflict of pride versus practicality, "And just so you know . . . the other children will never know." I breathed a sigh of relief, "Okay – that will help us out."

As I signed the form, he asked, "You're not from here, are you?" I replied, "No, we just moved here . . . in fact, we've rented a home across the street," as my embarrassment morphed into casual friendliness. "I'm originally from the Pacific Northwest." "Oh, yes . . ." he said, and he paused for a second before continuing, "I noticed that you are obviously Anglo. What brings you here – the college?"

I wasn't insulted, but it was the first time that I'd ever heard anyone refer to me as an "Anglo." I'm certain he was curious as over fifty percent of the population in Socorro was Hispanic. "I'm a writer and work at home, plus I have a small mail-order business. My partner and I decided that we wanted to live where it is warmer, so we chose the southwest," I explained, as I voiced a canned, partial truth. I could only imagine what he'd say if I told him that I had moved here to live in the Golden City of Gobean. He'd probably call the child protection agency.

"You excited?" I asked Carson, as the two of us walked across the schoolyard's green grass toward home. He thoughtfully looked at me and his brilliant blue eyes flashed as he nodded, "Mom, I think tonight we should call Len." I nodded back, and thought to myself, "Yes, tonight we'll call Len." When we called, Len presented us with the unexpected: "I have good news – I bought a ticket today and I'll be home in a week." I could hear genuine enthusiasm in his voice. I was so excited that my heart was racing, "Really?" And I repeated myself again, "Really . . . you're coming home?"

Carson and I shopped the day before Len's arrival. We bought fresh flowers and placed them in a vase on the dining room table. And we baked a pan of fresh brownies – Len's favorite, for his homecoming. When Len walked off the plane, I barely recognized him – he looked so tired. "Oh – I'm so glad to be back in the west," Len announced as we hugged, and then with a relieved sigh added, "I'm back home . . ."

We drove home to Socorro and spent a few quiet days doing nothing, and then re-established our routine as a family. Mornings started early, and I was often out the door at 5 AM for a quick forty-five minute ride with my bike-riding group, and I'd get home just in time to get Carson out the door for school. In mid-afternoons, Len would walk over to the school to shepherd Carson safely home, and then sit with him as they completed homework together. I often chimed in while standing in the kitchen and making a salad, peeling vegetables, or loading the dishwasher. Even though our beliefs might have seemed eccentric and unusual to many, our life together was extremely conventional.

I updated Len on the status of I AM America, and we packed and mailed orders by noon. I shared the idea for the book title, and Len agreed that it was perfect, so I began to search for an illustrator for the cover. Because it had been some time since we last channeled, Len was anxious for a session with his guru. The instructive portion of the session started with some interesting material regarding the second layer of Earth's First Light Body, the well-known troposphere of weather and its correlation to human emotion. The teaching, however, primarily focused on personal discipline and how that relates to the patterns of mind. To understand the patterns of mind constructs, and how they may hinder or harm the physical body and the Ascension Process, Saint Germain addressed diet.

He emphasized identifying addictive substances, including seemingly benign foods, which might alter perception. He qualified an addictive substance as one that "think(s) you into a stupor," and elaborated that "only you shall know that which you *think* harms you." He also emphasized identifying at least five of these substances, including: any type of over-the-counter drug, caffeine, sugar, and alcohol. Then he suggested consciously removing them from personal consumption for six weeks. He said that this would allow the body and mind to recalibrate and unite, and destroy negative habits and thought patterns. Essentially, he was talking about a physical and spiritual detox.

Fortunately, Len does not use drugs or alcohol. He doesn't even drink coffee! So it is obvious that for him, addictive substances would likely focus on specific foods. It is wise to remember, too, that this is an inner process to gain better restraint, self-knowledge, and self-control.

There were a few more personal disciplines that Saint Germain mentioned in this lesson, which are worth noting.

Kriya Yoga is a form of intentional breathing, better known as *pranayama* in Sanskrit. It is a spiritual technique that expands human energy. Saint Germain introduced a beginning breathing technique in this lesson, which is considered a form of Kriya Yoga: the *I AM Rhythmic Breath*. This breathing practice is recommended before entering sleep, and allegedly helps to integrate the I AM Presence with the human auric fields. Saint Germain refers to this as the *fiery breath*. Saint Germain also introduced a technique to purify food and drink; that of visualizing Green and Gold energy streaming from your ring finger, on your left or right hand, whichever you prefer. Apparently, this is a type of individualized energy that streams directly from your I AM Presence, and carries a unique vibration and blessing that alchemizes a distinctive and matchless elixir into your food and beverages.

Over time I've learned that when the Spiritual Teachers introduce a spiritual discipline, it is not a form of correction or punishment. Instead, their disciplines and techniques are meant to train and engender a new realization of self. More often, these create an opportunity to gain inner awareness through tried-and-true traditions, and prepare and ready our consciousness for a vital, new experience. The most important spiritual disciplines that they have shared are those focused upon spiritual liberation – the Ascension Process. Through years of working with many of these spiritual disciplines, I can say, with experience, that some of them are not meant to be practiced for years. In fact, many of them are specifically designed only to help us work through a specific physical or spiritual obstacle. Others are meant to be practiced until we achieve a certain level of spiritual adeptness; for example, those disciplines used in the field of astral travel, dream work, or during advanced work with certain chakras and auric layers.

Then there are the cherished, everyday spiritual disciplines such as contemplation, meditation, visualization, and the application of the Violet Flame. Each and every discipline plays a unique role in our spiritual growth; however, the latter, every day practices are perhaps the most valuable, and comprise the teachings that calibrate and define personal awareness, vibration and magnetism, and spiritual maturity. I often refer to this calibration process as *spiritual metabolism.*

I must admit, in the past, I'd often cringe when one of the teachers introduced a new discipline to our spiritual repertoire. I'd object for various reasons: time, energy, and the mere fact that I didn't want to change some personal habits. But I've learned through this process that the best approach is a gradual surrender to each new technique, adjusting my schedule accordingly, and then seeing what happens. Saint Germain has often said, "Don't believe anything that I tell you . . . take unto the laboratory of self."

I certainly got the impression, from this advice, that spiritual discipline is uniquely different for each person. And the overall goal is to engage in fresh, positive thought patterns that ultimately initiate the physical body into the new levels of spiritual growth and evolution.

The eighth electromagnetic field is an energetic field of harmonizing. So, Dear one, what is the second layer of the field of the first light body?

Response: "It is the weather layer and also the emotional layer."

So that is where the first disturbance occurs, the thunderstorms and the tornados, through the mighty Elohim Astrea. You must understand that the work of Ascension is indeed the work for your eternal freedom. Dear one, I ask for you to not worry about the sweat, or to not worry about the tears; for you see, that is part of the natural process, for this is indeed a work. It is important that you understand that they at times shall be your taskmaster and I am indeed of service to you. But the reward is in the process itself, as you have understood the work of service in Third Dimensional expression. You must understand that the end result is your eternal freedom and then you stand forth in service as a Creator. Do you understand?

[Editor's Note: For more information on the steps of Ascension, see "The Twelve Evolutionary Points," *Divine Destiny.*]

Response: "Yes."

You have studied the works that have been brought forth through my beloved Brothers and comrades who have brought forth the steps of Mastery. As it was stated in the Jurisdictions, or the fundamentals for the millennium, you have these paths to choose. In the eighth step of Ascension, you come forth in perfection. To come forth in perfection, one thing individualizes a path of Mastery, that is then expressed as the first step of Co-creation in this universe. We speak then of responsible Co-creation. Dear one, we shall start on this first step, which is the purification of the body. Are you ready to proceed?

Response: "Yes, I am ready."

It is then stated in your work with Beloved Saint Germain that there are essential dietary guidelines that must be adhered to, in order for the body to sustain a hold on this process. To interfere or to mix vibration within the system with animal life that has held conscious form, scatters the coding of patterns. Do you understand?

Response: "I am thinking. Ah, I see! It is another disruptive pattern that enables one to be less focused."

You are commanding in the name of I AM THAT I AM to hold continuous, individualized focused patterns.

Response: "Yes, this I understand."

To take into the body that which has held a focus of another conscious form or pattern that is separate from yourself is distracting to the energetic barriers in your system.

Response: "It is almost as though an animal, who has an ending which comes in a fear, as one eats that particular flesh, the fear pattern is absorbed also into the system of the one consuming it."

This is so, Dear one, for there has been held a focused pattern within the conscious life. However, Dear one, I request that you understand this information in its full context. All creation carries divinity. At no time should that which is the animal be judged as less. It holds universal principle and thought within its form. Dear one, it too shall evolve to the point of the human if it stays through choice upon this planet. It is indeed treated as a seed and should be seen and held as such. Do you understand?

Response: "In other words, our Brothers and Sisters of lesser consciousness."

Brothers and Sisters who have yet to increase the spin of subatomic particles around the Golden Thread Axis, of which you have been well educated. The purification of the body through dietary intake is the first essential step, for you to understand disciplines of energy.

We are of concern, not about chemicals in your body; however, it is the thought that you associate when you take in certain chemicals. We are concerned with that which alters the perception, or that which you have allowed to alter your perception. You know these in your world as alcohol or drugs. There are indeed even foods that have given an opiate effect. Just sift through your thoughts, Dear one, for that which we will discuss in later steps for purification. However, until you understand the purification of thought, we shall discuss the purification of the body, and ask for you to remove those substances that you, through sense of separation or loss, have a tendency to think yourself into a stupor. Do you understand?

Response: "It is what you think it is."

This is exact, and I ask for you to write those foods or drugs, as you would call them, on a sheet of paper. List the five most harmful to your body as you understand it. It is enough for us to sit and give you guidelines; however, it is most important that you individualize, for only you shall know that which you think harms you.

Response: "I understand."

Dear one, you have also known these guidelines as set forth from Beloved Saint Germain. They are guidelines on that which is the path of Mastery. The first step of the purification of the body contains dietary guidelines that are essential for you to proceed to the next step. As we have said, you are preparing the body to become receptive to patterns. Do you know, Dear one, that you are receptive to harmful thought upon yourself? It is my request that you write these down for a period of six weeks and abstain from these.

Response: "As you wish."

This will allow your body to become receptive to the idea that it can be patterned and that the thought itself can be broken.

Response: "This sounds like a test. I accept it."

It gives you discipline, Dear one, merely a discipline, and I ask for you to see within it the sense of joy for your eternal freedom.

Response: "I accept this."

Purification of the body also includes the air quality which you take into the system, for food and air and water are the three elements, the three things that the human form requires, and yet curiously, are very much within its world. Air is to be taken in through what is known as the continuous cycle. It is best to do what we know as, or as you know as, continuous breathing in the sunlight. Repetitions of twelve are ideal; however, if you find these harmful, or make you lightheaded, repetitions of eight will also serve the purpose. You have been taught the three types of breath work through Lady Master Venus and I ask for you to review these, Dear one.

Response: "Yes, this will be done."

It is best when you are ready to retire or to go into that time of sleep, that you purify your lung system to what we call, the exchange. You are to take your finger, cover one nostril, breathe eight repetitions, then cover the other nostril and breathe for eight repetitions. We would ask if you are male, to first cover that which is the male side [right]; if you are female, to first cover that which is the female [left]. This sets up timing and delivery within the system itself and the body while it sleeps, and has an easier time adjusting to the rhythmic breath that comes forth from the beloved mighty I AM Presence as the bodies separate during the hours of sleep. We can spend more time discussing breath work, but I am giving you the basic guidelines of purification of the body. There is much to understanding the fiery breath. Remember, Dear one, we are working on the physical body and it's receptivity to patterns.

Water! It is ideal to drink eight cups of liquid a day. This is difficult for you, I understand, but you should have no less than two per day. We ask for the water to be the clearest and cleanest that you can find. You have learned the technique for clarification and purity through the Green and Gold Rays, woven through the ring finger of the left hand. This should be charged by you and you only, for you are charging it with the cure of that acceptance that comes from the beloved mighty I AM Presence. The beloved Elixir of Life which we call this, is the same pure substance which Beloved Saint Germain presented to Godfrey. This is indeed the eternal Cup that you drink from, for Godfrey shall never forget. Do you understand?

Response: "Yes, I do."

16

Our spiritual evolution is calibrated by bodies
of beautiful, sublime light.

Ascension Alignment

Saint Germain
Serapis Bey

Autumn in the southwest was filled with the smell of roasting green chili, roadside stands with homemade signs – "Pinions for Sale," and the familiar bright oranges and reds popping out against the flowing, earthy landscape. At that point, my only major complaint was that many of the Hispanic families kept chickens in their yards, and a nearby rooster would proudly and loudly announce the morning sun *exactly* at dawn.

It was on one of these early, barely awake, pink-skied mornings that Andrew called from Santa Fe. As promised, he was on his way down to Socorro that day, and wanted to know if he could stay for a week. "Of course," I responded, not yet fully caffeinated, but excited at the prospect of seeing our old friend again. Then I noticed Saint Germain nearby, with a huge grin on his face. "Andrew," I interrupted, "Be prepared . . . I think we'll be receiving some new information." Andrew chuckled and thoughtfully replied, "I knew there was a reason for me to come!" Len and I spent the next several hours straightening up the house, and changing the sheets and towels in the upstairs apartment.

Later that evening, following dinner, the three of us lingered over cups of tea. Then I noticed, yet again, the faint image of Saint Germain shuffling up and down the hallway, with an almost urgent, pensive energy.

"Hey guys," I interrupted, "Did you notice who is here?" and I pointed toward the lighted, standing image, now displaying sparks of purple light next to the dining-room table. Len immediately recognized our Spiritual Teacher and exclaimed, "Guess we have some work to do!" Andrew, who had yet to see, but did sense the high energy, commented, "I wondered what that scent was. I've been smelling a faint fragrance of lavender since I arrived."

We scurried up the stairs to a small circle of chairs I'd placed on the far end of the room, where I had done trance sessions with Madge. After a quick session of decrees, I was in trance. We were greeted by the wondrous Master of the Violet Flame, accompanied by El Morya and Mother Mary. We were about halfway through the session when Len realized that in our excitement to speak with the Spiritual Teachers, we had forgotten to record the session! As a result, I've summarized some of that lesson's important points.

For the last dozen years, Andrew – like Len – had been practicing different energy techniques, primarily focusing on certain grids that exist in the Human Aura known as Axiotonal Grids. These unique and ethereal, energy ley lines exist on the Earth and mirror our human body, primarily at the Fifth Dimension. Using the information he had found and seriously studied in *The Book of Knowledge: Keys of Enoch* by J. J. Hurtak, Andrew then applied this "Axiotonal Energy Work."

The Master Teachers had elaborated about this profound grid of life. It could traverse the causal energies of the Fifth Dimension onward through the beauty of the emotive Astral Plane, into the physical plane, onto Mother Earth manifesting as Babajeran, and into our unique Human Aura. Accessing and activating this network of spiritual energy could assist our spiritual growth and evolution, and would be extremely helpful in initiating the Ascension Process.

Apparently this was the reason for the Masters' timely appearance. The following lesson shares their spiritual knowledge, which integrates teachings on the human energy field, the importance of these energy grids, and how we can work with them on a practical everyday basis.

As I emerged from the trance session, I could still see the energy fields of light that were explained and displayed by the Spiritual Teachers. Here is a quick review of the well known light fields of the Human Aura:

First Light Body: The *Electronic Blueprint* holds the electrical impulse in the light body; therefore, it is similar to the *Auric Blueprint*. It is charged with the energy of the Seven Major Chakras, the energy grids, meridians, and nadis. It resembles a grid, and is blue in color. This layer of the Human Aura contains a distinctive pulse that is synchronized with the individual's heartbeat, and lies within several inches of the physical body.

Second Light Body: The *Emotional Field* holds our instincts, feelings, and emotions. This light body is normally a vibrant pink in color. It is associated with the magnetism of the physical body. This light body is most affected by sound, especially mantras and decrees. Because varied emotions can change the characteristics of this light body, the light body can fluctuate in color. Extreme anger or violence can turn the light body dark red, while spiritual feelings of devotion can alter it to a visible light pink with hues of green. This light body is observed four to six inches from the physical body.

Third Light Body: The *Mental Body* carries our distinct thoughts, ideas, and perceptions. This energy field, to some degree, is associated with intelligence and our capability to process and implement information. This light body is associated with the color yellow, although some individuals display mental bodies that are vibrant gold. It is located six inches to one foot from the physical body.

First Three Light Bodies: The first three light bodies represent Action (electronic blueprint), Feeling (emotion) and Thought (mental). These three primary colors also represent the Unfed Flame of Power, Love, and Wisdom, respectively. The first three light bodies of the Human Aura endure throughout the Earthly incarnation, and dissipate with the death of the physical body.

Fourth Light Body: The fourth light body of the human is the *Astral Body*. This is the energy body that we use when we dream and travel at night, via different meditation techniques. It is varied in color, but often displays a rainbow of pastel colors: blues, pinks, greens, and purples. It is located a foot, to a foot and a half, from the physical body. Advanced souls often display a larger Astral Body of luminous white light, with iridescent pastels. This light body, along with the next three higher light bodies, survives the death of the physical body, and then resides in the Astral Plane for further spiritual development to prepare for the next incarnation.

Fifth Light Body: This body of energy is known as the *Auric Template*, and is similar to the Electronic Template. However, this field of vital energy gives form according to individual states of consciousness. It radiates approximately one and a half to two feet from the physical body. It is the energy layer from where a seasoned energy practitioner can detect and treat disease. The color of this energy body can vary depending on the individual strength of Ray Forces.

Sixth Light Body: This energy body carries the individual's aspirations and beliefs. Many refer to this energy body as the *Celestial Body*, but it is also known as the *Spiritual Emotional Body*. This body is often connected to feelings of bliss, unconditional love, and interconnectedness. It can be reached through meditation.

This layer extends two to nearly three feet from the physical body. It is colored with opalescent pastels. Some energy practitioners report a gold-silver light shining throughout this energy body. Master Teachers, Spirit Guides, and Spiritual Teachers often enter this energy field to communicate with an individual, or to revive and heal the physical body. The Sixth and Seventh Light Bodies hold varying levels of the Akashic Records.

Seventh Light Body: The *Causal Body* is the last of the human energy bodies. It is an egg-shape ovoid that holds all of the lower energy bodies in place with extremely strong threads of light that form a golden grid. This energy body is also known as the *Spiritual Mental Body*, and contains the *Golden Thread Axis*, also known as the *Tube of Light* that connects one to the I AM Presence. Energy practitioners allege that this energy body holds the Akashic records that are keys to past-life memory. This energy body extends approximately three feet around the body but can be larger, depending on the spiritual evolution of the individual.

As human spiritual evolution advances, we begin to develop new energy bodies of light, sound, and experience. The Spiritual Teachers mention that the HU-man, the developed God Man, can acquire eight new distinct energy bodies beyond the initial, primary Seven Light Bodies. The Fifteenth Energy Body propels the soul out of duality, free from both physical and astral restraint.

An Ascended Master contains and influences twenty-two light bodies. Apparently, Light Bodies Eight through Ten have the ability to contend with varying light spectrums beyond Third Dimension and can manage space-time, including time contraction, time dilation, and time compaction. But more importantly, the development of the HU-man Energy system implements the ever-important Ascension Process. The following information shares descriptions of the HU-man Energy Bodies Eight, Nine, and Ten.

Eighth Light Body: Known as the *Buddha Body* or the *Field of Awakening*, this energy body is initially three to four feet from the human body. It begins by developing two visible grid-like spheres of light that form in the front and in the back of the Human Aura. The front sphere is located three to four feet in front of and between the Heart and Solar Plexus Chakras. The back sphere is located in front of and between the Will-to-Love and Solar Will Chakras. These spheres activate an ovoid of light that surrounds the entire human body; an energy field associated with harmonizing and perfecting the Ascension Process. This is the first step toward Mastery. Once developed and sustained, this energy body grants physical longevity and is associated with immortality. It is known as the first level of Co-creation, and is developed through control of the diet and disciplined breath techniques. Once this light body reaches full development, the spheres dissipate and dissolve into a refined energy field, resembling a metallic armor. The mature Eighth Light Body then contracts and condenses, to reside within several inches of the physical body where it emits a silver-blue sheen.

Ninth Light Body: This body of light is known as *The Divine Blueprint*, as it represents the innate perfection of the divine HU-man. It is an energy field that is developed through uniting dual forces, and requires an in-depth purification of thought. In fact, this energy field causes the soul to face and Master those negative, dark, forces that the Spiritual Teachers refer to as a type of *mental purgatory*. This energy body processes extreme fears and transmutes them. The transmutation completely restructures beliefs, and purifies energies held in the lower mental bodies accumulated throughout all lifetimes. This produces an alchemizing, divine, HU-man Mental Body that develops approximately thirty-six feet from the human body. This energy field first appears as nine independent triangular-gridded spheres. Apparently, the nine glowing spheres grow in circumference and, inevitably, morph into one glowing energy body. As the Ninth Light Body develops, it is extremely responsive to telepathy and group thought, and progresses to act and influence collective thought and consciousness. In its early to mid-stages of development, this energy body emits a high frequency violet light that evolves into the alchemic Violet Flame. The Spiritual Teachers claim that the decree, "I AM the Presence of Collective Thought," is its energetic mantra. The refined energies of the mature Divine Blueprint inevitably contract and concentrate in a similar manner to the Eighth Light Body. As it draws its auric field closer to the physical body; within two to four inches, it radiates gold and then a bluish-silver light that reflects the strength of its protective shield.

Tenth Light Body: This is the final level of three protective HU-man light bodies, which is formed through the purification of desires, and is known as the *Diamond Mind*. Because this energy body gathers thought as light, it is a substantive and sizeable light body. The Spiritual Teachers often refer to the three protective HU-man energy bodies as the *Triple Gems*, and together they are strong enough to pierce human illusion. Combined with the four higher primal energy bodies – the Fourth Light Body to the Seventh Light Body – the total sum of these energy bodies produces the alchemic number seven. In this septagonal order, the Diamond Mind helps to produce the *Lighted Stance* and the inevitable attainment of the *Seamless Garment*.

The Lighted Stance is a state of conscious perfection – a precursor to Ascension. The soul's ability to manifest the Seamless Garment bestows the Master with the ability to travel and experience the Astral and Physical planes without spiritual corruption or physical disintegration. This mature energy body compacts itself to reside approximately six inches from the physical body, and is alleged to have the strength and brilliance of "ten-thousand diamonds." This energy body also exhibits complete Mastery over thought, feeling, and action – the first three primal human Energy Bodies, and can dissolve or manifest their physical presence at will; or, it can take form for whatever cause, circumstance, or "task at hand," without any limitation.

This lesson was extensive. We considered editing it, but came to the conclusion that embedded throughout even its shortest sentences were valuable insights and hints regarding spiritual growth and evolution. In fact, the trance session was so long and intense, we took a break, and Len stepped in to complete the session while I monitored. In short, the Spiritual Teachers introduced and explained the energetics of Ascension and the process of spiritual liberation.

I have read this lesson many times to extract the unique subtleties and nuances that good channeled material is known for. Remember that the instructions in this lesson are customized for a hands-on-healer or energy practitioner. Thus, some of the information may seem a bit technical. Whether or not you are healer, you will gain through the understanding of this knowledge.

For information regarding *Star seeds*, I created a table based on the knowledge of Jyotish – Hindu Astrology. The Rays are essentially the seven traditional planets, and vice versa. The term *Atma Karaka* best explains the science of soul and how it may connect to one specific planet. In Sanskrit, Atma means *soul*, and Karaka translates to *indicator* or *significator*. So literally, the Atma Karaka – which any competent Vedic Astrologer can easily recognize in an individual chart – metaphysically indicates the planet and Ray Force that you most identify with. I think this may also be the planet of your soul's origin or, minimally, it may play a significant role in influencing your entry into physical incarnation(s) in this solar system.

> *Table of Star seeds*
> **First Star seed:** Blue Ray, Saturn
> **Second Star seed:** Pink Ray, Moon
> **Third Star seed:** Yellow Ray, Jupiter
> **Fourth Star seed:** White Ray, Venus
> **Fifth Star seed:** Green Ray, Mercury

Sixth Star seed: Ruby and Gold Ray, Sun and Mars
Seventh Star seed: Violet Ray, Saturn

[Editor's Note: To date, the Spiritual Teachers have not given any detailed information regarding the Eleventh and Twelfth Light Bodies. However, for more detailed information on the Ascension Process, its relationship to the Eight-sided Cell of Perfection, and the Twelve Evolution Points, see *Divine Destiny*.]

~

Welcome Beloved chelas, I AM Saint Germain, and I stream forth on the mighty Ray of Victory, the mighty Victory Ray of Forgiveness. This Violet Transmuting Ray comes forth to this planet, this Earth Plane and Planet in Transition. It is this mighty Ray of Victory that assures that your freedom of Ascension shall come. Dear ones, this work of Ascension that we bring forth, discourse by discourse, is indeed also the work of service. We have explained to you that to expand into the energetic bodies, one must be ready to use this energy, to use it to benefit all in constructive ways, for it is in constructive use of your energy that brings you into the realms of the Ascended Masters. You see Dear ones, it is this work of Ascension that expands your energy into this work we know as world service. Dear ones, as usual, I must ask permission to come forth into your energy fields.

Andrew: "Beloved Saint Germain, welcome into our fields."

Len: "Beloved one, welcome into our fields."

I AM the mighty victory of the Violet Flame and I stream forth forever to the hearts of men. HOLY, HOLY, HOLY, as we have said, HUE, HUE, HUE, let this victory be forever sustained upon this planet you know now as Prahna. Dear ones, we welcome you to the inner circle of those of the Violet Robe. Let me hand one to each of you. Wear this mighty cloak as your cloak of protection, for as we go into this focused work, this work of Ascension, we shall explore the world of the ninth energetic body. This body has been built upon the principles of the Trinity, and within the Trinity itself, is also the process of duality. As one prepares to enter into this ninth energetic body, one must be ready to face the fears of eternal darkness. You would ask of yourself, how would this occur in this ninth body? This body is indeed again an alignment one. Do you remember how Beloved Sananda spent forty days in the desert? It was in these days that he accepted his ninth energetic body.

Len: "Yes, I remember it."

This ninth energetic body understands the collective thought and how it plays a vast momentum in all HU-man energetics. It is the ninth energetic body that is also known as the first collective body, and this body starts in simple communication. You have a conversation with one person. That person has the conversation back. The exchange of this energy carries a momentum. The focused thought, or momentum, is enough within one moment, to create a collective. You have known Sananda to simply state, "When two or more are gathered." However, remember the gathered thought must carry a gathered focus. The ninth energetic body holds the gathered focus, thus holding the gathered thought. It is this gathered thought that you carry with your Beloved I AM Presence and it is the gathering of the thought of the present that creates the space to fill this ninth energetic body. Beloved Serapis Bey has discussed the rate of spin and the parameters of the eighth energetic body. The ninth is unique, for this is where the thought becomes purified. How does one purify the thought?

Len: "In the focus."

This is true Dear one. One must understand that all is qualified to the Beloved mighty I AM. So you feel that you, yourself, have no control over this that shall be determined by a force outside of you. But it is not the same Dear ones, for it is this mighty Beloved I AM Presence which streams forth, ever eternal in this mighty victory, ever achieved, ever sustained, ever fulfilled, ever maintained. The eternal victory of the Ascension comes forth from God, which is known as the eleventh body. It is in this body that one is able to break out of the atmosphere of gravitational pull, the electromagnetic current of the planet itself. It is the ninth energetic body that then allows the purification of the thought.

One must understand what it is gathering to itself. The tenth energetic body also gathers thought to itself, but works more from the substantive basis. The ninth energetic body carries the purification, not up to the mental body that you carry in the current embodiment, but the mental bodies you carry from all previous incarnations. It is there that you make the choice to purify all thought that shall be gathered to you. This comes with close union or contact with the mighty Beloved I AM Presence. It requires a trust which you have yet to experience in human embodiment.

There are few who are willing to go forth in the name of I AM THAT I AM. We have the saying, "To do, to dare, and to be silent." What are we speaking about?

The one who has the courage to step forth in the silence of the I AM and to face the eternal victory. However, this work is not achieved alone, but in close communion with the beloved mighty I AM Presence. The ninth energetic body allows the sustaining energy to stream forth between the Higher Self and the mental body of the HU-man. There, all thought is gathered, purified, and cleansed.

Perhaps the best way to understand this is that the first eight bodies are gathered in a collective effort to the HU-man; the ninth energetic body is a collective effort between the mighty Beloved I AM Presence and the individualization of that Presence. You have the life stream, that streams forth to the beloved mighty I AM Presence. It is this Presence that sends its force into the universe, setting forth the creative way, made in the image and likeness of God, to the Divine World. The first seven energetic layers individualize this Presence, or the human expression. One decides to enter into world service and he is born again, the water unto the spirit. He steps forth with a mantle of consciousness to Co-create and the eighth energetic body is born. Let me assure that this Co-creative process shall be sustained and maintained by the purification of thought. Do you understand?

Len: "Yes! However, it is almost the understanding that there is a polarization or an equal energetic exchange that occurs once the ninth energetic body is accepted."

You understand how I introduced to you the concept of duality, where, as one takes on the ninth energetic body, one is faced with all the duality that comes forth to all human embodiment. The most treacherous fears are presented to the mind of such an individual. The most horrendous doubts are presented to the mind of such an individual. Your work in holding and sustaining the focus with your Beloved Brother or Sister as they take on this energy, is to remember that this occurs.

Len: "Are these not only occurring so they may be purified?"

It is the trial by fire. This has also been known as the purgatory, or hell, that has been created by mankind.

Len: "The ninth energetic body is the purification of thought and focus; the tenth is the purification of feeling and desire; and the eleventh is the purification of will?"

It is one way to language it Dear one; however, there is other strategic information that needs to come forth. It is one way to understand, that this too is indeed a purification concept; it is also the expansion of one's will and focus into cosmic service. You have discussed the idea for a process of physical immortality. Physical immortality is sustained and maintained by holding the eighth energetic body. One may live for five, six, seven, even eight hundred years with the expansion of up to eight energetic bodies. When following the dietary requirements and breath techniques that we have spoken of, this is easily obtainable. Even I, myself, have had the pleasure of this experience.

There comes that point in the focus of all embodiment, when one decides it is time to move on, and one begins to wonder, "am I to Master thought?" It is in the ninth collective body that the Mastery of thoughts begins. Dear one, you well know that practice is a building block of this universe. In the beginning, there was the Word, and the Word, as we know, is the light of God.

Dear one, please remember that this work is the work of experience. What we are giving you, are alignment procedures for Ascension. If you are to step forth in the mantle of consciousness, as one shall be Co-creative with your Brothers and Sisters, you must understand that it is the experience that shall build this body of work. This which we give you at this point Dear ones, is only the outline, or the foundation, or better yet, the skeleton, or frame. Now you must fill this vessel, have the experience, as Beloved Brother Sananda has spoken of, "what is the difference but the experience."

We will give you information up to the energetic bodies of eleven. After that, Dear ones, we ask for you to go forth and to have the experience. You then shall practice upon those who come to you. This work brings you the experience Dear ones. It is a work of world service and allows those who have offered themselves for this service to become the cosmic servant. Your Earth Plane and Planet in transition has allowed the dispensation of life to be sustained and maintained. This is the period of the millennium, or grace. In order for grace to be sustained and maintained, the cosmic pillars must be intact. Up to this moment, four Beloved beings have offered to serve as these four pillars; however, during this Time of Grace, four pillars must come from the planet itself, those who shall offer themselves to serve as mighty pillars of energy to this planet.

Those who have come from the planetary system of Troy extended their work of service to Venus. The beloved son of Kumara then offered this great Ray of Love from his heart to this planet. So, it was first decreed that it shall become the paradise of love in action. It is Venus that is love in expression, but it is this planet that shall become love in action. We realize that it has been very trying for you to experience your love in action, but it is time Dear ones, that action is made without any sense of blame or guilt, as action which is made truly from the forgiving heart.

I understand the limitations you feel in the human shell. Love in action shall stream forth as you expand your energy body. It's easier to sustain and maintain. It is easier to make the choice to shatter this illusion of flesh. What we want you to understand is that you truly have life in action, from the smallest particle of energy to the largest, the sun. It is our love that is in action on this beloved planet, for the great Cosmic Being Babajeran has offered her heart to be this for you and also Lady Amaryllis, who stepped forth and who lovingly put her love in action. All who have come to this planet have demonstrated love in action. All that shall be upon this planet is again love in action. Have faith Dear one, that this victory is assured, for there is no finer victory than the freedom of life. For life to be sustained and maintained, the victory of Ascension shall be. And now Dear ones, with your permission, may I introduce Beloved Serapis Bey?

Len: "Please come forth Serapis Bey, and thank you very much my Dear Brother."

He's walking over, a slight man, about 5'6", in a white tunic and shawl over his shoulder. He carries a staff, with a gold ram's head.

Welcome Beloved students, I AM Serapis Bey. I request your permission to come forth into your energetic fields.

Len: "Come forth Dear one, you have my permission."

Andrew: "Thank you for your presence, and we welcome you."

It is a great joy that I am here as we continue this work, step by step, one foot in front of the other, shall we say, as we direct these steps toward teaching the Ascension. Our Beloved Saint Germain has explained the intent of this work. Do you now understand what energetic work truly is?

Len: "It is all the focus of the Ascension."

It is love in action Dear one. All energy that you carry or hold on this planet is love in action.

Len: "Ah-h. That is because that is the vibrational intent of the planet's creation."

Precisely Dear one. As we have stated before, this work of Ascension is really quite simple; however, it would appear we have given you complicated procedures. But we understand that you deal with the manifestation of the human mind, the mind that must dispense this material and use it to further the love in action. Here I begin our discourse on the ninth energetic body. Do we have questions from the eighth energetic body?

Len: "Yes. Last evening, we did not complete, as far as my knowledge goes, the adjacent points of seven and eight."

The adjacent points of seven and eight come forth approximately front of the solar plexus, and in back, close to the tail bone, or the Sexual Wheel Chakra.

Len: "Then, the adjutant points do not exactly line up for seven and eight?"

These adjutant points are exactly parallel to the adjacent points running to the Will Chakra and the Heart Chakra.

Len: "In human physiology, we have an adjacent point between the hips in the back and just below the sternum in the front. Is this exact?"

This is precise Dear one, for you must understand that there is more energy housed by the human at this point.

Len: "I understand, and I accept it. Another question, there is something that you have that I may ask for?"

Proceed.

Len: "If I come closer to your energy field, will you place your hands on my head? I'm not sure why I'm asking this, other than it seems like I should. It seems to me, there will be a space there for me to more clearly understand you. Is this correct?"

You are asking for your alignment pitch?

Len: "Yes! Is it appropriate at this moment?"

Close your eyes.

Len: "I am with you."

Hold your own hands to your temples.

Andrew: "I would also be included, if it is appropriate."

It is appropriate Dear Brother.

Len: "Shall I do the palms or the fingertips?"

Palms. Do you not hear the pitch?

Len: "YES!"

Hum it.

Len and Andrew are humming.

Did you feel the alignment that occurred in your Kundalini energy?

Len: "Yes!"

Did you feel it rush to your feet?

Len: "Yes."

There are approximately 144 pitches in this universe. You have hummed one that aligns your system to your planetary system. Presently on this planet, there has been a dispensation of thirteen pitches. That pitch which you have hummed comes from the Star Gate. This Star Gate is what you shall know, would you come forth to the eleventh energetic body. If, at any time, you have a problem in determining your pitch, follow this procedure again.

The hands of light are encoded with love in action. How does anyone upon your Earth Plane or Planet put forth the mighty works or acts of life, but to reach the hand out in service. Hold these hands again to your temples, which is where the focus of your thought lies. As you can see, it forms a line perpendicular across the forehead. It is the arching of this energy from palm to palm that one then hears his own encoded pitch. The ninth energetic body, as you have called to your beloved mighty I AM Presence to come forth in perfection, do you not feel a tingling sensation that comes over your hands, into your throat, and down into your feet?

The ninth energetic body occurs with the collection of thought between the I AM Presence and the HU-man self. You have known the mental body of the HU-man to exist approximately in the third field, is this so?

Len: "Yes."

Times this, three times three, or exponential.

Len: "And we have another mental body."

It's the mental body of the ninth alignment field which qualifies thought. The mental body that you deal with now Dear ones, is only the filtering system. You have your brain that works to create your choices; however, this is a gathering body, the body that qualifies as the electromagnetic spin. The ninth energetic body exists approximately, at times, thirty-six feet around the human shell. It is through the beloved mighty I AM Presence that you pull this in tighter. In the beginning, the ninth energetic body carries within it the Golden Ray. As one pulls it closer to the body itself, it takes on a silvery sheen and is approximately two inches from the body itself. It comes forth to the decree of the Presence:

I AM THE PRESENCE OF COLLECTIVE THOUGHT.

Len: "The I AM Presence is a collective thought?"

It is what we shall call a grid that is spawned in triangles of threes.

Len: "You and I have the same I AM Presence?"

You contain your own beloved mighty I AM Presence. We all contain our own beloved mighty I AM Presence, but there are the grids that are shared to these that are known as the Presence and we collect thought mutually. Do you understand?

Len: "So, in a collective grid, we are the same."

Precisely.

Len: "The ninth energetic body, at this thirty-six feet, expanded, is the undisciplined focus of it?"

Precisely Dear one. When you begin and focus discipline, it appears that you are enlightened.

Len: "Ah-h. So what we are doing is gathering this thought-focus body, so that it filters through the lower rates of spin bodies of one through eight."

And qualifies one through eight as one body.

Len: "Now I understand, that is why it turns from the gold to the silver-blue?"

Silvery bluish sheen.

Len: "Is not the eighth also a silvery-blue?"

They all are Dear one, when they pull closer to the one grid.

Len: "So when they pull closer to the collective grid, then they take that harmonic which forms a unity and in this unity, even you and I are the same."

Precisely Dear one. This is the collective expression of Brotherhood.

Len: "I understand and see the energetic pattern. It will be very interesting to draw to this density expression. I thank you."

Now he is diagramming pyramids.

Do you see this pattern Dear ones?

Len: "This almost looks like the Trinity to me, these three pyramids."

This is the pattern that pulls the focused thought as one harmonic unit closer to the body itself.

Len: "Ah-h. This is what Jesus did in the transfiguration."

So then you understand that you carry within your body only thought.

Len: "Is there not also feeling?"

Feeling comes with the next energetic body.

Len: "I understand. The feeling is then re-qualified."

I AM always in service. I AM.

Len: "I AM in service to you too and I thank you very much."

After a break, all agree to return to the session, Len is channeling.

Welcome my Beloveds, I AM Saint Germain, and I stream forth to you on the Violet Transmuting Ray of Mercy and Forgiveness. I ask permission to enter your energy fields once again so that we may continue this discourse.

Lori: "Welcome Saint Germain, please come forth."

Andrew: "Welcome and come forth, please."

You have been given instructions in the eighth and ninth energetic bodies. We will continue and proceed. Do you have any questions that I may be of assistance?

Lori: "The ninth energetic body that we just discussed with Beloved Serapis Bey, when a healer is assisting in holding space for the ninth energetic body, how may we best be of assistance?"

Assistance is held in the focus. It is important that each of those who are in assistance, who are aiding in this alignment process, have a clear understanding of the geometric configuration. First, the geometric configuration must be held in tandem consciousness to be of assistance in this process. This is either done through the assistance of auric vision or through the focus of the mind and the understanding that this particular energetic body, very much differs from those that have been taught before. This first procedure of understanding these geometric alignments is very important. Do you understand that the holding of the focus is a primary concern?

Lori: "I am noting that there are nine spheres on this configuration. Does anything in particular happen with these points? Are they like an inherent point or similar to the eighth energetic body?"

They are exactly inherent points. For each of these spheres, there is a point of interconnection and expansion. It is in this sphering motion that movement to the tenth, eleventh, twelfth, and so on is always functioned. You will note, as we go further into the discussion of all energetic bodies, up until the twenty-second, that of these, there are always portals, energy-connecting points. The spheres allow for the expansion; they allow for the step by step process to move on in consciousness.

As for your question, as to what can to be done, these points will be spun in a manner very much as chakras; however, they will not be spun in a single dimension rotation. They will be spun in a clockwise, multi-dimensional rotation; using both hands, as though you were cupping a ball. When you are dealing with your client or patient, who is lying on the table, each of these will be done in a manner that you will go to each of these points.

Lori: "So, you are saying that the ninth energetic body, due to the psychological trauma that exists, that they should lie down?"

This would be most advisable. In the lying down, the energy clearing can be easily facilitated.

Lori: "Now, I have numbered the points on here, and if you would look at this, Beloved Germain, did I number them accurately and identify the points?"

The point at the top is known as Point 1; the point at your left is Point 2. . .

Andrew: "One moment, please."

When you hold this up, the channel's auric vision permits me to see that you have numbered these exactly.

Lori: "Thank you. Now, we have a plan view of this. In order to get a perspective view, does this rotate around the body in a clockwise position, or is the grid like a blueprint that lies over the top and runs through the body? What is the dimensional configuration on this type of grid perspective?"

Dear one, do you remember your visit in the mountains with the Dear one and the Eight-sided alignment focus?

Lori: "I see, the Eight-sided Cell of Perfection?"

It is the same thing, in variation.

Lori: "Is there a Golden Thread Axis?"

Yes, there are several Golden Thread Axes.

Lori: "So, the Golden Thread Axis runs through every single one of these. I see. . . okay."

But runs, as you would say, top to bottom, North to South; it runs East to West; it runs front to back. Again, it is three axes.

Lori: "Correct. Is there one from one to five, three to eight, and two to seven?"

Yes, there is. You are exact, for you are also Master of this information. Once again, I am only reminding you.

Andrew: "Where is the body here? How big is this?" The body is encased.

Lori: "I see. Okay. I'm not sure how I would draw this, then. How tall would you estimate we are energetically, when we stand in our slowest vibration at Fourth Density?"

Remember Dear one, you are still focusing from Third Density and expanding to Ninth Density, when you are accepting this ninth energetic alignment. Your perspective, dimensional perspective, is a multi-dimensional grid system.

Lori: "Yes, now I understand it. Thank you very much. Now, each of the points, there is still the sphere, the adjutant point, as you call it. Give me the dimensions of an adjutant point."

An adjutant point is 3.8 centimeters to 4.2 centimeters. The adjutant point pulses, it has an expansion and a contraction, as is necessary in its aligning frequency.

Lori: "Is this where the pitch is held?"

This is where the pitch is held; this is where the pitch is released. In the 3.8 centimeters, it is held; at the 4.2 centimeters, it is released. This adjutant point is a sphere. The centimeters are the diameter.

Lori: "So, it's 3.8 to 4.2 centimeters in diameter?" In diameter. Now, do you see that you have nine points in one plane; you have points in the other plane?

Lori: "This body compresses then, or collapses in a sense, as this is the first collective body. The diagram that we have here, outlined in feet, when it comes in, it envelops the body in a sense. Serapis Bey was showing it approximately two to four inches above the body itself. Is that correct?"

I would like to step back, and allow my Beloved Brother to continue in the explanation.

Both: "Thank you, very much."

I AM Serapis Bey.

Both: "Greetings Dear one."

Greetings Dear ones, I come forth on the Fourth Ray of the Archangel Gabriel. This is the way of Ascension. Do I have permission to continue in discourse?

Both: "Please proceed."

Then with your permission, I shall enter your energy field.

Both: "You have our permission."

In listening to your question, I will refer back to the two inches in close proximity to what you call the physical body. Please bear in mind that each layer of your energy body corresponds to a dimension and that everything is built in this dimensional grid system. In the alignment and focus of the ninth energetic body, the acceptance of all mental experience, from all embodiments, brings forth to your Ascension. All reflects back, even into the flesh, for has not the flesh carried a coding system that is energetically fashioned from lifetime after lifetime. Is this not also that which you desire, to purify in thought?

Lori: "What I desire is to bring forth in perfection."

It is in the purification of this thought that the perfection streams forth, for the thought focuses the space and allows the love in action. As we proceed further in the understanding of the ninth energetic body, we must bear in mind that each of these sections, or grid patterns that are then gathered unto the focus point of the I AM, are bringing with them coding systems of all embodiments. This is why our Beloved Brother Saint Germain has given to you that there is a time, or period, when you may find much stress, or much challenge, during this alignment.

Lori: "Approximately, how long does this take, particularly for a healer who is working with a client or patient. Of course, Sananda spent forty days. Is that what is required of a healer?"

For each coding system of each Star seed, there is a difference of time.

Lori: "So, can the healer start the process and then allow the client or patient to proceed with his or her own process alone with the I AM Presence. Or, what is the process that the healer serves here?"

The healer serves as facilitator in the understanding that this process will proceed in a step-by-step fashion. If you look at each of these patterns, you count in upper and lower pyramidal structure, four sections of two, which is eight for one plane, and four sections of two, which is eight for the conjunctive plane. You see, everything has a balance; everything has a polarization. There must be a conjunctive intercepting plane to create focus. Have you not read of this, brought to you by one of your other Brothers? Has he not said that in this conjunction, that there is a rate of spin which is then formed and a precipitation of an energetic pattern? So too, in the ninth energetic pattern, there is the conjunctive plane for the conjunctive axis.

To answer your question further, as far as time limitations, we would recommend first, that the individual who desires to take upon the ninth energetic body would, as prescribed before, fast for seven days. In this Time of Grace, of Transition, and time compaction, the forty-day period is no longer serving to facilitate the transition. The seven days of solitude; the seven days of meditation; the seven days of fasting; and one-half gallon of water per day is sufficient time for preparation of alignment. It is during this time that the individual, choosing to take on cosmic service, is then accepting responsibility for all Co-creative experiences to this point of creation. It is at this particular moment in the acceptance, that the individual, bringing and drawing forth this collective experience of all embodiments into this ninth energetic pattern, is then of an allowance of the Divine Will to work within.

We ask that the facilitator for each of these individuals treat this ninth energetic patterning on an individual basis until you have sufficiently Mastered the experience that each goes through. But sufficient experience will be acquired at the ninth, and then, again, at the eighteenth, and then still again, at the twenty-seventh. You will note in your personal experience, the great pattern that you so have. By the eighty-first client, you will have sufficiently Mastered, to the point that we would then ask a group of eighty-one be gathered for this alignment, and that each of the eighty-one follow the prescribed dietary regime of two meals a day, as earlier prescribed. We would recommend that you bring forth this information also, and make this available. The facilitator in the individual's experience would then have the sensation of the energetic pulse. There may be times when the individual client on the table is experiencing great discomfort. We would ask at this point that you step back and break. Allow this to happen in an easy manner.

The amount of time that one must see the facilitator depends on the individual. Each Star seed, each coding system, has a minimum requirement: first Star seed has a minimum requirement of seven visits; second Star seed has a minimum requirement of nine; third Star seed, eleven; fourth Star seed, fourteen; fifth Star seed, sixteen; sixth Star seed, eighteen; seventh Star seed, twenty-one. Now, you have noticed that as the numbers progress, so do the minimum-required visits to facilitator increase. This is because the world service alignment and the cosmic service acceptance grows exponentially. It is a momentum.

You will be able to identify each of these individuals when you place your hands on the temples at the first visit. You will hear in your heart of hearts each numbering; you will hear "a first Star seed," you will hear "a sixth Star seed," and you will hear the pitch when you place your hands just as you received guidance now; you will hear this. Keep the exacting, or log, for each of these experiences. At some time, in the very near future, you will very easily look upon one and be able to distinguish these Star seeds. It is unlikely that you will work on any of seven Star seeds; you will work mainly on one through six. However, for the energetic completion of the pattern, it was necessary to give this information. Are there any questions?

Lori: "At this moment, I don't have any. I would like to review this tomorrow and present questions."

Then I will proceed with one other process. In the group working, this will be done as described yesterday, with the standing up and the lying down. This will be done in a group section, and as the group consciousness forms a collection, you see how the double pyramid, based one to another, is formed on this ninth energetic body. So too will the group form this geometric configuration. It will facilitate, for the facilitator, the process of the alignment. When you walk from one end of the room to the other, it is simpler if this is facilitated while they are on the floor.

17

We are divine beings, having a human experience.

Disciplined Focus
Sananda
Saint Germain
Mary
El Morya

The next morning we awoke early and re-examined our drawings from the last channeled session with the Spiritual Teachers. Andrew was thrilled, as this gave him the additional clarity he had been seeking regarding his energy work. He was anxious to incorporate spiritual activation of the Eighth, Ninth, and Tenth Light bodies. Even though we were reinvigorated by the trance sessions, Andrew felt tired and tried to explain this to Len and me, "I'm uncertain just how to explain how I feel and why . . ." An unusual look of worry furrowed a deep line across his forehead. This was extremely unusual as Andrew is usually upbeat, hopeful, and while intense, always in a good mood. "I guess I've had some heavy karmic lifting lately . . . sometimes, I just don't feel like I'm getting ahead, financially, spiritually, and even in my relationships," he said.

We had known Andrew for several years now, and he always seemed to be surrounded by unique and interesting people. In fact, his home in Sedona was actually a large networking hub of New Age thinkers, visionaries, and healers. Len walked over, stood behind him, and began to massage his shoulders. Andrew sighed as Len began to move energy through him. Andrew said, "I know things will inevitably get better, but sometimes I feel like my work is futile." It was apparent he was in a slump; perhaps, a change of pace would be helpful.

I remembered the Mineral Museum, located at the college, "How about a late brunch, and before that we'll stop in to see some beautiful crystals?" I knew this would pique his energy – crystals were his passion. While viewing the beautiful cases filled with rows of unique specimens of gold, silver, and sparkling jewels, we discovered that some of the crystals hearkened from the unique provenance of El

Dorado – the Cities of Gold. From 1540 to 1542 Francisco Coronado marched around the southwest United States, searching for the alleged Seven Cities of Cibola – cities filled with riches and gold.

Spanish settlers followed and formed one of the first settlements in the New World near the Rio Grande River, where the Piro natives gave the newcomers assistance, food, and water. This settlement was later named *Socorro*, which translates to "help" or "aid." This unique treasury was known as "Coronado's Treasure Chest," and was collected by many of the conquistadors in their insistent search for the fabled Seven Cities of Gold. Now this collection rested on the glass shelves in front of us.

Coincidentally, it was now hundreds of years after the Spaniards' search that we were viewing their remnants, on a search of our own. Our journey to the Golden City was similar to the Spaniards' in some ways, and was also fueled by a desire to seek the unknown. Our journey to Gobean was indeed a physical journey, yet stark in contrast as our intentions were spiritual. We supplanted the greed and violence of the past with spiritual conquest; our goal was to explore and understand the vast planes of consciousness.

Afterwards, over sopapillas and honey at Frank and Lupe's Restaurant, I made a suggestion, "How about another session and you can ask the Spiritual Teachers why you've been down?" Andrew avidly agreed, and the next session became a transcript of a lesson from Sananda, Saint Germain, Mary, and El Morya.

The topics presented in this lesson were practical and yet, compelling. The first question was, "How do Lightworkers, after Spiritual Awakening, keep their joy and passion for their work, often their soul's mission?" And from a more practical point-of-view, we queried, "How do we continue, in that self-directed purpose, to support ourselves financially with success and inner joy?"

As suggested by the Spiritual Teachers, when life becomes too complicated, immediately slow life down and start to reflect inwardly. From the soul's stillness, we can retreat into the sanctuary of the I AM – the individualized presence of God where we can evaluate and make better decisions. Many newly awakened aspirants and chelas often comment, "I wish the Masters would help!" Unfortunately, that is not really their task. Sananda says, "We cannot do this totally for you, but we can share in this experience that we have, and it is an experience founded on love." Interestingly, applying the Law of Love becomes a critical nuance to our inner balance. The Masters suggested "eating" the calming, harmonizing fruit of love, a sweet, gentle food that can restore our spiritual metabolism. I referred to this anomaly in an earlier lesson as a way to self-gage our own inner peace, awareness, and vibration; yet, in this lesson, the Spiritual Teachers raised this phenomenon as a science, which is uniquely calibrated through the thoughtful disengagement of negative self-destructive emotions, primarily anger and fear.

To increase spiritual metabolism, the masters suggest using "chakra breathing" as a way to adjust your spiritual frequency. They also refer to this breathing method as a way to adjust "rate-of-spin." There are many different forms of chakra breathing, so I suggest you do some research and find the one that works best for you. In fact, this lesson does not even describe which is best. But for those who are new to this spiritual technique, here are some basics.

First, familiarize yourself with Chakra Colors and the location of the energy centers. The following is a guide, based on the I AM America Spiritual Teachings:

> **First Chakra** or *Root Chakra*: Red or Ruby, located at the base of spine – the perineum; the energy of this chakra flows between the legs downward and connects to Mother Earth.

> **Second Chakra** or *Sexual or Creative Chakra*: Orange, located in the lower abdomen, between the navel and genitals.

> **Third Chakra** or *Solar Plexus Chakra*: Yellow, located between the navel and base of the sternum.

> **Fourth Chakra** or *Heart Chakra*: Green, located at the center of the chest; the heart.

> **Fifth Chakra** or *Throat Chakra*: Blue, located at the throat.

> **Sixth Chakra** or *Third Eye Chakra*: Dark Blue or Purple, located above and between the eyebrows.

> **Seventh Chakra** or *Crown Chakra*: White or Gold, located at the top of or just above the head.

[Editor's Note: for additional information on the seven chakras, see *Light of Awakening*.]

Then, use the following method:

Close your eyes and inhale. On the first inhale, visualize a Ruby Color permeating the First Chakra. As you exhale, see the chakra light up with Ruby light. Visualize the chakra moving in a clock-wise motion. Continue to breathe while simultaneously visualizing colored light permeating the chakra. Use a total of seven breathes per chakra, comprising both the inhale and exhale. After you have finished the first set of seven breaths, continue onward to the Second Chakra, and to the color affiliated with it. Proceed to complete the process for each of the Seven Chakras and their unique color. A complete set of breaths will contain a total of forty-nine breaths – seven breaths for seven chakras.

The Spiritual Teachers ask that we understand what it is to be human, "You are being asked to understand the periphery of what it means to become a Master. You are here to Master the human experience." To paraphrase, this means learning to view humanity from the "periphery," beyond self-focus, and act accordingly. Perhaps some of the best advice from the Masters to come out of this lesson was, "Come rain, come shine – you are divine."

❧

We are in Socorro, New Mexico with a friend, who will also be asking questions. Len opens the session with a decree, then Saint Germain steps forward.

Welcome Beloved chelas, I AM Saint Germain, and I stream forth on this mighty Transmuting Ray of Mercy and Forgiveness. It is this Violet Ray that streams forth to the hearts of mankind, transforming all that is within, into the act of forgiveness. It is the act of forgiveness that shall stream forth into the hearts of men, assuring that Prahna will be restored to her original state of kindliness. Dear Ones, I stream forth and bring with me those whom you requested. To my left is Beloved Sananda; to my right, Beloved El Morya; to my back, Beloved Kuthumi and Beloved Mother Mary. We have all stepped forward Dear Ones, at your request and now, with your permission, may we enter your energy field?

Both: "Please come forward, we welcome you."

Welcome my Beloved students, I AM Sananda, and I stream forth on the Golden Ray. The swirl of changes that is brought to the Earth Plane and Planet at this time is a work of goodness. So what is goodness Dear ones, but finding that God source within yourself and extending it to your Brother and Sister.

There are times in your life that you feel that all is most complicated, but I ask if you will take one short break, one short minute, and in that minute, find the stillness in your heart, which assures that you are connected to your beloved mighty I AM Presence. This Presence is always with you, ever prevailing, ever Omnipotent. It streams forth from the Holy of Holies.

Do you remember Dear ones, as we sat and supped and all drank from this Cup? The Cup from which you have drunk has at times tasted bitter, but Dear ones, when this happens, I ask for you to stand back, take that short moment, catch your breath, and reflect within yourself: "Is this something that I should remove? Is this something that I should take out, or is this something that I should carry?" Dear ones, we all have a cross to carry. It is, of course, our choice as to how to interpret this cross we have.

Dear ones, all that you have in your life is not yours to bear, but is yours to bear with. It is the fruit of your labor which you shall be, in a sense, spoken of. This fruit which you bear constantly, taste your fruit. How is it Dear ones? Is it sweet or is it bitter? There are times, I know, within this work that you look at your feet and find them sandy and you think: "Is this even worth another step? The sun is hot and my throat is parched." However Dear ones, we must assure you that this work is indeed a work that streams forth with much joy.

This work that streams forth to the Earth Plane and Planet has brought forth a service to uplift the hearts of mankind forever. You are in the Seventh Cycle. What does this seven mean? This shall be the completion of all. And then we enter into the Eighth energetic Cycle, which assures that all shall finally be sustained and maintained. When I speak of the Heart of Desire or the Perfect Sound of Perfection, I speak of perfection finding an energetic that can be fulfilled, sustained, and maintained.

I am sorry if your drink is bitter Dear ones, or the fruit that you taste, or that which you are bearing, is not exactly as you would choose. Is this the wish you would fulfill? Is this what you wish to sustain? Is this what you wish to maintain? That is when you make the choice. If this fruit does not serve you, is it time for you to put your focus upon the ripened fruit in the field; or is it time for you to pour water onto your tree; or is it time for you to ask the sunlight to come forth to each of the branches? Dear ones, we cannot do this totally for you, but we can share in this experience that we have, and it is an experience founded on love. Do you have questions?

Andrew: "Yes, Sananda, I have a question. I would ask you if we are being obstructed in some way? All three of us feel very strange. I am feeling very lethargic and tired."

Virus indeed, very lethargic. But what does fear do, but stop you Dear ones? There are those who come to the Earth Plane and Planet to take advantage of the human's view of fear and anger. Do you understand?

Len: "It has been my observation that our coding systems carry this virus of fear and of anger. Is this an accurate observation?"

Perhaps it is more accurate to understand what happens to your world when you allow your thoughts to become focused on anger, on fear, for these allow your metabolic rate to drop instantly, or your rate of spin in each of the chakra centers. In the slowing down, or running down, as it is best stated, an energetic exchange occurs. Similar views that come from other dimensional expressions enjoy this type of activity; however, you must understand that you have allowed, through your implied agreement, for this to occur.

You must understand Dear ones, that our life is sacred, and our life is eternal, even that which comes from planetary systems that you are not familiar with. You must understand Dear ones, that this is a world, not only of procreation, but a world of Co-creation. All that is created is really of the Source, so that which comes, which seems to inhibit you, will come from that Source, the same as you. It is best that you understand what you must separate in order not to have unified disharmony, but to have unified harmony.

Len: "So what you're saying is, by redirecting the focus toward the fear, toward the doubt, toward the anger, then that is creating the energetic harmonic which allows those who resonate in that energetic to be part of your experience?"

The timing of the metabolic becomes distorted; the ratio of spin, which you are normally accepting into the chakric centers have a ticking, or timing, which becomes somewhat bent, or distorted. This process that occurs through anger, and also through the metabolic exchange of fear, allows the chakra to function in such a way that you would have an energetic coding, or the energetic fusion occurs. It is still this act of fusion that beings from dimensions puncture through and into this energy they are attracted to. This is known as possession. We have discussed this before Dear ones, regarding possession. It does occur; however, we ask that you not be in fear of this, for it is the simplest thing to remove. What you must do Dear ones, is to purify your body with water. That is indeed one of the most cleansing activities that you can do. Of course, we have always asked you to bathe, at least twice a day, once in the morning and once in the evening. However, since this has occurred, it is most important for you to find yourselves a body of water. It is also important for you to throw a bit of salt into this water, or to be near salt water.

As you have understood that the breath of life, or the breath that you are, contains your creative process. It is important then, that if you so choose, that you breathe into each of your chakra centers and adjust your rate of spin. Decree to the mighty I AM Presence to manifest in perfection. Demand and command Dear ones, for this is your Divine Heritage. Creation will adjust itself accordingly and lead. You see Dear ones, you are made and coded in the image and likeness of I AM. These are indeed the pitches, the key, that contain all within them for you to have full manifestation abilities in this universe. Do you understand?

Len: "Yes. So the step-by-step process is self-cleansing, self-allying, and self-focused."

Dear ones, it is important that you proceed without fear, for it is all part of creation.

Len: "This I understand. And you are asking us just to have an understanding and allowance of that, and to just go forth on this mission of choice, not be dissuaded one way or the other, and to stay on focus and purpose?"

Beyond staying on your cosmic identity, or your world service, or mission, which you have chosen to focus upon, it is important that you carry the winnings of creation, which is love.

Len: "So love should be the primary focus."

Of all that is, the greatest is love. If you should choose in your path, a world service which is not exactly the one which bears the fruit you wish to eat from, remember there is always the fruit you can choose to eat from that is the Law of Love.

Len: "I understand. Once again, we go back to choice."

All that exists in the world of service is the extension of choice. You must understand Dear ones, that even before you came to this of world service, you too made choices to get you to this portion of the path. So we think no differently of you if you choose your service or not.

Len: "I see; however, all has been set in motion in those agreements, has it not?"

It is important, in order for us to harmonize, that we first have our agreement.

Sananda is now sitting down and a lamb is at his feet.

Dear ones, I ask for your gentle heart to be expressed. In the mighty planet of Venus is the expression of love. Here on this planet of Prahna, it is the action of love. Act in gentle ways towards one another. Realize that no one is more and no one is less. As I have explained to you before, the difference is only experience. Let your experiences be gentle and sweet to one another. See Dear ones that this work that you bring forth, which is the extension of love to the Earth Plane and Planet in transition, is clearly and purely that. Beloved Mary has spoken of the Immaculate Concept. If you so choose, hold this work immaculately conceived in gentleness.

Len: "In our recent channelings, there was the inference of the four pillars and the sense that I received from that was that it was also a request, or it was being made known to us, that you were asking for those of us here in embodiment to act also in the capacity of the four pillars in a balanced harmonic. Was that correct?"

It is important for mankind to see himself always as a pillar of cosmic identity. It is important for him to take world responsibility. To become responsible, is to stand as the pillar, one who is firmly attached to the foundation, and yet one who reaches to the sky. Becoming the pillar assures that the foundation will be built and the structure will be maintained and sustained. Do you not see how we are all pillars in one fashion or another? There are, of course, those who step forth in this service, or this work who decide that they shall become pillars, in a sense. Have you not experienced pillars in your community? Pillars you have known in schools? Pillars you have known even in religious activities. In this work that we do, or this relationship that we have in a sense developed, we have asked that you become a pillar, if you so choose.

Len: "Since it has been my Heart's Desire my entire life to be as you are, if I am found acceptable, that would be my request, to stand in your place."

If you so choose to stand in my place, travel to where I am.

Len: "I so choose."

As you know Dear one, my work is in Ascension Valley, and my focus is carried at the apex of Shalahah. This is the work that I bring forth, my work of cosmic service through the millennium. This Dear one, is the work of serving as the pillar.

Of course, as in all things, many are asked, but you know that so few follow. Should others come to be of service with you, let them stand as pillars with you, standing on a firm foundation of the beloved mighty I AM Presence and reaching to the sky, taking a full course of their divinity and carrying forth with Co-creativity. This work is brought to bless mankind; it was never brought to bring division.

Len: "Sometimes our desire is interrupted when our focus is on fear."

You must understand Dear ones, these are truly natural ways of the human. You are being asked to understand the periphery of what it is to be HU-man; you are being asked to understand the periphery of what it means to become a Master. You are here to Master the human experience. And all of you contain, each and every one of you, the spark of divinity, and heritages that are rich from many planetary life streams. All of you, in a sense, are from many, many cosmic identities. This experience which you are choosing now, is to Master a human form on Prahna. To assist in this development, you have chosen, at the Time of Transition, the Earth itself, or Beloved Babajeran, to enter into her cycle of sustainment.

Len: "Yes, the cycle of sustainment. We would be most joyous if we could sustain this harmony."   Please see, this Beloved Babajeran is not much different from you, for she too has taken, in a sense, a human experience.

Len: "There are times when I see her actually as a human . . . as I appear, or as you appear to me. Then, there are other times when I see her as a planet. It is very interesting."

She contains at least seven individualized identities which stream forth for each transition.

Len: "Is each transition sponsored by a Ray?"

Of course Dear one, but the Rays play such a remarkable course in creation. This Ray that streams forth to begin the eighth sustaining period is the Golden Ray. I would like to take a short break, and then I shall return to continue our discourse regarding energetics.

I need to rest and Len continues by channeling Saint Germain.

Welcome my Beloved chelas, I AM Saint Germain and I come forth on this Violet Ray and ask permission to enter your energy field.

Andrew: "Please enter. You are welcome."

You have seen how your thought and feeling are truly Co-creative. You have, as we say, experienced that which you have energetically dismissed. We too experience instantaneous action without thought and feeling. This is the path that each and every one of us travel in this experience of Mastery of the human form. We would ask also in your consideration of your focus, that you come forward in a sense of true joy, for this service is of true joy.

This service that we share with you, we ask that you in turn share with others in a sense of true joy, as we are in this true joy. Many times you have called unto me; many times you have asked for your guidance. As Beloved Brother Sananda has said, "step back." Yes, step back into that moment of silence and ask for that I AM Presence, for in that, your true guidance and Mastery is; the expression of this union with your I AM Presence, is that you truly are the image and likeness of God, the I AM THAT I AM. We ask you just to remember this, for this is a very important part of your path. You will find that true joy in that space, that stillness. And now, I would like to ask if you have questions?

Andrew: "I have a question, Saint Germain. I am wondering what is stopping me from having a more direct connection with yourself and others on your level of being."

We would ask that you find that stillness in yourself. You see, each one of you is part of us, and we are part of you. We would ask that you sit in that silence and we will truly come and speak to you. You will hear us. We will come forth very softly in that stillness. It is remembering that stillness inside is the pathway that allows each and every one of us to have a harmony of focus. It is that space inside of you, that your I AM Presence comes forth; that your I AM Presence shares the experience of divinity. It is in this path that we come forth too. We cannot come to you without your permission, or your request. There is nothing stopping you Dear one. It's just holding the focus of the stillness inside and knowing that you are truly of great value, that you are truly a most Beloved one. We would ask that you come to us in your stillness, and there we are. Do you have questions?

Andrew: "I have a question that I am almost embarrassed to ask, but it's been bothering me for a long time. It is about what happened the other night with the flies and I often take the position that all life is sacred, like Sananda said just a few minutes ago. I am wondering, do we make exception for the pests, such as flies, and mosquitoes, and animals that would harm us, or is all life sacred to the point that you kill nothing?"

All is in energetic balance. All life carries divinity. The fly which you killed is of an energetic balance. All we ask of you is to find in yourself that sense that divinity pervades and is part of all creation. There is no judgment in the killing, as you will, of a fly, or of any animal that you perceive is of harm; however, in our experience of Mastering the HU-man form of thought and feeling, we, in a step-by-step process of working in the stillness, were able to eliminate the experience of fear and of anger; we were able to eliminate the experience that was even, as you perceived, necessary to kill the fly.

All of these experiences come up to you as you proceed on the path. It is as though you started in a soft meadow and then you traveled on through a forest and you traveled onward to foothills, until finally you come to the great challenge of self. And, as you climb this mountain of self, as you proceed to the summit in your great desire of self-conquest, you will always come across the rock that is loose to support here and you will come across the crevasse that you must traverse. It is part of the path. The fly is no different, nor is any other animal in the experience of your path, when you are climbing the summit of the self. Once you have reached the summit of the self, it will not seem so high or so difficult. You will then be able to traverse and climb the summit many times with great ease, and in that, the loose rock, you will then scamper across and the crevasse, you will just gleefully slide over one edge to the other. It will mean nothing. It will be nothing, for you have already Mastered the experience.

The moment will come when the fly will no longer cause a disturbance, will no longer be attracted. As Beloved Brother Sananda had said earlier, the focus of the anger and fear attracts the being. Do you think these beings have no influence over the fly? Or have no influence over your dog, or no influence over any other creature? They do interact, for each of these creatures has a connection with all of creation. And so, in the doubt, in the expression of your fear, or of your anger, these small parts of the path will be attracted to you electromagnetically. When your focus is only on that which you desire to create, then the periphery of these experiences will no longer sit on your path, they will be to the side, for they will not be part of your expression or your choice. With your permission, Beloved Mary would like to bring forward information on the desire of your heart.

Andrew: "I would welcome Mary with great joy."

Welcome my Beloved children, children of the Golden Flame of Desire, of Perfection. I come forth to you in the light of purity, in the light of understanding. I come forth to you, so that you will understand this Immaculate Concept. It is a discipline to keep your concept pure, to hold a focus of your true Heart's Desire. You are all part of the great family of creation; you are part of the great family of service. You have come here with the Immaculate Concept and the desire to bring forth service, so that the transition will be complete in a manner of peace and harmony.

This service is of great joy; this service is the most perfect concept that can be brought forth now in this transition. I would ask you to hold this focus, to see yourselves as the true lighted beings of radiance that you are. You are truly my children and I carry each and every one of you close to my heart. Hold this focus, this Immaculate Concept, that you are perfect in the eyes of God and in my eyes. And all those who assist you, see yourselves immaculately conceived in preparation of your service and to bring forth the pattern of your Ascension and to share this with your Brothers and Sisters. See this and focus. This is such a great joy, this work you do. You are bringing forth the understanding of the perfection that you truly are. See this joy, feel this great joy well up in your heart. Have that as your focus, have that as your Immaculate Concept, and all else will have the perspective as being a gentle breeze through the trees on a soft spring day. All else will come to you in this joy. Do you have questions?

Andrew: "I can't think of how to phrase my question, but I have a tremendous problem in maintaining a joyful attitude and happiness. I always feel burdened by, if not my problems, then there are always other peoples' problems, there are problems of the world, so there always seems to be something on my shoulders."

We would ask you to sit in the stillness of your I AM Presence and to make a choice of your true desire, and if your true desire is to create and share joy, then those who also desire this will come to you. We do not deny the inharmonic activities in your world. We do not go about our daily experience, unnoticing the disharmony that exists in your plane of consciousness. But we would ask that this Immaculate Concept, this joy and divinity that you are, be your focus. And as you focus on this, others will focus with you.

In a moment where you find difficulty, we ask that you step inside yourself, as Beloved Sananda has already instructed. Step inside and call to your I AM Presence, and breathe ever so gently. You will then be renewed, to bring forth this joy. You will then be revitalized to carry this Immaculate Concept of your divinity and joy forward. Others will, in essence, have the marveling after joy, and they too will desire to be as you are; your example, your radiance, will permeate all whom you associate with. No longer will they come to you in a manner of burdensome attitude, for they will only come to you in a sense of joy. You will be of service by bringing this joy.

Before you came here, you and I sat and we talked of this service, and we fashioned the most perfect Heart Chakra. We fashioned the most Perfect Cell for you to bring this joy. We asked what experiences you would choose before coming to this service, and you chose all of those experiences which would bring the sense of compassion to those who have no joy. All the experiences of your life have come to this moment, the moment of your world service. And now, I ask you to remember all of these experiences are but the tools you have chosen to finely hone your focus upon joy.

The Immaculate Concept of your divinity is a joy to bring forth, and all those who have experienced as you have experienced will come to you. They will, as bees to honey, sweet nectar that you are, and they will come away replenished, and bring forth their own Immaculate Concept of themselves and of their joy. This I ask you my Dear one, to remember you are always in my heart. I am always with you; the joy is always shared.

Andrew: "Is this joy that which is lacking in my work?"

The choice of the Immaculate Concept is one that each and every one on the path of Mastery comes to. It is, as the Beloved Brother said, one of the loose rock. We see no lack in your work. We only ask that you bring to your work the concept of your divinity; that you bring that in a joyful expression, with great excitement; that you may share that with others, so that they too will be of joy in the concept of their divinity. It is only natural in the human world, when one is excited and joyous about a new understanding of self and wishes to share that with others, that the excitement and joy is contagious. We ask you to have some laughter, for your enlightenment will radiate in that laughter, the inner light that you truly are, the joy that you are. When I look upon you, all I experience is joy. You are the joy of my heart. Bring that forward in all that you choose.

Andrew: "May I ask another question? This has to do with difficulties with finances, with attracting the ability to support ourselves and support our work. Sometimes I think I'm doing the wrong work if I can't support myself in doing it, or am I wrong in thinking that I must support myself with this work? Is it better to support myself with something else and do this work in addition? I would be grateful if you would comment on this."

I will take leave of you and allow Beloved Saint Germain to come forward.

Andrew: "Thank you for your help and blessing. Thank you for being there."

Greetings Dear one, I AM Saint Germain, and I come forth on this Violet Transmuting Ray. As usual, I ask permission to once again enter your energy.

Andrew: "Welcome."

Your question of self-support is heard and duly noted. Dear one, this Immaculate Concept which beloved Mary has most joyously brought forth is a focus, just as self-support is a focus. You are on the path of Mastery. This is duly noted in the records. You are also on the path of world service. In the path of Mastery and world service, there are certain agreements that each of you make to fulfill your material needs. One, is to decree daily for these fulfillments; Two, is to always carry the focus of what you truly desire clearly in your mind. Do not allow doubt, fear, or anger ever to come forward, for then the focus is clouded, and once it is clouded, that's what you draw, that's what comes to you. Because of this path of Mastery, there is instantaneous effects.

If I were to think in a doubtful manner, that any of you would ever not succeed in your path, this effect would be extremely disastrous to your path and to my own, for that focus would come unto me a thousand times fasters than any lightning. So in the Immaculate Concept that Mary has brought forth for each of you, I also carry this Immaculate Concept for each of you. I hold this focus of your success. There is no doubt you will succeed once you have chosen to hold clearly to your focus. I now ask to take leave of you and Beloved El Morya, the Master of focus, will come forward.

Andrew: "Thank you very much."

Greetings Beloved chelas, I AM El Morya, and I come forth on the Blue Ray of Truth, the Blue Ray of Wisdom. I come forth on the Blue Ray of Focus. Dear ones, do I have permission to bring my focus into your energy?

Andrew: "Please enter and welcome, and thank you for coming."

IN THE NAME OF I AM THAT I AM,
I CALL FORTH THE FOCUS OF CREATION.
I CALL FORTH THE TRUTH AND
THE WILL OF GOD TO BE MANIFEST IN PERFECTION.

These are the beginnings of my personal decree. It may sound as though this is a large job, to bring forward the focus of truth, the focus of the will of God; however, it is with the will that the focus is truly maintained and, as it is my assignment to align the will of all those who desire alignment to the divine, I too now speak of the will. The will, Dear one, is the active energetic participation that keeps the Immaculate Concept on focus and purpose. It is the agreement-committal-energy action that allows all that you desire to come forth. It is most sacred and beautiful to have a focus; it is most sacred and beautiful to have the desire; but it is the will that creates the action. I would ask you now to, on a daily basis, call forth your will into Divine Alignment and Service. Then, as you decree for that which you desire, it will come forward, for it is the will that keeps you on purpose.

We have spoken many times of these Co-creative energetic balances of thought, feeling, and will; the thought being the light; the feeling, the sound; the will, the action. That is Co-creative. You, Dear one, are on the path of Co-creatorship. That which you think, instantaneously manifests, whether it is fear, anger, or doubt. We ask you to hold this Immaculate Concept and in a moment when the Immaculate Concept is difficult, as Brother Sananda stated very simply, "step back into your I AM Presence." Step back, take your breath, find the joy and the true essence of who you are. Bring that forward with a determination and a focus will never, ever be bent. These are the energetic patterns that one must discipline on this path.

There is compassion always. For yes, you have stumbled. For yes, even I have, on this path in human form. But it was the determination that, in the stumbling, I once again regained my footing. I stood there for a moment, took the breath, stepped into the space of the I AM that is within me, brought forth that focus, held that as an Immaculate Concept, and brought that forth in joy, in the determination to always stay on purpose. When you follow these, as a step-by-step procedure, success is insured. All will come to you, whether it be a need for financial assistance, whether it be the need for help. All will come to you.

Decree in the same manner: step back into the space, define what it is you truly desire, and come forth and decree in the name of the I AM THAT I AM that this be manifest, fulfilled, and sustained. Then release that and know that it will be. We ask you, as we always have in these teachings, to come forward in this perfection. Do you have questions?

Andrew: "Yes, if I may, I have a related question. In the past three years, I have had three occasions when the sum of $12,000 was either stolen from me in the form of merchandise or money, and it keeps happening. Is this some kind of a Karmic repayment or is there a lesson that I am not learning, that it keeps happening? What is the significance of the number twelve? It's very distressing to me."

You, Dear one, are on the path of world service. The three times twelve is thirty-six and thirty-six is three plus six, which is nine. The nine is the ninth energetic alignment that is your world service. No longer will the pattern be repeated, if you accept this world service. This alignment is the service. You, Dear one, have come across others in your path who have volunteered, who have voluntarily come forth to be part of your "loose rock," so to speak; they have, in an active manner, set you for what you call a loss. In the loss, find the great gain, find the gain that you now are. That which you need will come to you, as you focus on your world service, and we will never leave you. In accepting this service to this planet, to this plane, to this humanity, and to this hierarchical structure, we too are of service to you. You may step into that space and call upon me anytime you desire, as I have stated to you before.

Andrew: "I do accept the service, and I thank you for your offer."

You are currently in the radiance of the Golden City that I am sponsoring. This Gobean City is for you to go beyond all that you have accomplished. Each who comes here goes beyond the self and expands in the great will, the great desire, and the great truth that is from the Source that has created all of us. I ask you to go beyond whatever you have done. I ask you to be as you are, my magnificent Brother, as we are all Brothers and Sisters in the I AM. I ask you now to come forward. Do you have questions?

Andrew: "Yes, would it be appropriate for me to change my location of where I live, or does it make any difference, since I'm traveling a great deal. Would it be better to be living here in this area?"

Your current location is just at the fringe radiance of this great city. We would ask that you consider being closer in the radiance as your home. We would also ask that you do travel to these Golden Cities, as these energetic alignments are most suited to these Golden City areas. These Golden Cities are worldwide, and in the completion of this work, you will have access to that information in exactness. We ask that you focus in the next session on the ninth and tenth energetic bodies, for you too will work with these. They are part of your path and your service. If you have no further questions, we would ask to retire.

Andrew: "I thank all of you for your great assistance and service. Thank you."

18

*Feel the radiance of the I AM Presence and its physical
acre of light. Each acre builds the ONE unified field.*

Awaken to a New Day
Saint Germain
Sananda
Kuan Yin
Kuthumi

Our beautiful autumn faded into winter, and before long cool temperatures and snow approached the high mountain desert. I was asked to speak again at the Gardenia Center in Sandpoint, ID, but planned to present the information without Len. He would return back to the East Coast, for several weeks of small talks and energy work. We decided that we would spend Christmas apart this year. That would allow Carson and me to stay for several weeks at my parents' ranch with the girls, and Len would spend the holidays with his children and parents.

Before departing from the Albuquerque airport, we sat holding hands, "You're certain you're coming back?" I questioned him, trying to joke to hide my insecurity. Len squeezed my hand and kissed my cheek, "It will only be for a couple of weeks." Carson and I waved goodbye to Len as he joined the line to board his flight. Several days later, Carson and I flew to Idaho and were greeted by my parents at the airport. I must admit, it was nice to be in familiar surroundings again. They both commented on how tall Carson was. It's funny how you don't notice things that are around you every day. Reunited with the girls, we basked in holiday traditions for several days, wrapping small presents, baking cookies, and helping my grandmother decorate her Christmas tree. It appeared that the three children were thrilled to be together again.

Before we had left Socorro, I had mailed an especially large box of presents that I knew I couldn't check on the flight. Carson and I had shopped for several weeks, looking for just the right gifts for Bryn and Kait. Finally, one day at the department store, we found them: two beautiful old fashioned dolls in Victorian dresses. The price was a little high, so I placed them on lay-away, and made the final payment a few weeks before we left. I filled out the rest of the package with some pajamas, a few new outfits for both school and play, plus two boxed bath kits – one for each of them. I was now getting anxious; it was Christmas Eve, and the package had not yet arrived.

I scraped together a little extra cash, and ran into the small farming town to find something to wrap and place under the tree. I decided on socks, underwear, and new barrettes and hair-ties. Not much, but hopefully, with the gifts from my parents and their dad – they wouldn't notice.

Hours after opening gifts on Christmas Day, I found Bryn in my bedroom with tears filling her eyes. "What's the matter honey?" I sat down on the bed next to her, and brushed her long brown hair away from her wet eyelashes. She was hesitant, and then I could see a well of emotion burst, "You didn't get us anything for Christmas!" "Oh god," I thought to myself, "You are the worst mother!" I carefully explained to her about the lost package, and that I had presents for both her and her sister, but they hadn't arrived. It seemed to calm her somewhat, but deep inside I was churning. Even though I understood my commitment to live in Gobean, at that moment I questioned the practical sanity of my choice between Gobean and family, and not being able to fully be there for my children.

Two days later the box arrived, damaged, and with half of the contents missing. Fortunately both dolls were intact, although the wrapping paper was missing. I gave them to the girls. They were somewhat pleased, but I could tell that receiving gifts several days after Christmas was a bit anticlimactic. I asked them several times, "Do you like the dolls?" They both nodded. However, at that point, I was insecure about my parenting skills, exacerbated by the fact that we were living too far apart from each other for me to attend to their immediate needs.

A week later, Carson and I boarded a plane to fly back to the southwest. As I settled into our seats, I caught a glimpse, across the tarmac, of Bryn and Kaitlin standing behind the glass in the waiting area, still waving goodbye. I quietly made a vow to myself that as soon as it was possible, we would all be together again.

Our return home was uneventful and as we drove from Albuquerque to Socorro, I noticed that the high desert was brown and almost as grey as Idaho in winter. Upon return, the answering machine was filled with over four dozen messages, some orders – mostly minutia – but with an interesting message from Athena in Long Island. "Called to wish you a Happy New Year, and as soon as you get my message, would you please call back?"

It had been about a month since we last conversed, and I enthusiastically updated her on the status of New World Atlas and the production schedule. "Do you need any help?" she asked. I paused for a moment. She had helped so much already and I couldn't imagine asking her for more. "Um . . . help?" I responded. "I think the book is about ready for publishing."

"No . . . help" she reiterated. "Do you need help in the office – you know, with orders, organization? I think I could be of service in some way." For a brief moment I was a bit stunned, and then replied, "Well, if you are ever out this way you know you are welcome to come and stay. In fact, we have an attached, private mother-in-law suite, with its own bathroom."

"I've received guidance to come out and help you – that is, if you will have me," she nervously giggled. "Is what I'm receiving accurate? Do you need help?" I reflected for a short moment. It would be no problem at all to have her with us. In fact, with Len's absence, I would certainly welcome the company. But I had concerns: at this point I was barely surviving financially, and there was no way I could afford to pay a salary, let alone an hourly wage. Athena sensed my struggle, "And just so you know, I don't expect to be paid – I offer myself in service . . . plus, I want to experience Gobean."

"Of course," I immediately answered, but then asked, "What are your plans?" It was obvious that Athena had given this quite a bit of thought, as she clicked off a list of things that she needed to accomplish, including shipping her beloved car, fondly known as, "Little A." She continued, "And I'm thinking of taking the train out – that way I can stop and see a few friends along the way and enjoy a leisurely trip to the west." Before the conversation ended she added, "I think I will be there at the end of March."

After we hung up, I marveled at her inner courage to embark on a spiritual journey from the East Coast to the rural southwest. Yet, in some ways, it was no different than the same journey I had made just a few months earlier. And I had no doubt that she was inwardly directed by her Master Teacher, El Morya – the spiritual teacher who assists the development of the will and the Blue Ray of Gobean's light. The month of January was a bit bleak. Carson and I filled the quiet days by renting movies and making our weekly trip to Denny's Restaurant for dinner and dessert. Overall, he seemed to be doing well with his schoolwork, but was missing Len about as much as I was. Len's calls were sparse, and I sensed Len was in some type of crisis that he would not share with me. His calls, which used to come on a daily basis, diminished to about once a week, and then become more sporadic.

At times, I was reluctant to even leave the house, a bit apprehensive that I would miss his calls. And if he called and I called back, it was rare that he was available or could promptly return my call. A part of me knew that he might never return to Socorro and to our dream of living together and experiencing a Golden City; yet, another part of me intuitively knew that we were connected beyond the physical, and that our vows of spiritual partnership would continue, despite any form of separation.

Earlier that autumn, I made a connection with a friend-of-a-friend who had been involved with Ascended Master studies for many years. After a few telephone calls, Len and I invited him to stay for a few days, which he did. Before he left us, he insisted that we should meet his friend and spiritual philanthropist, Fred Segal. Fred called one late February afternoon to say he would be driving through Socorro in a few days – could we meet for coffee?

Unfortunately, I'd be out of town that day. Before Len had left for Philadelphia, we had been working on a feature video of the I AM America Map and its prophecies, and I had finally found someone who could give us a hand with the production. However, the videographer lived in Santa Fe, so we agreed to meet in Albuquerque, about halfway. On the day that Fred would be arriving, I would be with the videographer.

I apologized to Fred, "I'm sorry, but I have a business meeting that day – and I need to be back before my son is home from school." Fred sounded disappointed and asked, "Any chance you can see us after your meeting for a few minutes?" I figured, "why not?"

On that day, Fred and his partner patiently sat in a booth, about thirty feet away from where I was discussing the possible video with the Santa Fe producer. After the meeting concluded, I walked over, introduced myself, and apologized, "I'm so sorry about this."

I scooted into the booth, and Fred immediately put me at ease, "Actually, you did a great job with the negotiation. But I think his price is a little high, and I'd like to help you out." Again, I was a little dumbstruck as Fred took over the conversation. He shared his background, how he started his now famous retail store, and his eyes lit up when he spoke about the creation of his "Peace Park." He extended an invitation to me: "I'd like you to come to the Peace Park to visit – I will arrange all of your travel plans – plus I'd like to help you with your new video and distribution of the I AM America Map."

This was a huge offer. His kindness and generosity were overwhelming. And no doubt, we could certainly use this type of help. Yet, in the pit of my stomach, I felt apprehension. Before we departed, he handed me his phone number, "Just call when your schedule is free . . ."

A few days later Len called and I relayed the details about the meeting and the offer. He was quiet, and after a moment of reflection he asked, "What does the boss say?" "Boss" is Len's affectionate term for Saint Germain. I respond, "I haven't heard anything just yet. But if and when I do, I *will* listen."

About a week later, I was awakened in the early morning hours. I heard a male voice, commanding and compelling. His words permeated the room, yet when I opened my eyes I realized that the message had likely come from the spiritual ethers. In three-dimensional reality, the room was quiet and the gentle light of dawn peeked through the blinds of the east window. The message was certainly not a whisper or suggestion, and it radiated subtle power and assuredness with its simple verbiage: "Not yet." Apparently, like it or not, I had received my answer . . . at least for now. Reluctantly I call Fred, and declined.

Back then, I had wondered why my teacher from the inner planes had stalled what seemed to be an obvious opportunity. In fact, I was disappointed. Later, with the benefit of hindsight, and several more decades of maturity, I realized that at this juncture in my spiritual mission, even though I was deeply devoted to I AM America, I was still a novice. Exposure to the gross public can be extremely difficult, even when one is properly prepared. Simply stated, I was not ready.

According to the Ascended Master Tradition, there are several steps in obtaining the vital training of self-mastery. The first level is the *aspirant*. These aspiring students are beginners and excitedly hopeful about their acquisition of spiritual knowledge. At this level, the students aspire to spiritual knowledge; however, they have yet to discipline their energies through adopting the spiritual techniques that are assigned through, and monitored by a *guru* – a spiritual teacher. If the aspirants apply the discipline to their spiritual growth, they advance to *chela* – a Sanskrit term for disciple – the second level of spiritual growth. Since the chelas receive guidance and direction from their spiritual guru, when the teacher deems the students ready, the chelas move onto the third level of initiation, the *initiate*. The guru gives initiates an important task, or service, to specifically perform for the guru. It is the chelas' choice to perform or not, and upon acceptance of the mission the chelas literally graduate as initiates, through ritual and the vital process of overshadowing. At this level, the spiritual teacher enters the mind of the initiates to give constant guidance and direction. It is literally a melding of consciousness.

There are many levels of spiritual development in the stages of chela and initiate. Each stage of evolution is marked by wonder, intensity, joy, awareness, and spiritual wisdom. [Editor's Note: There are many steps of spiritual development and instruction that precede the pledge of the initiate. To learn more regarding the phases of spiritual development in respect to Ascension, see: *Divine Destiny*.]

Len called several days later, and I told him the news, "Don't worry," he said. "I've booked a flight and will be home in several days. We'll find someone to help us complete the video." That was the best news I'd heard in months. We hadn't seen each other since before Christmas, and it was now February.

He arrived the day before Valentine's Day, and I was a bit giddy – almost like a schoolgirl. Recently, the weather had been sunny and in the mid-60s, so I packed a basket filled with fruit, homemade cookies, and snacks, with the hope that we could find a park someplace for an intimate lunch together. After we left the airport, we located a park and stopped for some quiet time. I sat next to Len on the park bench, and he wrapped his arm around me as I unloaded the food from the basket and placed it on a tablecloth. "You went to too much trouble," he said, "But I love it." He smiled and he kissed me on the cheek. In some ways, it reminded me of our first days together in Asotin. Here we were again, like old friends who had never parted.

Len's efforts on the East Coast were paying off. He was offering complimentary one-to-two hour living room talks, which led to participants signing up for energy sessions. In fact, he was attracting a bit of a following. Several of the students were interested in Ascended Master Teachings, along with the energy work, and had begged him to start some sort of training. So Len asked me "Will you come out and join me . . . everyone is excited to meet you, and I know your presence will add so much."

I was flattered, and Len was almost begging. But I knew that for now, while Carson was in school, going to the East Coast was not possible. Perhaps after Athena arrived I could; that is, if it was okay with her.

Within days after his return, Len made about a dozen phone calls and found a video studio in Albuquerque that could handle all of our video production. I gathered my slide presentation and several changes of clothes, and after Carson was safely off to school, we left early on a Monday morning to begin filming. Of course I was excited, but a bit anxious. Len was assuring, "There is nobody as well prepared, or who knows this material better than you." I appreciated his vote of confidence. I marveled over how well we worked together creatively. Our relationship, which seemed a bit frayed for months, was again cohesive and cooperative. When we were not separated by economic need, the spiritual work united us as ONE. When we were in this artistic, productive state, our spiritual partnership seemed solid and my past feelings of hesitation and uncertainty disappeared.

After a week of filming, constant editing, and making multiple decisions, the video production was complete. We decided to name our new film, *Moving into Our New World*. With the *New World Atlas* book close to publication, and the upcoming video release of the I AM America Map prophecies, several of our most important goals were close to completion. Yet, we still needed to compile the multiple maps that contained the global Earth Change prophecies, and while we had received the cartography and outlines for the world map, we'd yet to channel the information surrounding the prophecies and the vital accompanying spiritual messages for China, India, Australia, Japan, Europe, Africa, and the Middle East.

I knew how grueling this process would be. Receiving the information for the I AM America Maps required about eighty channeled sessions and transcriptions! Hopefully, with my evolved skill set and Len's ability to fill in, if needed, this process could be somewhat shortened. But more importantly, I had deep concerns about how we would create a map model for the new world map.

Dan had created the first model, and before I had left the Pacific Northwest I had asked him if he could help on the project. He was hesitant, but after reconsideration he handed me an estimate for almost six thousand dollars. It was obvious his intentions were monetary, so I decided to wait. Surely if the Spiritual Teachers wanted the world map produced they would make it clear and obvious just how and who would be involved, right?

This was the question that I posed to Athena, shortly after her arrival. Carson and I picked her up on a bright, sunny March afternoon at the train station, and we loaded her bags into the back of the Grand I AM. After settling her into the small apartment at our home at Socorro, and providing a welcome Southwest dinner at Frank and Lupe's Restaurant, she asked, "How far are you on the world map project?" A bit frustrated, I responded, "I'm a little stuck . . . I don't have a clue who will help with the map model, plus after that I need to find a good photographer and then a printer!" "Who created your first map model?" she asked, unaware of my previous efforts. I briefly explained why using that same person was not possible, and she quickly replied, "I'd write and ask him again. Maybe he'll change his mind."

Athena was remarkably easy to live with. After Len left us, again, for work in Philadelphia, it was nice to have company. And because Athena had just left Long Island, and was biologically still several hours ahead, I awoke every morning to a freshly prepared pot of coffee. Plus, she was organized! In several days, she had mastered the computer system, caught up on filing customer invoices, and took over my almost daily trip to the post office. This allowed me to finish the final proof, and polish off the final layout of *New World Atlas*. Then I mailed it express delivery to the printer.

Several weeks later, Athena excitedly entered my office and handed me a large envelope. I tore open the package to find the finished book. Together, we inspected the front and back cover, and turned several of its pages. As if it were a new baby, we each took turns holding it, feeling its dimensions, its width and bindery, the smooth glossy cover, and the crisp, white interior.

After our initial excitement, Athena pointed to a letter addressed to me, found within the pile of mail that had arrived that day. It was a letter from Dan. A week before, I had taken Athena's suggestion and written him to ask, yet again, if he would consider working on the world map model for a reduced amount. This time I added that if he could not, "would it be possible to ship me the I AM America Map model?" I reminded him that I had paid for it, and that its return would be helpful for another artist to examine it for design purposes.

I nervously slit open the letter and read his response. I was shocked. Apparently, there was no model to return – he had thrown it out with his last move. Obviously, in my asking, I hit a raw nerve. His last sentence read: "You need to let go." I handed the letter to Athena and when she read about this unwarranted and thoughtless action, her dark eyes flashed with exacting insight, "We'll discuss this later tonight." No doubt, that was a soul dampening moment. It was like giving birth to beautiful newborn twins where one lives and the other is stillborn. I thought about the model and all that it represented. I could barely comprehend why he had made the choice to destroy it.

That night after dinner and dishes, Athena and I sat out on the patio in the cool spring air. The sky was lit with stars, and their vast beauty almost made me forget the loss I felt in my heart. Yet I knew that somehow I would traverse this obtuse closure – if you could call it that – and a new door would open that I would surely travel through. My inner thoughts were interrupted by Athena's voice, "Do you have Dan's letter?" I replied, "Umm . . . yes, of course – it's still on my desk."

Athena continued, "I've been thinking about it – and I think you should burn it." I nervously laughed, "Burn it?" "Yes," she replied, adamantly. "It is filled with the negativity of the past, and you need to embrace the future. Besides, Dan's a jerk." We both giggled a little.

I left the patio and quickly returned with the letter. Athena grabbed a book of matches. Together we placed the letter on the ground and lit it afire. And then something unusual happened: the fire suddenly turned an intense purple. Then, a flickering, alchemic Violet Flame engulfed the letter. We both stared in disbelief at the flame, and in seconds the flame vanished, along with the letter, with little to no ash remaining. Our eyes silently met, in astonishment, at this self-affirming experience. The Violet Flame had intervened, not only spiritually, but physically.

Carson was on a school break, and we all had a serious case of spring fever. So we decided to pack the car and drive to Arizona for a few days. Fortified with a thermos of French Roast coffee, we drove across I-40, through Winslow and Flagstaff, and arrived at Andrew's home, in the red rocks of Sedona, a little before 2 AM. Andrew was always the perfect host. Even with such short notice, he had arranged a talk for me, scheduled for the following evening at his home.

That evening, I updated a small group of people regarding Earth Changes and spiritual changes, and focused on new insights regarding energy fields and humanity's Ascension Process. After the talk we mingled, while Athena viewed Andrew's extensive crystal collection. The collection was, perhaps, one of the best in the southwest, with many large and rare crystals, collected specifically for their spiritual energies.

After spending an additional night in Sedona, we left early the next morning. Then we spent one night in Payson. This was my third trip to the beautiful Gobean community, located on the edge of one of the world's largest pine forests. I was anxious to see what Athena's insights were regarding the area, especially since we'd had discussions about possibly moving there. More importantly, I wanted to experience the sublime energies of the Western Door of Gobean, distinctively different than Socorro, Gobean's Eastern Door.

Athena and I had a unique friendship, unlike any other I'd experienced. We were blessed with a true telepathic rapport, a connection likely forged through lifetimes together. As we drove into the small town, Athena immediately remarked, "What a quaint town . . . what is the rental situation like?" Obviously, she was also feeling the high but subtle force of the primary ley line that pulsed through the town.

I intuitively blurted out, "There is another primary convergence of ley lines to the east, and yet another junction about forty-five miles south." Quickly she responded, "I was just about to ask — and you've answered my questions. The energy here is lovely and I think this is the right place for I AM America." She confirmed what I had sensed on my first trip here, about a year earlier.

Have you ever experienced a series of events that come together with such ease and effortlessness that you know they are meant to be? We stopped into a realty office. They had a three-bedroom condo, suitable for Len and me, an office space at an extremely affordable rate, and a small home that was perfect for Athena. That evening in the motel room, I was able to call Len, and explain the situation. "What do you think?" I asked. Without hesitation he replied, "Go for it."

That too, was extremely rare. I had learned that Len often needed time to think things through, sometimes for weeks. Also, in this case, there were no economic restraints, and with our limited income and budget, that, too, was unusual. So without uncertainty or reservation, it became obvious that is was the right time to move. When we returned to Socorro, I gave notice to vacate the home we were renting, and we readied ourselves to move four weeks later, at the end of May. By the time Len returned from Philadelphia, Athena and I had most of the home and office packed in boxes.

After loading our furniture into the truck, I found myself, yet again, following Len as he drove the moving truck across the beautiful lands of Gobean. We crossed the Plains of Saint Augustine, and drove onward to the New Mexico border, into the Round Valley of Arizona. It was here that I noticed the greatest shift of Vortex energies, due to the intense influence of the center of the Golden City Vortex, also known as the "Star." We entered the rolling hills of the Southern Arizona Colorado Plateau, traveled from Show Low, AZ, to Heber, AZ, and crossed portions of the Apache-Sitgreaves National Forest, onward to the biologically diverse Tonto National Forest that surrounds the "Rim Country" of Payson.

As we drove down the Mogollan Rim, I was churning with both excitement and fatigue. I intuitively knew that I might live for many years in the expansive beauty of the Gobean Mountains and its forests.

After unpacking a maze of boxes and organizing their contents, we became somewhat settled in. The girls would arrive in less than a month. I decided to travel two weeks before they arrived, with Len, to help him teach a large class in his hometown of West Chester, a suburb of Philadelphia.

With the excitement of moving and exploring our new home, Carson seemed sullen. Len and I were both a little perplexed about this. However, we realized that he was almost twelve and about to enter the throes of adolescence. Plus, he was probably a bit anxious about entering Junior High School in a totally new environment and having to face, yet again, the challenge of finding new friends. After several conversations with him, we decided that a few weeks at the farm were in order, plus, it would give him much needed time with his dad and sisters. So we purchased a ticket for him to return to Idaho.

As we stood in line at the luggage check-in counter, I noticed that he was now almost as tall as I was and he was no longer a child. When we had first arrived in Socorro, he was still a little blond-haired boy. Throughout the previous, time-compacted year he had suddenly matured.

Several days later, Len and I left Phoenix for Philadelphia. This was my second trip to the East Coast. My last had been my trip to New York the previous summer. I was excited to meet many of the new students studying the Ascended Master traditions. When I entered the classroom, it was impressive. There were at least eighty students and Len was speaking to them, on a small stage, through a microphone. I purposely sat several rows back to get a sense of the ambience and energy. I listened for about fifteen minutes, and then I realized Len was explaining material that we had taught together in our small classes in Lewiston, ID! In fact, much of the content came directly from our many channeled sessions together in Asotin. For a minute I was shocked – how could he?

We had always taught this information together; in fact, I had considered our spiritual partnership a sacred pact. I had never thought Len would teach or even mention the material that we had channeled and developed together without asking me first. True, I had known he was teaching. But I had genuinely thought that he was teaching information he had gleaned through his years of study of the Human Aura and alternative healing processes. I purposely quelled an inner spark of jealousy and continued to listen and observe.

Then I noticed that the young man, who was sitting next to me, was avidly listening, chuckling at Len's humorous antidotes, and obviously enchanted with his presentation of the material. I glanced across the room, and noticed dozens of faces lit up in loving adoration. And then it occurred to me, "Len is an aspiring guru!" I was stunned by this truthful realization.

In the past, through many of our thoughtful, intimate, and philosophical conversations together, Len and I had openly agreed that this type of teaching could become alarmingly diluted if we made ourselves cult-like gurus of this information. We agreed that our roles as physical, Spiritual Teachers of the I AM America Teachings would, perhaps, be best grasped as a *way-shower* – that of seasoned guides or mentors. We would show aspiring students the inner path toward the individual, magnificent light – the Mighty I AM Presence – because in truth, the divine guru is within.

Yet, the search for the inner guru often requires an outer guru; one who can maturely share his or her experience with love and compassion for the human experience. And we were both of the opinion that in our western culture, many spiritual students quickly give their identities and power away to spiritual gurus – a dark reality we wanted to avoid. Was Len crossing the line?

As I sat through the next hour of Len's presentation, I felt an odd mixture of many feelings beyond cursory jealousy – admiration and joy, mixed with darker emotions of loss and betrayal. By the time Len was ready for a break, I knew for certain that I was both annoyed and a bit confused. Even more frustrating was that I was certain the young man sitting next to me didn't even know who I was at all, and for a bleak moment I felt completely insignificant.

Only then did I realize why Len had been so conflicted and withholding over the past year. It was obvious that without me he had created an entirely different world, solely as a teacher of the material. And even though we once taught together in this classroom, it was now apparently his and his alone, and was now an entirely foreign domain to me. In fact, I was uncertain if I would ever again feel comfortable teaching by his side. Even worse, if I did teach with him, I questioned if I would even be welcomed?

Throughout the day, I was able to cover up the feelings that clashed about within me, but later that evening in our hotel room, I finally mustered the courage to comment, "I'm a bit surprised that you are presenting the I AM America teachings without me." I hesitated for a moment, felt the hard swollen lump in the back of my throat, and although I was too frustrated for tears I finally blurted out, "I feel a bit left out. Are you sure you want or even need me here?"

It was apparent I had caught Len a bit unguarded, and he immediately responded, "What do you mean – I always wanted you by my side." In that moment I realize that the fresh, glistening sheen of our newfound partnership had worn thin. We now faced one of the most typical problems in any relationship – *communication.* Metaphysically, I instinctively knew that students would benefit best through both a masculine and feminine interpretation of the teachings.

He continued, "Don't feel insecure . . . tomorrow I will officially introduce you, and I'd like you to present the information on the Earth Changes and Golden Cities." Len's voice was far from placating, and I sensed his genuine sincerity. For the moment I was relieved. However, realistically, I also knew that there were still multiple issues to work out and clarify as our teaching and spiritual partnership matured.

As Len promised, the next day I gave my presentation to a welcoming and eager audience. I honestly felt a little better about my predicament, and for several moments throughout the next day of teaching, I again felt our unique comradery. Yet, while the students were genuinely focused on the Ascended Master tradition, it was also obvious that they had forged an indelible bond with Len as their teacher. My entrance into this mix might challenge Len's authority and the students' devotion and respect for his leadership. It was apparent that for now, the strength of our partnership would lie in other arenas, and not in teaching together – at least in this capacity.

I decided to take a few days off while Len finished his class and completed his scheduled energy sessions. Since the energy sessions were scheduled at a student's residence, we would move there for a week. Our host, Rachel, was a lovely Lightworker and local networker who lived in the suburbs of Philadelphia, in Jenkintown, PA. Her home was also a hub for many students in the class. It was filled with activity where students would come and go, along with those clients who would wait for their appointment with Len. That gave me a chance to meet a few of the students personally.

I encountered a personable woman, Penny, who shared her thoughts with me through a series of thoughtful and insightful questions about the Ascended Masters, their teachings, and the experience of channeling. "Would you like to get out of here for a hike?" she asked, probably sensing my need to break away for some quiet and a little exercise. "Sure," I said, and I ran upstairs and slipped on some walking shoes. We meandered down a gravel road and if I hadn't known any better, I could have been anywhere in rural Idaho, with locusts singing and wildflowers growing along an old wire fence. "Oh, here it is . . ." Penny said, and we walked toward an entrance hidden in a grove of thick fir trees.

Penny Greenwell was an artist professor at a local college, but it was obvious that she was also a nature enthusiast. We walked along the trail that edged a meandering creek. It playfully dove and dipped along the forest of green trees, brush, and undergrowth. As we walked, she shared her story with me about her life as a single mother with four children, her experiences as an artist and sculptor, and the profound Spiritual Awakening that she experienced after she literally fell off a cliff. While falling sixty-five feet down into a dry creek bed when hiking in the Catskills Mountains, Penny experienced her life in slow motion. "At first I thought I was dreaming, and I spread my arms out like I was flying in the air, diving head-first," she explained to me. But when she realized she was literally falling, for some unknown reason, a memory of her daughter's twisting body in gymnastics practice captured her consciousness. She physically twisted her tumbling body just enough so that her head would not take the impact of the fall. Her back slammed into the rocks breaking four vertebras, two ribs, and dislocating her hip. At the emergency room she was accidently given morphine with ephedrine for pain, and the allergic reaction stopped her heart. Penny was dead for twenty-seven minutes. Then she experienced a NDE – more commonly known as a *Near Death Experience.*

As we walked along the narrow trail, my eyes glanced downward toward the rambling, water-filled creek, about twenty feet down an embankment. I shuddered at the thought of even falling or sliding that far down, and she had fallen three times that distance! I stopped in my footsteps, "What happened on the other side?" Penny recounted her experience very matter-of-factly: "At first, I floated to the top of the hospital room, and I saw my body lying below me. And then my grandmother – who had passed away many years ago, suddenly appeared. We flew together into the ethers, above the hospital, throughout the atmosphere, and then above the Earth. There she asked if I'd like to see my grandchildren." At that time Penny was barely forty years old, with no grandchildren; in fact, her two younger daughters were in high school and her two older children had just started college.

"We circled the Earth" – very typical for an out-of-body experience. Then she chuckled a bit, paused for a moment, and her intense blue eyes widened. "I saw a river – a silver river. It was the viscosity of mercury. Together, my grandmother and I moved into it . . . Then I distinctly saw Africa, Madagascar, China, the United States, and South America. These were the countries where my grandchildren, ages forty and older, worked and lived. And each of them [was] helping Earth through some sort of a crisis – one was working with water reclamation, while others were helping with overcoming the pollution of the environment."

I wondered if, indeed, this was a vision of the future, or if Penny had viewed the souls of her grandchildren before their births? So naturally I asked, "Had we [already] experienced Earth Changes?" On this point Penny was unsure, but she remarked that the encounter had left her with, "Hope." Then she explained, "I have no doubt that humanity will survive the Earth Changes and we will help to rebuild and regenerate [the Earth's] fragile systems."

We hiked in silence to the end of the trail; it was a lot to absorb. There was a unique energy about Penny, one that I can only describe as family, or *spiritual family*. No doubt, I felt like I already knew her well, and I was at ease in her company. As we retraced our steps along the steep incline of the trail, she began to recount her journey back into the physical, Earthly world, and it was not pleasant. She faced months of excruciating pain, walking on crutches and overcoming addiction to painkillers. Yet, it was through this journey that she inevitably became spiritually reawakened.

Unable to walk without help, a friend frequently checked in on her. And through word-of-mouth, members from an entirely new community entered Penny's world: acupuncturists, massage therapists, herbalists, and healers. Before long she was walking, and after a profound experience with a Reiki therapist, her body became pain-free. Yet she still wondered about her spiritual experience, and why she was given a unique glimpse into the future.

"A friend invited me to one of Len's living room lectures – I'll never forget it. It was on January 11th . . . I decided that I would sign up for a healing session, and it blew my mind." "What happened?" I asked. I was curious.

Penny replied, "Well, at first I felt a tremendous amount of healing energy and my body was recharged. Then Mother Mary appeared and she literally rearranged my energy. After the session, I told Len, and he responded, 'You are a healer.' I guess at that point I wasn't sure what a healer was... but now I know that Mother Mary began to reconnect the dots within, and validated that I am a spiritual being with a mission . . ."

Penny's voice faded for a moment, and then she candidly revealed her motives for our hike together, "I knew at that moment that for this man to so clearly understand the energy of the Master Teachers, he had to be with a strong spiritual partner. And I wanted to meet that woman."

For a moment, I was a little shocked, but somewhat relieved with her openness and candor, "I'm really glad that we met Penny," and then I spoke honestly, "I feel like we've known each other before." She immediately responded, "Yes, it's like we're sisters." At that moment I telepathically heard Saint Germain chime in, "You *are* sisters."

After our hike, Penny and I sat in Rachel's living room, enjoying a cup of tea. Penny continued her discourse. "I'm fascinated with the Map and the prophecies of Earth Changes." Her voice broke the silence in the room. "In fact, I can't help but wonder if my near death experience is related to the prophecies, and perhaps I play some sort of role to help others to make positive change." And then her voice changed, and it almost deepened. "I think I could help build a Map model for the World Map."

I wondered if she was channeling and my interest was piqued. No doubt Penny had the experience and the knowledge to properly execute the project. My only question was, would this be okay with the Master Teachers, especially Saint Germain? Even though we had a deep and unique connection, in reality we had just met. "I'll talk to Len and see what he thinks," I quickly responded. She answered, "No problem . . . in fact, I will see you tomorrow," and added, "I've scheduled an energy session."

That night Len was tired, in fact, whipped. He'd seen over a dozen clients that day, had worked through lunch, and had finished a little before eight in the evening. "Is there anything I can do?" I asked, as we settled into bed for the night. He thought for a moment and said, "Well maybe . . . Any chance you could help me out with the sessions tomorrow? I think I have about ten slots scheduled, and then I'll be finished for this trip." Without hesitation I answered, "Sure" and kissed him on the cheek. "Sleep well," I said. He was already asleep.

I laid in bed, serenaded by the rhythm of Len's breath and an occasional snore, while the thoughts of the day flooded over me. I reviewed the rush of new faces eager to become acquainted with their own ethereal light; the hike in the magical, green forest; and the visions from Penny's story – her horrifying fall and the wonder of her redemptive spiritual awakening and consequential physical healing. I wondered if she could indeed construct the model for the Map, and if she could, would it look as professional as the one Dan had constructed nearly three years before?

Before long, the dawn's delicate light streamed into the eastern bedroom window. My body yearned to sleep, but the excitement of a day helping Len with energy work prompted me to get up. I tip-toed into the guest bathroom; the mirror was covered with steam and Len was in the tub.

"Are you awake enough to talk?" I quietly asked. The water stirred, and I heard his sleepy voice respond with his own question, "Are you still going to help me today?" I quickly responded, "Of course – in fact, I'm looking forward to it." I was a little timid to interfere at that moment. I knew this was Len's time alone to meditate. Len then asked, a little more alert, "How was your day yesterday?" I spoke gently, but my words were jammed with excitement, "I think we may have found someone to build the World Map model."

Len and I worked throughout the morning. Similar to our days in Asotin, there was a heavenly collaboration between us and the many different guardian angels, Spiritual Teachers, and personal spirit guides who would often make an appearance during each healing session. Typically, one of us would stand at the top of the patient's shoulders, with the other holding the ankles, until we established a sufficient course of light energy. Then we'd start the energy balancing, while repairing certain chakras or charging weak energy fields. Sometimes, what we'd need to do for each patient was apparent, and streams of light energy would pour through our hands to the weak area. Often, this light easily and readily adapted to each individual and easily absorbed throughout their chakras, sub-chakras, energy meridians, and nadis.

For tough cases, however, Angels and Spiritual Teachers would preside, carefully instructing us or reaching through our hands to apply a specific light Ray, repair a grid, or selectively overhaul one or two energy fields. After each session, the energy in the healing room could be so intense that we'd often open a window. We'd witness the nature devas of the air and wind cleansing the room, quickly readying it for the next person.

It was late afternoon when Penny arrived for her session. She rested on the healing table, eyes closed. I stood holding her ankles while Len began to run energy starting from her shoulders. When I closed my eyes, I begin to hear a sublime sound; faint at first, but growing in distinct intensity. A bell from the ethers was chiming. I cannot easily describe its pitch and tenor. At first I thought I was hearing the sound clairaudiently, but when I opened my eyes, both Len's and Penny's eyes were open. Clearly, the three of us heard a tone that had pierced the spiritual ethers and entered the physical plane. My eyes glanced around the room to see if anything was generating the high-pitched frequency – but there was nothing to explain its presence. The heavens had opened, and the healing frequency filled our ears, our bodies, and the room. It lasted for about three minutes, and as subtly as it had started, it began to fade.

Afterward, a high-frequency energy permeated the room. For a minute we were silent, and then a smile erupted on Len's face, "Well, we know who is going to work on the Map model!" We all giggled like children. To this day, I have never experienced a physical phenomenon as unique as this one. The message was as clear and inspiring as the tone of the celestial chime; we needed to finish the World Map of Changes. We made plans for Penny to return with us after our one-week trip of teaching and energy work with clients.

Penny returned with me on a flight from Philadelphia to Phoenix. While the plane queued its flight, I said, "I can hardly believe that you are coming out to build this model and work on the Map." I hesitated for a moment to find the right words and continued, "You don't know how excited I am, and grateful for your help." Penny slowly sipped her coffee, and after a few thoughtful moments replied, "After the last couple years of my life, at this point, I could believe almost anything."

The next lesson is from a session with Saint Germain, in the presence of Penny. Sananda and Kuan Yin joined in on this teaching to reiterate the importance of our individual thoughts, feelings, and actions, and equally, the importance of their Co-creative contribution to the world that we perceive and experience. It is interesting to note that Kuthumi chimed in at that time and mentioned the contributions of the celestial chorus. I wondered, "Was the chorus responsible for the chiming sound that we had heard during Penny's healing session?"

Penny was contemplating a move to the Golden City of Klehma. It would be a big move for her to leave the East Coast, where she has lived for many years. She had asked the Spiritual Teachers that if she, or anyone, were indeed guided to move, should it be to a Golden City? Their response was that if she felt the instinct to move, then by all means she should. Yet, they also encouraged her to consider the "supreme glory of light" that is held within, and its ability to serve and heal others during this transition. The teachers shared a decree with her to engender the inner light, "I AM a force that is ONE with my Brother. I AM a force that is ONE with the mighty I AM Presence."

At that time, I personally, felt for Penny. I understood the hard work, emotional turmoil, and physical grit that were required to move away from all that she had known, into the unknown, solely based on the heart's inner desire for spiritual growth.

After reading and rereading this transcript, I am of the impression that we have spent many lifetimes preparing for that moment in our souls' history to consciously serve the light and unite with others, as ONE, in our service. The Spiritual Teachers claim that through our personal cultivation of the light through service to others, "great treasures await."

At the end of this short lesson, Saint Germain mentioned an "acclimation process" that often occurs once you move from one geophysical locale into a Golden City Vortex. Apparently, there are additional levels of spiritual adjustment to be made; those of energies and frequencies. No doubt, those energy adjustments take deep inner trust and knowing, and I can't overemphasize this important process.

This reminds me of an old saying from the 1940s that was generally said to those who were making a major change or move. They were wished safe passage – "on a wing and a prayer." I revised this saying for current circumstances, "on an angel's wing and a celestial song." [Editor's Note: To learn more about *Spiritual Migration*, the intentional, physical movement into the Golden City Vortices, see *Points of Perception*.]

Saint Germain begins to speak.

Beloved chelas, it is with great joy that we stand here today, Brother to Sister, arm in arm. We hold our hand to you and ask for you to join our circle. We have given you much instruction and realize at times, you are boggled with so much data and information at this Time of Transition. But you see, Dear ones, we have offered it in many ways and in many voices. Do you not see that there is one message that comes through this? Unify! And to come together through unification, it is most important for you to address the crisis upon your planet. You have that of the economies; you have crisis of war and engaging in conflict with one another; you have crisis at your family levels; you have crisis that has occurred within your house system; you have crisis that is occurring at every avenue of your life. Will you not wake up and see this? Does it take an Ascended Master to step forward and shake you by the nape of the neck?

You see, Dear ones, it is not our position to judge you. It is indeed our position to guide you and direct you. We have mastered Third Dimension reality. It is indeed our pleasure to offer this instruction to you. But you see, Dear ones, it is not a matter of escape or running to hide. It is a matter to face your responsibility of choice, that which is your true creation, that which has come forth through the dispensation of your own energies. My Dear ones, realize that there is a way, a guiding force and a guiding path that is through the celebration of harmony and alignment, attunement with that of the mighty I AM Presence. For you see, Dear ones, throughout the cosmos, beings are banding together to come to you, to come to remind you that you are indeed the Divine Inheritors of this planet that you walk upon.

You search for your homes and your Star seed groups but do you not see that you have been brought to this Earth Plane to Master the Earth Plane, also known as Terra? Beloveds, come forth in the Light of God that Never Fails. We have given you instruction in the cellular awakening for you to come forth in unification. We have planted within you, the use of the Violet Flame for purification of the physical body. We ask for purification, not only of the physical body, but that of the mental body and the emotional body. For you see, Dear ones, these are the solidification of the physical body.

That which you think upon, do you not become? That which you feel through, does this not affect your thinking world? See how they are all connected. See how they manifest within your world. Your feeling body is brought to you for survival, survival when you existed in a linear, genetic code. You have risen above this. Your feelings are not to be controlled. Emotion, at some particular level, while in physical embodiment, is brought to shield the physical body and is known as instinct. Do you have questions?

Question: "We can control everything on a personal level, just by how we think and feel, is that correct?"

It is important for you to understand, your feelings are brought to protect the physical body. Your feeling world enters into your thinking world. Your thinking world commands your physical body. It is important for you to understand this. And so your feelings, yes, may be controlled. This occurs through your thinking world.

Question: "Is there almost a war at the mass consciousness level?"

Has this not come through the reactive phase of the emotional body, set upon survival standards of fear? Has their Father, the Beloved I AM Presence, not provided for them? You are Creation, my Dear ones. You have been brought forth into this world, all that you need is here, Dear ones, nothing less, nothing more.

Question: "Is it necessary to move to safe areas? If we're guided, if we feel like moving, should we not move?"

My Dear ones, if you instinctively feel a need to protect your physical shell by moving to an area, we encourage this. We also encourage those who step forward to say:

> "I will be of Divine Service,
> I will step forth to heal mankind,
> I will step forth to raise my vibratory action,
> I will sit in the supreme glory of light,
> I will manifest harmony in my world,
> And extend this to the world of those around me.
> I AM a force that is ONE
> With my Brother.
> And I AM a force that is ONE
> With the mighty I AM Presence."

He is moving a torch.

I light this torch for Justice and Freedom. For you see, Dear ones, free will has been brought to you to enable you to make the choice. Each second of time, as you have understood it, you make the choice. Each day, you come forth to say "I make the choice to be free. I make the choice to be happy. I make the choice to live in harmony." And indeed, there are those who say "I make the choice to be in fear. I make the choice to have pain. I make the choice to live my life with very little." In living your life with very little, you are living your life abandoned and separated from your mighty I AM Presence. We ask for you to feel its radiance about you, for it is indeed your Divine Seed. It has been brought forth to allow your embodiment in the physical, to provide an acre of light within your world.

We invite you to come and to share these other worlds with us, and we challenge you to Master your feeling and thought of Third Dimension. For it is our hope that you will gain the ability to move within the Third Dimension effortlessly, for there are great treasures that await.

Sananda is stepping forward.

Dear Brothers and Sisters, as I have stated, when you live in a world of turmoil, have you not chosen this turmoil? When you live in a world of peace, have you not chosen this peace? How long will you live in turmoil? How long will you live in peace? This is your choice, Dear ones. It is a matter of choice. I would like to introduce to you, my Beloved Sister Kuan Yin.

Kuan Yin comes forward.

Come forth in brilliance; come forth to extend your hand in compassion to your Brother. See within his face, your face; see within his home, your home; see the food he eats as your food; the flowers in your garden are his. You are Children of Creation and will remain as such. Extend your world of Creation and come with us. You are not abandoning anything; you are accepting your role as a creative being and inheritor of your Brother and inheritor of your Sister. You are indeed the caretakers and we ask for you to see your role as such. For if you are Creation, is not Creation part of you? If you are compassion, is not compassion you? Look to the fruit of the garden and taste its sweetness or its bitterness. Is this not what the garden is? From the East come winds and they blow a time to sow. Should you beat your harvest from this wind? Or turn your back to such?

Kuthumi comes forward.

I come forth to represent an Elemental Life Force that exists within your body, which has been brought forth through the Elohim to offer its life spring to you. You contain within your body the Beloved spirit of these forces and your Earth contains this as well. This celestial chorus is that which awakens the Elemental Life Force in your early morning hours. Do they not seem to awaken this life force? This is the music of being. This is the music of Elohim.

Saint Germain comes forward.

Beloveds, we have worked on many projects with you, but among all of these is this project, brought forth for you to recognize and reach within your being to the creative force. We may speak of structures and we many speak of products that align yourself. But of all, what is most important is your desire. We ask you to look within your heart and to follow your desire. If you wish to move to a safe location, there are ways to prepare and align your body for such. For you see, you are not allowed to live in certain areas with your linear structures. We are asking, if you live in one area, to align yourself to it. It is most important that you see yourself as an extension of the Earth in the area that you live, that you not aimlessly run about, to plop yourself in the middle of an area. Each energy varies in density and vibration and you must become sensitive to the area that you live upon. Do you understand?

Question: "I think so. So this new place I'm moving, I should sensitize myself to the new house?"

And align yourself accordingly. You see, you affect the vibration of the planet itself and she affects you. See yourself working together as ONE. She offers herself as a nurturer and you too must respond as a caretaker. Children, wipe your tears from your eyes. Wipe your tears and smile with joy, for your time of rest is over. It is time to open your eyes and awaken to a New Day.

19

*In all experiences, both good and bad, the ONE is present.
Oneness moves us into Co-creative acts of harmony and Unity.*

Law of ONE
Saint Germain

The girls returned home, again, to live with us in Payson. They were quite impressed with our little condo – it had a swimming pool. The sweltering summers on the farm had required a twelve-mile drive into town for a cool dip at the community park pool. So for them, farm kids, a pool was a luxury. Those hot and sunny Arizona days were filled with lots of poolside time, and my office window overlooked the pool area where I keep a motherly, watchful eye on the girls. Carson stayed with his father for the entire summer. He was learning how to drive a hay and grain truck on the family farm. And he had asked if we'd let him stay for the entire school year. I was a bit disappointed, as I had hoped that all three children would live with us in Payson. Plus, Carson and I had forged a unique bond during our time together in Socorro, and I missed him terribly. His father and I had officially agreed that the girls would remain with me and start school that fall in Payson. Carson would stay in Idaho, where he would begin Junior High School. Penny had been inordinately valuable in helping me to understand this unusual family dynamic. She has been divorced for many years, and had personally witnessed and experienced her children shifting from one parent's home to the other, contributing to each child's unique and changing needs. "He is at an age where he wants to get to know his dad," she assured me. "He had his time with you, now he needs time with him. It's crucial to his development." I hoped we were making the right decision, and in reality, if it didn't work out, the situation could be changed. Penny had now traveled to Payson several times to work on the World Map Model, and it was near completion. Len had created a workspace for her at the office, so I occasionally dropped in to see how the model was progressing. Through this process we'd become great friends. We'd cooked together, ridden bikes on the red-rocked trails in the pines, shared our experiences of raising children, and thoroughly examined the Ascended Master teachings and the presence of the Spiritual Teachers in our lives.

Before we had started the process, we had gathered all of the various maps from our channeled sessions in Asotin and decided that the information would best be presented on one map projection. We chose the Robinson Projection; a projection originally designed in 1963 by cartographers to convey the globe as a flat image for map publisher Rand-McNally. Penny carefully scribed the various trance session map information, including the I AM America Map information, onto the new projection, and glued it onto the model. Then she began the painstaking process of creating the model with sheet rock mud, squeezing the mud out of small bottles, letting each new layer dry, with constant sanding and carving.

Her sculpting ability was profound and exact: she used dental tools for the minute details of the underlying cartography. "Sometimes the Earth looks like it is angry," she commented, pointing to new areas where new lands had risen, "And other days, it feels innocent and gentle – like a newborn baby. Maybe it reflects my mood!" I responded, "Well, it is metaphor, to some degree, right?" And we both stood back and stared at the model, a little in awe, and, in reality, a bit shocked at the degree of the prophesied changes.

On my previous trip to Philadelphia, I'd had a few moments to explore a bookstore where I had bought a used copy of the book, "*The Ancient Aramaic Prayer of Jesus*," by Rocco Errico. I was captivated by his research of ancient Hebrew Prophets who, according to Errico, would never translate a Prophecy's meaning with one simple literal interpretation. Instead, the Prophecy was analyzed three times: literally, metaphorically, and mystically. This is called a "Mitzrah" tradition. The Jews use this to reapply ancient interpretations to modern-day events.

After this process, the Prophecy was taught and applied for spiritual insight and knowledge. This method not only intrigued me, but made practical sense. I applied this method to the World Map Prophecies and decided to write about my new interpretation of the I AM America prophecies. This would be published as a small book to accompany the World Map.

I introduced the first pages of the *World Map Prophecies* book with definitions of "Prophecy" and "prophesy;" the spelling dependent on whether you use the word as a noun or a verb. Even though I was raised in a traditional Christian home, had two years of formal catechism, learned traditional prophecies, and had presented the I AM America prophecies professionally for over two years, I was still confused regarding specific word usage. I consulted an old dictionary that listed the differences.

Here are formal definitions from my 1937 Webster's Dictionary:

Prophesy: (prof' e si) verb, 1. To speak as a mediator between God and man or in God's stead. 2. To teach religious subjects or material.

When you use the word "prophesy," that is the act of speaking or teaching while receiving this type of spiritual information.

Prophecy: (prof' e si) noun, 1. Divinely inspired utterance. 2. Utterance under the inspiring influence of religious experience. 3. Inspired declaration or revelation of the divine will including moral teaching by warning, consoling, exhorting, giving an example of fellowship with God and the like.

The word "Prophecy" is not so much the actual act of speaking the information, it defines the actual information that is given. So for the most part, the I AM America Map and transcripts are indeed prophecies.

And just so you know, here is the definition of Prophet.

Prophet: (prof' it) noun, 1. One who speaks for another, especially for God. An inspired revealer, interpreter, or spokesman. One whose office it is to deliver a message. 2. A preacher who is distinguished from a priest.

I don't consider myself a Prophet, but I do consider the Ascended Masters prophets – especially Saint Germain. In fact, they are not shy about this at all and have stated this fact, albeit in esoteric terms.

About twenty years ago, Saint Germain had ended one of his teaching sessions with this phrase, spoken in an angelic tongue: *Om Manaya Pitaya Hitaka.* I had never heard this terminology before, and had wondered what it meant. We once asked Saint Germain, in a channeled session, about its meaning, and he said we could interpret it as "I AM the Light of God." The word "Hitaka" is yet another angelic utterance that means, "So Be It." This is similar to the western word "amen." I never thought about it again until about twelve years later. I was participating in a traditional Hindu ceremony known as *Navagraha Puja*. The puja is a fire ceremony performed by a Brahmin priest. The priest chants in perfect Sanskrit to invoke the nine classical planets of our solar system: Sun, Moon, Mercury, Venus, Mars, Jupiter, and Saturn, including the Moon's Nodes, Rahu and Ketu. This ceremony is to remove the negative karmas that we may suffer, as predicted through our astrological charts. The Navagraha Puja blesses the planets, and increases benefic results from their energies.

During the ceremony, I heard the priest often repeat the partial phrase I had heard before from Saint Germain: *Manaya Pitaya*. Although I'm unsure of its spelling in Sanskrit, I noticed the same pronunciation used by the Hindu priest: *Maw nae' uh Puh tie' yuh*. After the ceremony, I asked the priest the meaning of the phrase. He scratched his chin for a moment, and translated the phrase into English, "the seer of the Lord." So the phrase *Om Manaya Pitaya* also means: "I AM the Seer of the Lord."

I questioned just what to title the new World Map. I'd been researching other Ascended Master teaching traditions and discovered a wonderful anthology of teachings compiled by Tellis Papastavro, "*The Gnosis and the Law.*" Those teachings are apparently from a well-known Ascended Master channel, Geraldine Innocente, who led the formation of the "Bridge to Freedom," from the mid-1940s to 1961. Those earlier teachings from El Morya, Saint Germain, and other Ascended Beings referred to Earth, in its ascended states, as "Freedom Star."

After several personal sessions with Saint Germain, he agreed that this was appropriate for the prophetic map. So the world map of Earth Changes was christened, *Freedom Star World Map*, and I named the new booklet of interpreted prophecies *Freedom Star*. Through this process, I felt a vital spiritual shift within myself, including a shift in how I viewed the I AM America Prophecies.

At the end of that booklet, I condensed new insights. I offer this summary:

> The Earth and humanity are ONE physiology: a light and energy system that cannot be disconnected. Our lives comprise many sensitive systems that are interrelated and Co-created through an underlying metaphysical hologram of thought, feeling, and action.

> Every individual thought, feeling, desire, and action creates a Collective Consciousness.

> Collective Consciousness influences the outcome of events, and is projected through communal effort in prayer and meditation. This can change a cataclysmic hurricane into a gentle summer rain.

> If you live with fear, you will create fear. If you live with love, you will create love.

We are living in a Time of Change. This period is evidenced by tremendous changes in our society, cultures, and world politics, in tandem with individual and collective spiritual awakenings and transformations. These events occur simultaneously, with the possibilities of massive global warming, climactic changes, and seismic and volcanic activity – Earth Changes.

Our positive inner change and transformation help to change society, governments, and the environment. Our conscious choices influence the possibility of Earth Changes, and can change, ameliorate, or avert cataclysm. The three monikers of positive shift are: choice, change, and consciousness.

This is an important time on Earth. The time is now!

[Editor's Note: For more information see the *Freedom Star Booklet*.]

It was July. Len was on the East Coast, absorbed with his class schedule and energy practice. I'd been organizing files in my office and catching up on housework. One particular morning my phone rang. It was Athena, who urgently said, "I think you should come immediately to the office – something's come up." Then she added, "It's best if you come alone." Her voice sounded intense, almost cryptic – I couldn't imagine what the problem was, but I sensed stress in her voice, "Okay," I said. "I'll be there in five minutes."

"You won't believe this . . ." said Athena, and then her voice was calm, almost measured, "I just got off of the phone with Len's ex-wife." This news startled me for a minute. Len had been divorced for many years and I couldn't imagine what the problem would be. "Is Len okay?" I pensively ask. Athena continued, "Oh – he is just fine," but I could tell from her tone that she was annoyed. "Apparently he is involved in helping her build a house. And she has just learned that the two of you are together . . . do you know anything about this?"

For a moment I was stunned, in fact almost breathless. As far as I had known, Len and I had shared everything – I couldn't imagine that he would withhold something this important from me. Plus, I was shocked that his ex-wife had just *now* been informed about my presence – Len and I had been together for almost two years! Athena sensed the shock I was feeling, and purposely suppressed her own irritation, "Something's going on and you'd better get to the bottom of it." I was physically shaking as I drove home.

I barely slept that night. And in the morning, I reached out to Sherry. If anyone could figure out the spiritual motive and energy surrounding a moment of emotional chaos, she could. "Let's see what the cards have to say," she said. I heard her shuffling the cards as I anxiously clasped the phone. "You know he loves you, but has been afraid to make a commitment to you . . . interesting, hmmm . . ."

She was quiet for a moment and I could feel uneasiness swirling in my gut, as she said, "You will still be receiving spiritual information and working together." I could almost hear her flip over the next card, "He has been confused and has past commitments that he must fulfill . . ." Her voice faded, and I knew she was likely in trance, receiving information that would help. Meanwhile, I struggled to understand.

"I'm going to stop this reading for a minute to explain something to you," she said. "He has not betrayed you and is certainly not a cheat. But you need to understand that before he came to live with you and help you with your spiritual work, he had a life, and he must deal with past obligations." Then Sherry became inordinately practical, "You need to remember that there is no one on Earth who will understand your spiritual path more than Len. And the cards say that he loves you and cares for you, and remember, *no one* is perfect." She sighed, "All relationships are work. And I think this is a relationship worth working for." Sherry's words somewhat relieved me, and if anything else, it was just good to hear the voice of a trusted old friend.

Later that day, Athena called to check in, "How are you?" I could tell that she knew I was a mess. I responded, "I seem to be okay. I talked to Sherry earlier and she did a reading for me. It helped." I could tell from her lack of immediate response that for some reason she was still annoyed. She finally broke her silence, "I don't think Len treats you right." I immediately replied, "I know, and I'm not going to make excuses for him. But I have deep concerns [that] if I react to this information in a negative way, not only will it impact my personal life but it could affect my spiritual work."

What I didn't say was that I had been in this precarious place before and, above all, I didn't want this to financially impact I AM America. "Well," Athena quickly answered, "I'm sure it already has [impacted and affected you] to some degree. Maybe you should ask the Masters and see what they want?"

So that night I prayed. I asked for clarity regarding my relationship with Len and for guidance with my spiritual work. I didn't get any direct response or a bolt of Violet Flame from the heavens, but I did feel the gentle and loving overshadowing of both Saint Germain and Sananda.

The phone rang at 10 AM the next morning and Athena was on the line. "I have something that I think you should hear," and she turned up the office answering machine so I could hear. "Well hello I AM America." It was a voice I hadn't heard for some time, but would always recognize – it was Dan's. His voice hesitated for a moment, and then I heard a tenderness that was almost apologetic. "I called to ask if you'd like to work together again. I know this must seem odd, but I had to ask. I miss you. Please call." At that moment, I swear, I could have been blown over by a feather; a call from Dan was the last thing I had expected.

It appears that for whatever reason, Dan's call was likely the result of my prayers. Our relationship, as flawed and dysfunctional as it had been, seemed to always be there when either one of us needed help. Our lives were unusually, yet indelibly, connected to a flowing web, and it seemed that if one of us tugged on one of the ethereal strings of this web, the other inevitably felt the pull and vice-versa.

Years later, I discovered the esoteric meaning of this in my Jyotish – Vedic Astrology – studies. These types of relationships are often marked by an exchange of nodal energy and are inordinately karmic. This type of connection and rapport is often immediate and intense, but it is unusual that these types of relationships endure, at least in a conventional manner. After the two have fulfilled their karmic duties to one another, the relationship often ends as quickly as it began. Yet, there is a deep-rooted psychic link between both persons. For this reason alone, I called Dan back.

I'm glad that I did. His voice was warm and friendly, and there was no mention whatsoever about the destruction of the I AM America Map model and his somewhat abrupt letter to me. "You've been on my mind for months now, and I knew we had to talk," he explained. "And I was really hoping that you'd think about moving back here, and consider working together again." And then he excitedly went on to explain his new ideas about marketing the Map and how he could help with the World Map.

I must admit, it was a bit surreal. This was the old Dan I had known several years ago, who loved spiritual work and the Ascended Masters. And even though, at one time, he had loved me, I wouldn't go so far as to say that he did again. But at least for now, it appeared that he liked me. Truthfully, I was certain that something had recently become unbalanced in his personal life, too, but I didn't ask. I purposely kept it light and said, "You probably noticed that my phone number has changed and that I've moved." He quickly responded, "Yes – I got your office number through the spiritual center."

"I've just moved to a small town in Arizona – Payson – we're about an hour or so away from Phoenix . . ." I paused for a minute, I couldn't find the words to tell him that I had no desire whatsoever to leave Gobean, and above all, regardless of whatever circumstances Len was personally experiencing, my heart was with Len. I continued, "Hey, good news, I've found someone to help me with the Map model . . . an artist that I met in Philadelphia, and so far she's really done a terrific job." I could tell he was disappointed when he replied, "Oh . . . umm . . . that's good!" "Yes," I quickly replied, "We're using some of the techniques you developed when working on the first model."

From that moment on, our conversation went a little flat. I think he realized that there was no reason for us to revisit our business relationship, nor would I be returning anytime soon to live in the Pacific Northwest. And I realized something that was vitally important – the fact that whatever problems I was facing with Len, I had an inner faith that some way, somehow we would work it out.

When Len returned from Philadelphia, it took me several days before I confronted him with the news of his ex-wife's telephone call. I asked him, "What's going on?" Len took a deep breath and tears welled up in his eyes, "I don't know what to say, and I'm so ashamed." He held his head in his hands and murmured, "I would never want to hurt you ever, but I'm afraid to lose my children!" I had never seen Len this way. He was always so self-assured, and now he was sobbing.

So, it was true. It all began to make sense. My mind flashed back to the past: his emotional withholding our first night together in Long Island, the long absences and his inaccessibility – sometimes for days. It was a lot to absorb, and the emotional pain stabbed and seared in unstoppable waves. And even worse, I thought I could be calm about this when, in reality, I was also furious. Perhaps Athena was right – he had not treated me right at all and maybe I *should* leave.

We spent several days in silence. I wanted to talk, but I needed our communication to be meaningful. I had learned in my relationship with Dan that emotional drama was exhausting and useless. I even thought about calling Dan back to rescind every word of our "light" conversation, and beg him to drive down and help me move me back to the safety of Asotin. Yet again, after each intermittent spin of inner turmoil, I was comforted by a feeling that I would be okay, and I certainly *did not* need Dan to save me. And in the quiet stillness, when I'd query my heart, the answer was always Len. For good or for bad, the reality was that my heart was wholly his. But how could he betray me, our life together, and our spiritual partnership?

Now, twenty-five years later, I can look at this with mature insight. Intentional spiritual work – which is *real inner work* focused on self-development and knowledge of self (both light and shadow), alongside helping and assisting others on their spiritual path – is indeed difficult. In fact, at times it can be downright overwhelming. In many cases there are sacrifices that seem inordinately unfair, almost unbearable. The Master Teachers often say, "Our work is hard, but the reward immeasurable."

We finally spoke, and Len revealed that he and his ex-wife had never really separated, at least not in a conventional manner. They had, however, been legally divorced for many years, and both had other relationships from time to time. But they still found friendship and comfort with one another and loved and adored their children. He explained to me that he felt like he was abandoning them, and could not in good conscience create a life with me without knowing they were all okay. So he was helping in whatever way he could with extra money, and finding contractors to help build them a small home. "I've never fallen so deeply in love with someone as I have with you . . . it scares me," he stated. Yet simultaneously, he was losing everything he knew; all that mattered in an Earthly sense, including his connection to his children.

That experience of confliction is common in Spiritual Awakening. As we move to a new vibration, those that we love and cherish often do not. So we need to move forward and leave them behind.

I meditated upon and contemplated my dilemma. I sought guidance from the Spiritual Teachers, but inside I knew that this was my independent decision and action. On a quiet morning while Len was watching the girls, I drove to the office to meet with Athena. "Do you have Len's ex-wife's telephone number?" I asked. She seemed startled, "Umm… yes, I do. Are you sure you want to do this?" She handed me the number written on a pink message slip. I was extremely nervous, but knew that this call was important.

She answered the phone – an assertive, yet welcoming voice. I responded, "Hi, this is Lori. I understand that you asked for me to return your call." She sounded surprised, "Oh . . . I'm glad you called." I continued, "I want you to know that as far as I knew, the two of you were divorced and lived separate lives. I would never, ever, be involved in separating a family." I spoke my words with certainty – this was my truth.

She quickly responded, "Until Len returned home, we [the family] didn't know that you were part of Len's life." I cleared my throat, "Yes, he has told me that, and I want you to know that if you want him – that is, if you love him . . . I will pack his things, buy him a ticket back to Philadelphia, and promise to never see him again."

Undoubtedly she was shocked, and said, "Well, just so you know, I'm not in love with him."

My heart skipped a beat . . . could this be true? And after a short pause of disbelief, I asked, "You are not in love with him?" "No . . ." she said, and she began to rattle off a litany of criticisms. I interrupted with a purposeful question, "So, you don't want him?" She responded, "No, I don't think so . . . not at this point." Countering this, I replied, with certainty, "I do."

Again, my direct response and declaration of love for Len, in spite of the tenuous circumstances, caught her off guard, "Well . . . wait . . . maybe." "Okay," I responded, "Then I will send him home to you." She was quiet, yet again. "No – don't. It is over between us."

When I finished the conversation and opened the door, Athena was standing there, almost breathless, "How did it go?" "Well," I responded, "I guess she is not in love with him." Athena stood there, a bit puzzled. Fortunately the office phone rang, and I quietly waved good-bye and left. I'd had more than enough drama for the day. Later, I confided with Penny and she commented, "You did the right thing. Until that moment, she was never certain if she wanted him or not."

Len asked me to marry him, yet I was a bit uncertain and could not say "yes" or "no." I wanted to make sure that this was not an emotional, knee-jerk proposal. My inner guidance was to give it some time, so I responded, "When Saint Germain says the time is right – then we'll get married." Len chuckled about this, "Oh, I see – an arranged marriage."

Unfortunately, Athena could not resolve her conflict over Len's situation and decided to leave. In reality, those events were a catalyst that influenced her personal spiritual growth and changing needs. The I AM America office had become a bit too isolated for her. I was now working at my home office and Len was traveling back and forth from Philadelphia. I knew that the time she gave us was inordinately generous and helpful. I would certainly miss her and her amazing organizational skills.

Almost immediately after her departure, a team of volunteers appeared from the Payson Lightworkers community to help manage the office. Several began to roll and package Maps, and two of them offered to come in and handle the front desk a couple of days per week until we found another secretary. That took the pressure off of me while Len was away, and when he was home, he, too, filled in at the office. Len and I, who had been a bit isolated in our work, welcomed this sincere offer of service, and enjoyed working with them. Plus, it was nice to begin to know others in our local community. In a short amount of time, Payson began to feel like home.

In early September the girls started school. They had the option of walking to school or catching the bus, but more than often I'd drive them the several blocks in the morning, and they'd walk home after school. They both seemed to be adjusting well to their new environment and both asked to bring new friends home for play dates.

We were considering moving. The condominium was a bit too congested for Len; we needed a garage to store extra books, and a yard would be nice for the girls, although I knew they'd miss the pool. I found an affordable three-bedroom, two-bath brick ranch home, with a stunning view of the Rim. We would move in October.

Penny arrived in Payson for her last working session with the Map model. On this trip she flew out with Rachel, who had continued to volunteer as an organizer and scheduler for the Len's school and energy sessions. Since attending classes with Len, Rachel had become inordinately absorbed in Ascended Master teaching, and no doubt she was passionately stirred within – a full-fledged aspirant. Like so many others that awaken into vital spiritual experience, she was seeking the appropriate discipline that would lift her to her next level of growth – the chela. She had received inner guidance to visit Gobean and felt the draw of its steward and Master Teacher El Morya. Rachel also wanted to camp out in the Gobean forest for a few days by herself, to absorb the energies of the Golden City Vortex, and hopefully receive guidance regarding her next move in spiritual growth and evolution.

Penny was concerned and shared with me, "I don't understand why she has to go camping – if she'd meditate she would be able to contact him." I assured Penny that the campgrounds were relatively safe in the area, with restrooms and running water. I'd learned that for some adepts, meditation is not the best spiritual discipline. In fact, I'd come to understand that while meditation is a sublime and expeditious spiritual technique for some, it can often be difficult for others. I had also learned, through my Jyotish practice, that the individual's chart best defines the spiritual disciplines that one may apply, and there are many: stillness, prayer, visualization, and contemplation; decree and mantra; hatha yoga and body prayer; ritual and ceremony; and breath work – also known as *kriya yoga*.

Each individual has a unique and distinctive spiritual path. Often, physical approaches to spiritual growth are needed as well. I had no doubt that this was part of Rachel's passage into her own union with self and the I AM Presence. But just to be sure, I promised a session for both Penny and Rachel so they could personally ask. My guru Saint Germain appeared, and provided a lesson about the ONE and the Oneness that we all share, especially in Co-creative processes. For further understanding of this next transmission, I'd like to share the definitions of ONE and Oneness.

The ONE is indivisible, whole, harmonious unity. Oneness is the personal experience of the ONE; therefore, it is the combination of two or more, including the communion with a Spiritual Teacher or guide, which creates the whole. Perhaps, what impressed me most about the following transmission, is that in the tempest of our life – often rife with dysfunctional relationships including our search for perfect love, and the inner longing to know self – is often achieved through the dualism of loyalty and betrayal, love and attachment, service and selfishness, anger and pacifism, and the many other pairs of opposites that define the breadth of human experience. Again, these conflicts are common in Spiritual Awakening. The Law of ONE quells their separation into harmony and light, with our wondrous return to Unity.

Saint Germain reiterates this great law and seeming paradox, "For all it takes are two to pierce this illusion, and heaven and Earth are created." Interestingly, neither Penny nor Rachel asked any questions. This was a compelling and complete lesson on the ONE, and I suggest that you take your time when you read this lesson. It contains many subtleties and nuances on the Spiritual Teacher's viewpoints, including one of the most amazing definitions I've yet to read about our collective forgetting – *the Law of Forgetfulness*.

❧

Welcome, my Beloved chelas, I AM Saint Germain and I stream forth on that which is that mighty Violet Transmuting Ray of Mercy and Forgiveness. As usual, Dear hearts, I request permission to come forth into your energy fields.

Response: "Please, Dear one, come forth."

This work of transition upon the Earth Plane and Planet known as Prahna, and indeed known as this Beloved Star of Freedom, is a time where one makes that choice to put these lessons into a disciplined activity. This disciplined activity is for the chela who truly does the choosing, for in the choosing of All That Is, is the true being of the Source. As each and every one of you has sought your individuality, you each indeed, in a paradox, search this that is the collective. For as we have instructed, it is this collective that knows no boundaries and yet, it is only through the individualization that then, one understands the need to let down all. As you have understood, it is time to let the little self be and allow what is this larger Self, to disseminate. This is what we call this Law of Oneness. For this Law of Oneness allows the Divine Will to stream forth into the hearts of men and then your heart is indeed softened. For it is then willing to serve with grace, a grace that transmutes beyond all human creation and into the heavenly realms. This Time of Grace that comes to the planet is a time when this collective shall beat the heart of ONE great being.

This Law of Oneness, as you have all known, is indeed founded upon the principles known as the Jurisdictions for the Planet Prahna. However, it is the deeper reasoning of such that leads one into harmony. This perseverance of the soul too comes from this great collective Source, as in this breath that is the out-breath. The time has come for the great in-breath and you are all brought back to that fiery Source, that which you call as Helios and Vesta, but that which we know is the Source of all Source for creation of your universe. This Time of Transition is where one chooses: shall I return to this Law of Oneness? Am I willing to dissipate my boundaries of individuality and allow a great Collective to supersede my consciousness?

The time has come, Dear ones, for you to make this choice. For you see, we are all truly ONE. Do you not feel my energy at this instant and moment, for we are truly ONE? Do you not feel the hardness of where you sit? For your body and that object from whence it is placed, it is truly ONE. As you eat, do you not take this nourishment into your system and you are truly ONE? Find all the examples in your life which merge you to the great collective Law of ONE. You search for your Mastery upon this Earth Plane and Planet and yet, so few have touched into this known as the Collective. For all it takes are two to pierce this illusion and what shall be created, but heaven on Earth.

To anchor in the Golden Cities of conscious light, one must be willing to consciously merge their being with that of the Earth Planet itself. To prove to be an anchor of light, one must have a stalwart heart and perseverance of the soul. One must find within their being, that great Pillar of Light that is anchored so firmly within their heart, that they call upon it in reservoirs, where the seeming famine would be.

This time has come, Dear ones, for each of you to prove, inside, that you are this Law of ONE. In the collective forgetting, as we would call it, each and every one of you came, in a sense, as a group, proving the Law of Forgetfulness; proving that boundaries and separation could indeed exist; proving that individuality could create a great mass ego; proving that all of this could even produce such a sinister force, it could rule with such confusion. The time has come for you to prove, in this great in-breath, that you are a God-Free Creation, made in the image and likeness of light and sound.

From this, that is the holographic universe, you are patterned. As it was said, even the hairs upon your head are patterned. You are brought here not only to Co-create but to disseminate and assimilate simultaneously. Disseminate this great Law of Oneness and assimilate it, as in this great in-breath. Disseminate your goodness and being of heart and assimilate your spiritual contact. Know, Dear hearts, at all times, divinity streams forth through your being as you share in your collective choosing. Know that as you choose, you choose too for your Brother and Sister. Adopt a sense of collective reasoning and then you shall understand how collective thought is held. Adopt a practice for collective experience and then you shall understand how science and molecular structures are built upon these concepts of collective reasoning. Adopt a sense of collective philosophy. Adopt a sense of collective theology. Find within yourself, a monotheistic reason and you shall return to that which is a unity of self. In this great in-breath, you have been asked to take this most challenging step, a step that will catapult you into the unity and harmony you so seek. You and each and every one of you have asked for your bliss and to follow your Heart's Desire, but this time, it comes to the planet and comes to the stalwart one who says: "I shall be small, I shall be as little as that, for this too contains the inherent power of creation." You are Co-creators, yes, and Co-creators of great thought and movement. Use your thoughts to Co-create. Use your hands to Co-create. Disseminate and assimilate.

Know that within each of your beings is this great Law of Union and ONE, working to bring eternal peace and gladness to every man, woman, and child upon the Planet Prahna. Speak with glad-tidings, which means to speak as one who pulls the breath back to the Source; act as one who has Co-created from a fruitful desire;

be one who shows, through this method of action, a reverence for this Law of ONE. You remember being this blade of grass, this movement of wind, this drop of rain and so becometh, to anchor this Time of Golden City Vortices upon the Earth Plane and Planet. One must understand collective reasoning to hold collective thought, to allow the Divine Will to stream forth in the obedience to the Law of Truth. Adopt a way to understand. If you have to use methodology, apply a method that appeals to you. This is of course, your individual choice.

20

*Every individual thought, feeling, action, and desire
creates the world in which we live.*

Come Forth in Your Light

Saint Germain

This book closes with a final lesson from Saint Germain. It was received by Len, via automatic writing, but for some reason I'm unsure just where or when it was written. Perhaps it was received after our inspiring hike on Mount Shasta in the moonlight; or after a calming rainstorm in the Hells Canyon, which tempered the feminine heat of the sands of Asotin. Maybe these words settled into consciousness, provoked by a swift wind over the high desert plains of Gobean while the sunset playfully painted the sky with hues of pink and blue, as angels recited the Violet Flame. The simple words of this teaching are perhaps the most practical and healing for our fields of light and the everyday moments that uniquely create our lives, "Upon what you focus, is that which creates . . ."

This lesson, in basic terms, reiterates a spiritual guideline for achieving wholeness, light, and Ascension. The basic premise is that it is up to each and every one of us to consciously raise our own vibration, through the calibration of our everyday thoughts, feelings, actions, and desires. Why? Because today and tomorrow this precious world is in need of your "light and love." Because, undoubtedly a "Change of Heart *can* Change the World."

Greetings in the Breath, Sound, and Light of the Most Radiant One! I AM Saint Germain and I come forth to give you discourse, to bring the Light of God that Never Fails. Do I have permission to enter your energy fields of consciousness as you read this? "Beauty is in the eyes of the beholder." This age-old saying is a truth and as truth, it is unlimited, for as beauty is beheld, so too is light and dark. It is the focus that creates the reality and the focus is guided by the intent. To those who behold dark, it is dark that they fear and see in everything. In the intent to eliminate the dark, the focus gives the dark a power that feeds the fear and doubt. So in this dark, they see only a focus of dark and judgment that is carried to all they contact and to all with whom they speak. For the thought and the word are the tools of creation. Again, upon what you focus, is that which you create and recreate.

To those who behold light, it is the same. The light begets light. In the intent to create light, the light is the focus and is expanded to the consciousness that is carried to all and so, the cycle is in a perpetual expanding motion for everyone to enjoy. To create a focus of light, one does exclude all focus of dark. Your thoughts, feelings, actions, and desire for the Divine Will of the God Source are the key to the vessels that you all are, in this plane of conscious activity.

Consider again, as you speak, that creation is responding to your creation of word. The word is the power of creation in this plane and planet. You, as creators, are creating this world, word by word, thought by thought. Your feelings and actions are given power by your focus of thoughts, and your words create space for the action to manifest. Your feelings intensify your words, which expands the space that, in turn, quickens the action. You are the Love of God that Never Fails. You are the Light of God that Never Fails.

The time is now, that your thoughts, feelings, actions, and desires truly manifest who you are in this schoolhouse of divinity. The focus of your personal peace and your personal light are the Love of the Mother/Father God that Never Fails. Take this to heart, for the world is in need of your light and your love. You are all the foundation of Creation. Come forth in your light and expand to all those around you. Speak the words of light; act the acts of love; feel the love in action, for you are as God is, Creators! Go forth and create the Light of God that Never Fails and be as the Love of God is: truly nonjudgmental; unconditionally loving; grateful of all; and of fruitful service.

I AM ONE with you. I AM Saint Germain.

Epilogue

On a sunny December morning I am awakened by Saint Germain gently tapping my consciousness, saying, "Today is the day." Half-asleep, I repeat his message several times to myself, then realize that today was the day that our beloved Spiritual Teacher had chosen for my and Len's wedding day. Months before we had taken out a wedding license, and Len had purchased two wedding bands. "How do you feel about getting married today?" I ask, while I sit down at the kitchen table where he sips his morning tea. A sleepy look immediately leaves his face and his eyes widen, "Well yes. Today is a perfect day." A smile glints across his face.

I call the Town Hall to see if the judge is available. "Yes, she might be," her assistant states, then asks, "Can I call you back?" In the meantime, I iron a white shirt for Len and decide that I will wear a white wool jacket with some casual slacks. The phone rings, and it is the judge's assistant, and although the schedule is tight that day, she can squeeze us in around two to two-thirty that afternoon.

We walk into City Hall at exactly two PM, check in at the window, and leave our names. The receptionist points to a few chairs in a waiting area. I choose a chair with a poster taped above it, probably for drug awareness, with big bold letters that state, "Sit and think . . ." I point to this, and Len and I both giggle. We had both been sitting, thinking, and waiting for this moment since we first met, certainly a few more minutes wouldn't hurt.

Eventually Judge Little steps out from her office. Bearing resemblance to her name, she is a short, petite woman with bright red hair, "Mr. Toye and Ms. Wilkins?" We both stand up, and she asks as we follow her into her chambers, "Did you bring a witness?" This is one detail we hadn't thought of, and immediately her assistant volunteers. Our vows are complete with the exchange of rings, two gold bands designed to hold inlays of vibrant purple sugilite – a symbol of the Violet Flame. The Judge and her assistant cry as Len and I join hands, now husband and wife. That day was several decades ago, December 3, 1992.

Since 1992 we have seen many changes with I AM America. In the mid-nineties the I AM America Map received publicity regarding its prophecies, and features of the Map were aired on FOX, NBC, UPN, London's Carlton Television, plus given coverage in the *Washington Post* and the *New York Times*. We have published three more Prophecy maps, including *Freedom Star World Map* and *Freedom Star Booklet*, and three volumes of prophetic information regarding possible Earth Changes – *New World Wisdom Series*, the *Golden City Series*, and the *I AM America Trilogy*. Several new titles containing instruction from the Spiritual Teachers are currently in process for publication.

I AM America is not a church, religion, sect, or cult. There is no interest or intent in amassing followers or engaging in any activity other than what we can do to publicize the information we have been entrusted with. In the early 2000s we were given direction to build the first Golden City Community. Since Golden City areas hold a high spiritual energy, plans are underway to build a sustainable community in Gobean, using solar energy alongside classical feng shui engineering and infrastructure.

Most of Len's time is now involved with the community, and he still manages the I AM America office and fulfills orders for maps and books. I work as a writer and spiritual teacher. In 2013 I began to mentor students in the Ascended Master tradition and I AM America Teachings, and still offer Vedic Astrology consulting. And from time-to-time I interview with various radio and internet radio talk programs, including *Coast to Coast* and others.

Our children are grown and all have families of their own. We currently have five grandchildren – one for each Golden City of the United States!

I would be remiss to not mention some of the amazing people I have met along my spiritual journey and written about in this trilogy. But before I do this I must again express my sincere gratitude and appreciation for the unique contribution that each of them made so that this work could be available to the public. This, of course, came through their deep commitment for the spiritual growth and evolution of others, yet for some of them it was an expression of their love and service to the Ascended Masters. We all owe them a great debt.

Our good friend Andrew left Sedona, AZ, in 1998. He became dissatisfied with U.S. politics and government (Saint Germain suggested this in "A Teacher Appears"), and so he decided to return to Europe, where he spent some of his childhood. He now lives in the Golden City of Afrom, which is a spiritual focus for the White Ray and the energies of Ascension. We email often, and he is still an avid Lightworker and networker. He is involved in mentoring youth in Africa, recently lectured in Egypt, and is currently renovating a building for a Light Center that features high vibrational art. He invited us to come and present our material, translator included. As the consummate host, he wrote, "Also note that you do not have to present or do anything to stay here. You can come just to get away. Reboot, write, swim, walk in the woods, and vegetate."

Throughout the years Sherry and I remained close. We often caught up on the phone, or visited in person when we could, and in fact the last time I saw her in Scottsdale, AZ, she laid out her Tarot Cards on the café table as we chatted. With the exception of Len, Sherry was perhaps one of the greatest advocates of my trancework, and she continued to play a role, helping in sessions. In fact, she sat as questioner and guest in two chapters of *Points of Perception*. Her presence often addressed more common-day problems and she was truly an advocate for the conventional thinker. She wrote the foreword for *Sisters of the Flame*, enjoyed reviewing the first drafts, and helped with ideas for the cover art. Sadly, Sherry passed away six months after its publication. Today, she is always with me in heart and mind, and I feel her standing over my shoulder, guiding me with loving encouragement to continue my work. "Your stuff is the real thing," she would often say to me, "Don't ever turn down an opportunity to speak or share."

For years I lost contact with Miriam; I assumed that she remained in Montana in the sanction of the Golden City of Shalahah. Surprisingly, I recently heard from my old friend. Health issues had forced her move to Iowa. In the Vietnam era she had been exposed to Agent Orange chemical poisoning. The eternal optimist, she wrote, "God is taking care of me and I AM on the mend . . . all will be well."

Madge drifted out of my life, almost as swiftly as she appeared. Since our days in Socorro, NM, I have never heard from her again. Yet, I am still grateful for her service, light, and friendship during a somewhat lonely time in my life.

Athena is a Naturopathic Physician, and her medical practice is located in New York State. We saw each other again in 1995. She was a volunteer at the *Philadelphia Prophecy Conference*, sponsored by I AM America. When we hugged good-bye she reminded me, "If you ever need my help again, I am a call away."

Like I suspected from our first meeting in 1992, to this day Penny and I are still dear friends and we often share, analyze, and explore our many spiritual experiences and adventures. In 2011 she wrote the foreword for *Light of Awakening*, the second book in the Golden City Series. We spent several weeks together in 2014 while Penny worked on yet, again, another I AM America Map – the *Map of the Ancients*. We also hiked, cooked together, and shared stories about our grandchildren. Penny has lived in the mountains of Colorado since 1995 and enjoys the expansive energies of the Golden City of Klehma. She is an extraordinary artist and has won several juried art shows and still teaches art part-time.

After we discontinued the Philadelphia classes in 1994, we lost communication with Rachel. We have learned however, that she lives in New York State where she owns and operates an Eco-Holistic Educational Center.

For years I enjoyed telephone calls with David, and we continued to passionately discuss contemporary Theosophy and Ascended Master Teaching. David, Len, and I spent time together in 2006 in the White Mountains of Gobean, and toured the lands of our community project. He was avid about his charitable causes, took seriously his vows as a World Server, and oversaw a successful non-profit that provided free of charge medicine and medical supplies to third-world countries. He passed away in 2007 after a brief illness. In our last telephone conversation, he confided to me that as soon as he regained his health, the Golden City project would be his number one priority. I'm certain he is helping from the other side.

Dan continued his spiritual growth and pursuits, and after a near fatal heart attack wrote a book about his spiritual journey. He mailed me a copy in 2012, and it arrived the same day I received the first drafts of *"A Teacher Appears."* Dan later wrote me that he had decided not to sell the book, and that he preferred to stay anonymous in his efforts with the Ascended Masters. He is happily remarried, is retired, and lives in the Southwest United States.

Spiritual Lineage of the Violet Flame

The teachings of the Violet Flame, as taught in the work of I AM America, come through the Goddess of Compassion and Mercy Kuan Yin. She holds the feminine aspects of the flame, which are Compassion, Mercy, Forgiveness, and Peace. Her work with the Violet Flame is well documented in the history of Ascended Master teachings, and it is said that the altar of the etheric Temple of Mercy holds the flame in a Lotus Cup. She became Saint Germain's teacher of the Sacred Fire in the inner realms, and he carried the masculine aspect of the flame into human activity through Purification, Alchemy, and Transmutation. One of the best means to attract the beneficent activities of the Violet Flame is through the use of decrees and invocation. However, you can meditate on the flame, visualize the flame, and receive its transmuting energies like "the light of a thousand suns," radiant and vibrant as the first day that the Elohim Arcturus and Diana drew it forth from our solar sun at the creation of the Earth. Whatever form, each time you use the Violet Flame, these two Master Teachers hold you in the loving arms of its action and power.

The following is an invocation for the Violet Flame to be used at sunrise or sunset. It is utilized while experiencing the visible change of night to day, and day to night. In fact, if you observe the horizon at these times, you will witness light transitioning from pinks to blues, and then a subtle violet strip adorning the sky. We have used this invocation for years in varying scenes and circumstances, overlooking lakes, rivers, mountaintops, deserts, and prairies; in huddled traffic and busy streets; with groups of students or sitting with a friend; but more commonly alone in our home or office, with a glint of soft light streaming from a window. The result is always the same: a calm, centering force of stillness. We call it the Space.

Invocation of the Violet Flame for Sunrise and Sunset

I invoke the Violet Flame to come forth in the name of I AM that I AM,

To the Creative Force of all the realms of all the Universes, the Alpha, the Omega, the Beginning, and the End,

To the Great Cosmic Beings and Torch Bearers of all the realms of all the Universes,

And the Brotherhoods and Sisterhoods of Breath, Sound, and Light, who honor this Violet Flame that comes forth from the Ray of Divine Love—the Pink Ray, and the Ray of Divine Will—the Blue Ray of all Eternal Truths.

I invoke the Violet Flame to come forth in the name of I AM that I AM!

Mighty Violet Flame, stream forth from the Heart of the Central Logos, the Mighty Great Central Sun! Stream in, through, and around me.

(Then insert other prayers and/or decrees for the Violet Flame.)

Glossary

Adjutant Point: A secondary point in a Golden City Vortex, which gives aid and assistance to primary points and ley lines.

Agreement Formation: The sacred meeting of two minds that reflects our intentions and commitments. The result of our agreements with others mirrors our choices and our responsible actions, which define our life force. Since our actions illustrate our motivations, agreements reflect our ability to effectively Co-create with others, and produce the level of harmony we enjoy from the interaction.

Amaryllis: A deva of both the Plant and Elemental Kingdom. She is also known as the Goddess of Spring and a Spiritual Teacher of the Mental Plane. She is affiliated with the Green and Gold Rays and the spiritual qualities of resurrection, beauty, love, and the supreme victory over death. She travels throughout the Nature Kingdom of Earth, and blesses the planet with the Christ Consciousness of love and beauty. It is alleged that the gnomes, fairies, undines, and sylphs of the Elemental Kingdom trail behind her on this sacred mission.

Angel: A celestial spirit-being who attends to the needs of creation and humanity, especially as a guardian, or messenger of God.

Angelic Realm: The hierarchy or organization of Angels that includes Archangels, seraphim, cherubim, thrones, dominions, virtues, powers, and principalities. According to the Ascended Masters, seven unique Angels assist and protect each individual in their spiritual growth and evolution. This is referred to as the Angelic Host.

Apollo: A God of healing, truth, music, and Prophecy. This Ascended Master is a venerated scholar of the Ascended Master tradition and is considered a guru, or Master Teacher, of many contemporary Ascended Masters.

Archangels (*the seven*): The seven principal angels of creation. They include: Michael, the Blue Ray; Jophiel, the Yellow Ray; Chamuel, the Pink Ray; Gabriel, the White Ray; Raphael, the Green Ray; Uriel, the Ruby Ray; and Zadkiel, the Violet Ray.

Astral Body or Plane: The subtle light body that contains our feelings, desires, and emotions. It exists as an intermediate light body between the physical body and the Causal Body (Mental Body). According to the Master Teachers, we enter the Astral Plane through our Astral Body when we sleep, and many dreams and visions are experiences in this Plane of vibrant color and sensation. Through spiritual development, the Astral Body strengthens, and the luminosity of its light is often detected in the physical plane. Spiritual adepts may have the ability to consciously leave their physical bodies while traveling in their Astral Bodies. The Astral Body or Astral Plane has various levels of evolution and is the heavenly abode where the soul resides after the disintegration of the physical body. The Astral Body is also known as the Body Double, the Desire Body, and the Emotional Body.

Ascended Master: An ordinary human being who has undergone a spiritual transformation over many lifetimes. He or she has Mastered the lower planes – mental, emotional, and physical – to unite with his or her God-Self or I AM Presence. An Ascended Master is freed from the Wheel of Karma. He or she moves forward in spiritual evolution beyond this planet. However, an Ascended Master remains attentive to the spiritual well-being of humanity; inspiring and serving the Earth's spiritual growth and evolution.

Ascension: A process of Mastering thoughts, feelings, and actions that balance positive and negative karmas. Ascension allows entry to a higher state of consciousness and frees a person from the need to reincarnate on the lower Earthly planes or lokas of experience. Ascension is the process of spiritual liberation, also known as *moksha*.

Atlantis: An ancient civilization of Earth, whose mythological genesis was the last Puranic Dvapara Yuga—the Bronze Age of the Yugas. Its demise occurred around the year 9628 BC. Esoteric historians suggest three phases of political and geophysical boundaries: the Toltec Nation of Atlantis (Ameru); the Turian Nation of Atlantis (the invaders of the Land of Rama); and Poseid, the Island Nation of the present-day Atlantic Ocean.

The early civilizations of Atlantis were ruled by the spiritually evolved Toltec. Their spiritual teachings, ceremonies, and temples were dedicated to the worship of the sun. According to Theosophical thought, Atlantis' evolving humanity brought about an evolutionary epoch of the Pink Ray on the Earth, and the development of the Astral-Emotional bodies and Heart Chakra. Ascended Master provenance claims that the Els—now the Mighty Elohim of the Seven Rays—were the original Master Teachers to the spiritual seekers of Atlantis. Atlantean culture later deteriorated through the use of nuclear weapons and cruelty towards other nations, including the use of genetic engineering. The demise of Atlantis was inevitable; however, modern-day geologists, archaeologists, and occultists all disagree to its factual timing.

Ascended Master teachings affirm that Atlantis – a continent whose geophysical and political existence probably spanned well over 100,000 years – experienced several phases of traumatic Earth Change. This same belief is held by occult historians who allege that the Earth repeatedly cycles through periods of massive Earth Change and cataclysmic pole shifts, which activate tectonic plates and subsequently submerge whole continents, creating vital New Lands for Earth's successors.

Awakening Prayer: Ascended Masters Saint Germain and Kuthumi offered this prayer to more than 200 people at the 1990 Global Sciences Congress in Denver, Colorado. Group and individual meditation of the Awakening Prayer encourage a heightened spiritual consciousness and Cellular Awakening.

Great Light of Divine Wisdom,
Stream forth to my being,
And through your right use
Let me serve mankind and the planet.
Love, from the Heart of God,
Radiate my being with the presence of the Christ
That I walk the path of truth.
Great Source of Creation,
Empower my being,
My Brother,
My Sister,
And my planet with perfection,
As we collectively awaken as one cell.
I call forth the Cellular Awakening.
Let wisdom, love, and power stream forth to this cell,
This cell that we all share.
Great Spark of Creation, awaken the Divine Plan of Perfection.
So we may share the ONE perfected cell,
I AM.

Aura: The subtle energy field of luminous light that surrounds the human body.

Babajeran: A name for the Earth Mother that means, "Grandmother rejoicing."

Blue Ray: A perceptible light and sound frequency. The Blue Ray not only resonates with the color blue, but is identified with the qualities of steadiness, calm, perseverance, transformation, harmony, diligence, determination, austerity, protection, humility, truthfulness, and self-negation. It forms one-third of the Unfed Flame within the heart – the Blue Ray of God Power – which nourishes the spiritual unfoldment of the human into the HU-man. Use of the Violet Flame evokes the Blue Ray into action throughout the light bodies, where the Blue Ray clarifies intentions and assists the alignment of the Will. In Ascended Master teachings, the Blue Ray is alleged to have played a major role in the physical manifestation of the Earth's first Golden City, Shamballa. Six of fifty-one Golden Cities emanate the Blue Ray's peaceful, yet piercing frequencies. The Blue Ray is esoterically linked to the planet Saturn, the development of the Will, the ancient Lemurian Civilization, the Archangel Michael, the Elohim Hercules, the Master Teacher El Morya, and the Eastern Doors of all Golden Cities.

Breathwork: The conscious, spiritual application of breath, often accompanied by visualization and meditation. Ascended Master teachings often incorporate various breathing techniques to activate and integrate Ray Forces in the Human Aura and light bodies.

Causal Body: The Fifth Dimensional Body of Light, which is affiliated with thought. Its name is associated with "cause," and is alleged to be the source of both the Astral and physical body. The Causal Body is also defined as the *Higher Mind* – superior to the Mental Body.

Cellular Awakening: A spiritual initiation process activated by Master Teachers Saint Germain and Kuthumi. Through this process, the physical body is accelerated at the cellular level, preparing consciousness to recognize and receive instruction from the Fourth Dimension.

Chakra: Sanskrit for wheel. There are seven separate spinning wheels that are human bioenergy centers. They are stacked from the base of the spine to the top of the head.

Chohan: Another word for Lord.

Choice: Will.

Co-creator: To create with the God-Source.

Compassion: Sensitivity and understanding for another's suffering and the desire to give aid to relieve human pain, distress, and anguish.

Conscious: Awake, aware, and thoughtful.

Consciousness: Awakening to one's own existence, sensations, and cognitions.

Creator: Fully empowered God-Source, affirmed through human thought, feeling, and action.

Cup: A symbol of neutrality and grace. The Ascended Masters often refer to our human body as a Cup filled with our thoughts and feelings.

Decree: Statements of intent and power, similar to prayers and mantras, which are often integrated with the use of the I AM and requests to the I AM Presence.

Desire: Of the Source.

Deva: A shining one or being of light.

Dharma: Purpose.

Divine Heritage: The possession of providence and an innate connection to the God-Source.

Divine Inheritor: Successor and progeny of the inner God-Source.

Divine Plan: The outcome of creative and Co-creative processes that provoke spiritual growth and evolution. From a traditional viewpoint, the will of God.

Divine Will: The idea of God's plan for humanity; however, from the perspective of the HU-man, the Divine Will is "choice."

Dove of Peace: A symbol of universal peace; however, the Ascended Masters teach that the dove is also the symbol of one age shifting into a new one.

Earth Changes: A prophesied Time of Change on Earth. This includes geophysical, political, and social changes, alongside the opportunity for spiritual and personal transformation.

Earth Ray: A Ray of energy-induced light produced by the Earth. This influences other planets in our solar system.

Earth Plane and Planet: The dual aspect of life on Earth. The Earth Planet is a reference to Earth as a conscious evolving and sentient being.

Eight-sided Cell of Perfection: An atomic cell located in the human heart. It is associated with all aspects of perfection, and contains and maintains a visceral connection with the Godhead.

Elemental: A nature being.

Elemental Kingdom: A kingdom comprising an invisible, subhuman group of creatures who act as counterparts to visible nature on Earth.

El Morya: Ascended Master of the Blue Ray, associated with the development of the will.

Elohim: Creative beings of love and light that helped manifest the Divine Idea of our solar system. Seven Elohim (the Seven Rays) exist here. They organize and draw forward Archangels, the Four Elements, Devas, Seraphim, Cherubim, Angels, Nature Guardians, and the Elementals. The Silent Watcher – the Great Mystery – gives them direction.

Energy Body: A distinct mass of energy that can be singular or independent; or dependent and interconnected to other diverse bodies of energy.

Energy Field: Distinct and definable layers of energy that exist around all forms of physical life: mineral, plant, animal, and human.

Energy-for-Energy: The transfer of energies. To understand this spiritual principle, one must remember Isaac Newton's Third Law of Motion: "for every action there is an equal and opposite reaction." However, while energies may be equal, their forms often vary. The Ascended Masters often use this phrase to remind chelas to properly compensate others to avoid karmic retribution, and repayment may take many different forms.

Enlightenment: The act of gaining spiritual wisdom and insight. According to the Spiritual Teachers, this process literally increases the light of the Human Aura. From a Buddhist perspective, it is a final state of spiritual growth and evolution, and is defined by the lack of desire and human suffering.

Fifth Ray: The Green Ray.

First Ray: The Blue Ray.

Fourth Ray: The White Ray.

Gabriel: The Archangel of the White Ray.

Geometric Language: A symbolic communication through sacred shape and symmetrical form.

Great Central Sun: The great sun of our galaxy, around which all of the galaxy's solar systems rotate. The Great Central Sun is also known as the Galactic Center, which is the origin of the Seven Rays of Light and Sound on Earth.

Green Ray: The Ray of Active Intelligence. It is associated with education, thoughtfulness, communication, organization, the intellect, science, objectivity, and discrimination. It is also adaptable, rational, healing, and awakening. The Green Ray is affiliated with the planet Mercury. In the I AM America teachings, the Green Ray is served by the Archangel Raphael and Archeia Mother Mary; the Elohim of Truth, Vista – also known as Cyclopea and Virginia; and the Ascended Masters Hilarion, Lord Sananda, Lady Viseria, Soltec, and Lady Master Meta.

Golden Age: A peaceful time on Earth prophesied to occur after the Time of Change. It is also prophesied that during this age, human life spans will be increased and sacred knowledge will be revered. During this time, the societies, cultures, and governments of Earth will reflect spiritual enlightenment through worldwide cooperation, compassion, charity, and love. Ascended Master teachings often refer to this Golden Age as the Golden-Crystal Age and the Age of Grace.

Golden City of Gobean: The first United States Golden City located in the states of Arizona and New Mexico. Its qualities are cooperation, harmony, and peace. Its Ray Force is blue, and its Master Teacher is El Morya.

Golden City of Shalahah: The fourth United States Golden City, located primarily in the states of Montana and Idaho. Its qualities are abundance, prosperity, and healing. Its Ray Force is Green, and its Master Teacher is Sananda.

Golden Flame: An energy field of spiritual enlightenment. The teachings of the Golden Flame are said to originate from the Pleiades.

Golden Thread Axis: Also known as the Vertical Power Current. The Golden Thread Axis physically consists of the *Medullar Shushumna*, a life-giving nadi comprising one-third of the human Kundalini system. Two vital currents intertwine around the Golden Thread Axis: the lunar Ida Current, and the solar Pingala Current. According to the Master Teachers, the flow of the Golden Thread Axis begins with the I AM Presence, enters the Crown Chakra, and descends through the spinal system. It descends beyond the Base Chakra and travels to the core of the Earth. Esoteric scholars often refer to the axis as the Rod of Power, and it is symbolized by two spheres connected by an elongated rod. Ascended Master students and chelas frequently draw upon the energy of the Earth through the Golden Thread Axis for healing and renewal using meditation, visualization, and breath.

Great White Brotherhood and Sisterhood (Lodge): A fraternity of ascended and unascended men and women. It is dedicated to the universal uplifting of humanity. Its main objectives include the preservation of the lost spirit, and the teaching of ancient religions and philosophies of the world. Its mission is to reawaken the dormant ethical and spiritual sparks among the masses. In addition to fulfilling spiritual aims, the Great White Lodge pledges to protect humankind against systematic assaults on individual and group freedoms, which inhibit self-knowledge and personal growth.

Golden City Vortex: According to the prophecies, areas of safety and spiritual growth during the Time of Change.

Gold Ray: The Ray of Brotherhood, Cooperation, and Peace. The Gold Ray produces the qualities of perception, honesty, confidence, courage, and responsibility. It is also associated with leadership, independence, authority, ministration, and justice. The Gold Ray vibrates the energies of the Divine Father on Earth. Its attributes include: warmth, perception, honesty, confidence, positivity, independence, endurance, and vitality.

The Gold Ray is also associated with the Great Central Sun, the Solar Logos. Our Solar Sun is a Step-down Transformer for its energies. According to the Master Teachers, the Gold Ray is the epitome of change for the New Times. The Gold Ray is the ultimate authority of Cosmic Law, and carries both our personal and worldwide karma and dharma (purpose). Its presence is designed to instigate responsible spiritual growth and planetary evolution as a shimmering light for humanity's aspirations, and for the development of the HU-man. The Gold Ray, however, is also associated with Karmic justice, and will instigate change: constructive and destructive. The extent of catastrophe or transformation is contingent on humanity's personal and collective spiritual growth and evolutionary process as we progress into the New Times.

Heart Chakra: Known in Sanskrit as the *Anahata*. The location is in the center of the chest. Its main aspect is Love and Relationships, and includes our ability to feel compassion, forgiveness, and hold our own Divine Purpose.

Heart's Desire: The wellspring of abundance, love, and creativity. By identifying activities that yield personal joy and happiness, we may discover our Heart's Desire. Eastern philosophy often refers to this principle as the soul's specific duty or purpose in a lifetime, or its Dharma. The Heart's Desire is analogous to the principle of desire – the Ninth Jurisdiction. This evolved perception of desire is based on the true etymology of the word. *De*, is a French word that means *of*, and the English word *sire*, means forefather, ancestry, or source. From this context, Sanat Kumara teaches, "The Heart's Desire is the source of creation." Since the Heart's Desire is one of the most influential principles underlying humanity's spiritual development and unfoldment, Ascended Master teachings give it utmost importance. It is considered a physical, emotional, mental, and spiritual presence that raises the unawakened animal consciousness into human consciousness, and then onward, to the awakened aspirant and the devoted chela.

The Ascended Masters claim that the physical presence of the Flame of Desire lies within the heart, nestled inside the Eight-sided Cell of Perfection. As students and chelas perfect the Co-creation process, some teachings suggest the Flame of Desire evolves alongside the Three-Fold or Unfed Flame of Love, Wisdom, and Power into the Four-Fold Flame. In this physical, progressed state, the Flame of Desire develops as the fourth White Flame of Creation.

Helios and Vesta: The masculine and feminine deities who reside in the heart of our solar sun. In Ascended Master teachings, they are perceived as the divine parents of our solar system. Helios emits the quality of illumination for spiritual knowledge and enlightenment, while Vesta emanates energies of spiritual truth for self-actualization.

Higher Self: The *Atma* or *Atman*. This is the true identity of the soul, which resides in the spiritual planes of consciousness. Although it is energetically connected to each individual in the physical plane, the Higher Self is free from the karmas of the Earth Plane and from identification with the material world.

Holy of Holies: The inner chamber of a temple or sanctuary.

HU or HUE: A sacred sound that, when chanted or meditated upon, is said to represent the entire spectrum of the Seven Rays. Because of this, the HU powerfully invokes the presence of the Violet Flame, which is the activity of the Violet Ray with its inherent ability to transform and transmit energies to the next octave. In Tibetan dialects, the word HUE or HU means "breath." However, HU is also considered an ancient name for God, and it is sung for spiritual enlightenment.

HU-man: The God-Man.

I AM: The presence of God.

I AM Activity: A religious movement centered on Ascended Master teachings, founded in the 1930s by Guy Ballard and his wife Edna.

I AM Presence: The individualized presence of God.

I AM THAT I AM: A term from Hebrew that translates to, "I Will Be What I Will Be." "I AM" is also derived from the Sanskrit Om (pronounced: A-U-M), whose three letters signify the three aspects of God as beginning, duration, and dissolution – Brahma, Vishnu, and Shiva. The AUM syllable is known as the *omkara* and translates to "I AM Existence," the name for God. "Soham," is yet another mystical Sanskrit name for God, which means "It is I," or "He is I." In Vedic philosophy, it is claimed that when a child cries, "Who am I?" the universe replies, "Soham – you are the same as I AM." The I AM teachings also use the name "Soham" in place of "I AM."

Immaculate Conception: A spiritual teaching and energy initiated by Mother Mary. It creates purity and virtue of mind to enable conceptualization of the Co-creation processes.

Judgment: The act of forming negative assumptions and critical opinions, primarily of fellow human beings.

Kali Yuga: The Age of Iron, or Age of Quarrel, when Earth receives twenty-five percent or less galactic light from the Great Central Sun.

Karma: Laws of Cause and Effect.

Kuan Yin: The Bodhisattva of Compassion and teacher of Saint Germain. She is associated with all of the Rays, as well as the principle of femininity.

Kundalini: The coiled energy located at the base of the spine, often established in the lower Base and Sacral Chakras. In Sanskrit, Kundalini literally means coiled, and *Kundalini Shatki* (shatki means energy) is claimed to initiate spiritual development, wisdom, knowledge, and enlightenment.

Kuthumi: An Ascended Master of the Pink, Ruby, and Gold Rays. He is a gentle and patient teacher who works closely with the Nature Kingdoms.

Lady Master Venus: The Ascended Master and Goddess of Love, who is said to be the Divine Complement of Sanat Kumara. She is a feminine archetype from the planet Venus who allegedly holds the heart chakra of our solar system.

Lemuria: A continent that primarily existed in the Pacific Ocean before it was submerged by Earth Changes. It is deemed to have been the remaining culture and civilization of Mu – an expansive continent that once spanned the entire present-day Pacific Ocean. It is alleged that the lands of Lemuria, also known as *Shalmali*, existed in the Indian and Southern Pacific Oceans, and included the continent of Australia. Thus, it is believed to have integrated with the Lands of Rama, and is considered one the earliest cultures of humanity. Sri Lanka is alleged to have been one of the empire's capital cities. Esoteric historians theorize that the tectonic Pacific Plate formed this lost continent. *Asuramaya* is one of the great Manus of Lemuria's Root Race.

Some esoteric writers place the destruction of Mu around the year 30,000 BCE; others place its demise millions of years ago. According to Theosophical history, the Lemurian and Atlantean epochs overlapped. The apparent discrepancy of these timelines is likely due to two different interpretations of the Cycle of the Yugas. It is claimed that the venerated Elders of Lemuria escaped the global tragedy by moving to an uninhabited plateau in central Asia. This account mirrors Ascended Master teachings and Lord Himalaya's founding of the Retreat of the Blue Lotus.

The Lemurian elders re-established their spiritual teachings and massive library as the Thirteenth School. Spiritual teachers claim that the evolutionary purpose of this ancient civilization was to develop humanity's Will (the Blue Ray of Power). Lemurian culture also venerated the Golden Disk of the Sun and practiced the Right-hand Path. It is claimed that these teachings and spiritual records became foundational teachings for the Great White Brotherhood of the mystical lands of *Hsi Wang Mu* (the Abode of the Immortals) and the Kuan Yin Lineage of Gurus.

Present-day Australia – once known by Egyptian gold-miners as the ancient *Land of Punt* – is considered the remainder of the once great continent of Mu and Lemuria, which likely existed in the time period of Dvapara-Yuga, over 800,000 years ago.

Light: "Love in action."

Light Body: An energy body.

Logos: Wisdom.

Love: "Light in action."

Mantra: Certain sounds, syllables, and sets of words that are deemed sacred. They often carry the ability to transmute karma, spiritually purify, and transform an individual.

Master Teacher: A spiritual teacher from a specific lineage of teachers, or gurus. The teacher transmits and emits the energy from that collective lineage.

Mastery: Possessing the consummate skill of command and self-realization over thought, feeling, and action.

Michael: The archangel of the Blue Ray. Archangel Michael is the protector of chelas and initiates of the Ascended Master tradition through the activity of the Blue Flame.

Mother Mary: Ascended Goddess of the Feminine who was originally of the angelic evolution. She is associated with the Green Ray of Healing, Truth, and Science, and the Pink Ray of Love.

ONE: Indivisible, whole, and harmonious unity.

Oneness: A combination of two or more, which creates the whole.

Perception: Awareness and intuitive recognition.

Pillar of Light (Tube of Light): A tube of protective light, impenetrable to anything not of light. It surrounds the subtle light bodies and the physical body.

Pink Ray: The energy of the Divine Mother, associated with the Moon. This Ray is affiliated with the qualities of love, nurturing, hopefulness, heartfeltness, compassion, consideration, communication, intuition, friendship, humanity, tolerance, and adoration. In the I AM America teachings, the Pink Ray is served by: the Archangel Chamuel and Archeia Charity; the Elohim of Divine Love Orion and Angelica; and the Ascended Masters Kuan Yin, Mother Mary, Goddess Meru, and Paul the Venetian.

Pleiades: A seven-star cluster that exists in the Taurus Constellation near Earth, in the same Orion Arm of the Milky Way Galaxy. The Pleiades cluster is also known as the *Seven Sisters*. Its seven stars are called: Sterope, Merope, Electra, Maia, Taygeta, Celaeno, and Alcyone.

Portal: A gateway to another dimension, often accompanied by a natural Vortex.

Prana or Prahna: Vital, life-sustaining energy; also known as orgone or chi. The Spiritual Teachers often refer to Earth as *Prana*.

Prayer for Golden City Purification:

Golden Service Prayer
Beloved being of light that I AM,
Stream forth these Golden Rays into my being.
I AM resonating with all my focus, all that I AM,
Into the Golden Light that streams from Divine Creation.
Together we dance in the joy of being ONE.

Prophecy: A spiritual teaching given simultaneously with a warning. The teaching is designed to change, alter, lessen, or mitigate the prophesied warning. This caveat may be literal or metaphoric as the outcomes of these events are contingent on the choices and the consciousness of those willing to apply the teachings.

Purification: A clearing process, especially in spiritual practice, which frees consciousness from cumbersome or objectionable elements.

Raphael: Archangel of the Green Ray.

Ray: A force containing a purpose, which divides its efforts into two measurable and perceptible powers: light and sound.

Rate of spin: A measurement used to indicate either an adjustment or acceleration of spiritual vibration.

Root Chakra: The chakra that is located at the base of the spine, the perineum. The energy of this base chakra flows between the legs, downward, and connects to Mother Earth.

Saint Germain: Ascended Master of the Seventh Ray. Saint Germain is known for his work with the Violet Flame of Mercy, Transmutation, Alchemy, and Forgiveness. He is the sponsor of the Americas and the I AM America material. Many other teachers and Masters, affiliated with the Great White Brotherhood, help his endeavors.

Sananda: The name used by Master Jesus in his ascended state of consciousness. Sananda means joy and bliss, and his teachings focus on revealing the savior and heavenly kingdom within.

Sanat Kumara: A Venusian Ascended Master, and the venerated leader of the Ascended Masters. He is best known as the founder of Shamballa, the first Golden City on Earth. He is also known, within the teachings of the Great White Brotherhood, as the Lord of the World, and is regarded as a savior and eminent spiritual teacher.

Second Ray: The Pink Ray.

Serapis Bey: An Ascended Master from Venus who works from the White Ray. He is the great disciplinarian who plays an essential role in humanity's Ascension. He works closely with all unascended humans whose focus is Ascension. Serapis Bey is the Master Teacher for the Golden City of Klehma, located primarily in the United States of Colorado and Kansas.

Seventh Ray: The Violet Ray.

Sixth Ray: The Ruby-Gold Ray.

Solar Plexus: The navel chakra located between the navel and the base of the sternum.

Soltec: An Ascended Master of science and technology who is affiliated with the Green Ray.

Spiritual Hierarchy: A fellowship of Ascended Masters and their disciples. This group helps humanity function through the mental plane with meditation, decrees, and prayer. The term Spiritual Hierarchy often refers to the Great White Brotherhood and Sisterhood. However, the term also connotes the spiritual-social structure for the organization, its members, and the various states of member evolution. The hierarchy includes the different offices and activities that serve the Cosmic, Solar, Planetary, and Creative Hierarchies.

Spiritual Metabolism: The spiritual vibration and degree of concentrated energy held in the energy bodies of the Human Aura.

Star seed: Souls and groups whose genetic origins are not from Earth. Many remain linked to one another from one lifetime to the next, as signified by the *Atma Karaka*, a Sanskrit term meaning "soul indicator." Star-seed consciousness is often referred to by the Spiritual Teachers as a family or soul group whose members have evolved to and share Fifth-Dimensional awareness. Star seeds can also contain members who have not yet evolved to this level, who are still incarnating on Earth.

Step-down Transformer: The processes instigated through the Cellular Awakening rapidly advance human light bodies. Synchronized with an Ascended Master's will, the awakened cells of light and love evolve the skills of a Step-Down Transformer to efficiently transmit and distribute currents of Ascended Master energy—referred to as an Ascended Master Current (A.M. Current). This metaphysical form of intentional inductive coupling creates an ethereal power grid that can be used for all types of healing.

Subatomic Particle: Any variety of matter smaller than an atom.

Swaddling Cloth: An area of over a million square miles located in Brazil, South America. According to the Ascended Masters, this area is the primary prophesied physical location for the incarnation of the children of the Seventh Manu. The Swaddling Cloth is protected by the Ascended Master Mother Mary.

Terra: Earth.

Third Density: Third Dimension.

Third Eye Chakra: Also known as the *Ajna Chakra*. This energy center is located above and between the eyebrows. The Third-eye Chakra blends thought and feeling into perception and projection for Co-creative activity.

Third Ray: The Yellow Ray.

Time Compaction: An anomaly produced as we enter into the prophesied Time of Change. As our perception of time compresses, time seems to speed by. While the unfolding of events accelerates, situations are jammed into shorter periods of time. This experience of time will become more prevalent as we get closer to the period of cataclysmic Earth Changes.

Time of Change: The period of time currently underway. It includes tremendous changes in our society, culture, and politics, in tandem with individual and collective spiritual awakenings and transformations. These changes occur simultaneously and can also include massive Earth Changes: global warming, climactic changes, and seismic and volcanic activity. The Time of Change guides the Earth to a new time, the Golden Age.

Time of Grace: A time of worldwide peace, neutrality, and calm. This period is prophesied to occur after the tumultuous Time of Change and simultaneously with the Age of Cooperation.

Time of Transition: A twelve-year period when humanity experienced tremendous spiritual and intellectual growth, ushering in personal and global changes.

Twelve Jurisdictions: Twelve laws (virtues) for the New Times that guide consciousness to Co-create the Golden Age. They are: Harmony, Abundance, Clarity, Love, Service, Illumination, Cooperation, Charity, Desire, Faith, Stillness, and Creation/Creativity.

Unfed Flame: The Three-Fold Flame of Divinity that exists in the heart and becomes larger as it evolves. The three flames represent: Love (Pink), Wisdom (Yellow), and Power (Blue).

Vibration: The moving, swinging, or oscillation of energy. In Ascended Master teachings, vibration is associated with light's movement during physical and spiritual activities, as well as in the presence of the Masters.

Violet Flame: A flame that burns violet. The Violet Flame is used and can appear during the practice of balancing karmas of the past through transmutation, forgiveness, and mercy. The result is an opening of the Spiritual Heart and the development of *bhakti* – unconditional love and compassion. The flame came into existence, during the Lemurian End Time, when the Lords of Venus transmitted a Violet Flame, also known as the Violet Fire, to clear the Earth of negative forces and energies within the etheric and psychic realms, as well as in the lower physical atmosphere. This paved the way for Atlantean usage during religious ceremonies, and for use as visible markers in temples. The Violet Flame induces Alchemy: because violet light emits the shortest wavelength and the highest frequency in the light spectrum, it induces a point of transition to the next octave of light.

Violet Ray: The Seventh Ray, which is primarily associated with Freedom and Ordered Service alongside Transmutation, Alchemy, Mercy, Compassion, and Forgiveness. It is served by the Archangel Zadkiel, the Elohim Arcturus, the Ascended Master Saint Germain and Goddess Portia.

Vortex: A polarized moving body that creates its own magnetic field, aligning molecular structures with phenomenal accuracy. Vortices are often formed where ley lines (energy meridians of the Earth) cross. They are often called power spots because the natural electromagnetic field of the Earth is immensely strong at these types of locations.

Yellow Ray: The Ray of the Divine Wisdom, which is primarily associated with the planet Jupiter. Jupiter is also known as the Divine Guru. The Ray is affiliated with expansion, optimism, joy, and spiritual enlightenment. In the I AM America teachings, the Yellow Ray is served by the Archangel Jophiel and Archeia Christine; the Elohim of Illumination Cassiopeia and Lumina; and the Ascended Masters Lady Nada, Peter the Everlasting, Confucius, Lanto, Laura, Minerva, and Mighty Victory.

Zadkiel: Archangel of the Violet Ray.

Appendix A

Twenty Lessons: A Review

1. Creative Reflection. This universe mirrors and reflects thoughts back to the one creating the thoughts. We are creative beings and our thoughts and focus are our creations. Consider discrimination as judgment. That judgment keeps us at a distance from each other. Discrimination is based on fear, fear of being wrong or wronged, and there are only two choices that we are faced with, Love or Fear. Love is a state of being and allowing; it is not an emotion. Love is the state of pure creation, the first law of this universe, and the reason for all existence in creation. Love binds all creation together and is the reason we exist. By seeing light in all those around us, we become more lighted and release our Karmic darkness, from which all darkness currently comes. This makes space for more light in all realms of creation.

When we focus on darkness, we attract it. We were all ascended from before the time of Lemuria, but have all collectively chosen to forget, and we recreate the darkness in embodiment after embodiment. Judging is breaking the first Law of Love. Love is tolerant and allowing, and does not bind another to any fear, thought, or discrimination. By allowing all to be where they are with their loving thoughts and outlooks on life, we can be ONE in creation. Do this by decreeing the Violet Flame three times per day, seven times, seven each time. Sunrise, noon, and sunset are the times of clearest, precise alignment.

2. Pleiadian Ancestors. All those who step forth to sponsor the creation of a planet form an energetic pattern, a creative wave that is duplicated or expanded upon. This process of duplication is the basis of the genetic code formed by the Elohim and the Archangels. From the Pleiades, a planet of origin for many of us, harmony, beauty, and balance is the pattern and there is no place for disturbance.

3. Work of Ascension. It has been the work of the Spiritual Hierarchy of the Great White Brotherhood to move the Ascension work forward, move it from what is known as the Eastern culture into the Western culture, for it needs to be accepted by all races. The work of Ascension is to step forth to every Star seed. It is founded on the premises of freedom and choice.

4. Time Theories. Time Compaction is basically the compaction of sequential events, grouped on top of one another. This occurs during the End Times, long ordained from the creation of this universe. At the end of any creative pattern of duplication, there is a period of choice before reaching the apex, to access the Portals of Entry. At the end of one cycle, there is a moment to choose to continue the duplication process, or to go on to expand, store, or block the event. Triangular energy is the geometric form for duplication and at the right corner is the access to the center apex and the core energy, which one may use to go to the realm of expansion.

The End Times are a very large window of choice. All the events that have been stored within our Third Density world are being brought to the forefront. Before we enter into Creatorship, we must Master choice. We enter a time warp, which is the bending of experience by how we perceive it. Since it is our feeling that holds the shape, we have faced these choices before. These choices represent duplicated, rhythmic patterns, set up within the energetic life stream, which are incomplete because they did not align with the universal laws of our particular planet.

When faced with the duplication of energy, eighth, ninth, and tenth energetic bodies have the ability to deal with time compaction and time warp. In thought and feeling worlds, we may successfully use up to fourteen energetic bodies. It is the fifteenth level where we step forth, out of the world of thought and feeling as Creation, a state of being. To create is to serve all, and a lasting work comes through on the vibration of choice. Time compaction, plus choice, equals time warp. There are many threads which make a cloth and weave this work. This work is a collective woven effort.

5. Decree of Light. Time is a relative experience; relative to the metabolic rate of each and every life stream in expression. Our metabolic rate is a function of the imperfection of our present genetic coding, decaying the energetic pulse of the I AM Presence anchored in the Heart Chakra. Radiating through the energetic bodies, this imperfection then precipitates through our DNA coding, as a structured blueprint of the physical body.

At one time, the human expression was perfection, but the sustaining of perfection was a loss we chose. The original DNA structure was perfect and sustainable. The difference now in DNA structures is that the human metabolic rate is slower than in the time of the alignment to the sun of this solar system. Now that mankind has turned its face from the Light of God that Never Fails, the light energy is blocked in the DNA and the metabolism has slowed, affecting the human body. In this present Time of Transition, when we remember that we are lighted beings, our light will resonate within and without.

The light is inside and brought through our energy bodies and into our physical. But our ability to absorb and use the Light of God that Never Fails is blocked by our own thoughts of being less than we are. Lifetime after lifetime, we have created a pattern of forgetting and separation. It has become the focus of our lives.

The Violet Flame Dispensation is the gift to change and transmute the darkness we create. We can lift the self-created Veil and flow in our own light with the continuous use of the flame. We can lift our Karmic blocks and fears, which we hold fast to our energy and physical bodies using the Violet Flame Dispensation. Decree the Violet Flame three times per day; in the dawn, when the stillness of God announces the light; at the midday, when the light is at the fulfilled radiance; and at sunset, when the stillness promises the return. Do this seven times seven times, equaling forty-nine times, three times per day. That would be seven times for each of the seven chakras of each of your seven energetic bodies. This is a perfecting practice to realign with the Light of God that Never Fails.

6. Serving the Divine Plan. Continual rhythm, such as the setting of the sun and the rising of the sun, assures that the lapses in time, which we see as interruptions, are overcome. Seeing interruptions as disruptions is only a perception. Events are timed and brought to us as a choice, so we can act according to the Divine Plan. To turn our lives and wills over to the mighty I AM Presence aligns us with this Divine Plan. If an event appears to disrupt, we can take a moment and ask the I AM Presence to allow the Divine Plan to come forth in full manifestation that instant and forever! At that moment, the Divine Plan is revealed so that step by step, we can participate. When the Divine Plan works in our life and in the lives of others, there is an orderly timelessness to it, and it includes Divine Beauty and Divine Form. Divine Cooperation joins the Divine Plan, for a Divine Plan is the end result of the unique timing of events. The focus of allowance and the synthesis of cooperation are the middle way, the way that always harmonizes and balances.

Prophecy is that portion of the Divine Plan that is yet to unfold. Prophecy, and that which is free, combines to form the Divine Will, for Prophecy contains within it several steps of manifestation. Prophecy is a form of creative flow, for as a man thinketh, so he becomes; as a man decrees, so he is. Creative focus and free will combine to form the Divine Plan. And then there is the pivot point of the Divine Plan, the point at which the Creator of the universe then chooses that this shall be. For it is the will of the Creator of the mighty universal laws that have been set forth, that all is and all shall be.

We have been brought here to share in our Creatorship. Understanding the principles of creation is a step-by-step process of the acceptance of responsibility. When two or more are gathered in the name of I AM THAT I AM, an Ascended

Master shall be there. It is then the choice of those two who have gathered, if they shall listen or not, shall be guided or not.

Creation is that which shall be allowed to perpetuate, as we and the universe inhale and exhale. To inhale, the breath expands inside and circulates throughout the system. As we understand this work, we have breathed and expanded this into the very core of ourselves. We take it inside, internalize it, accept what it is, then exhale. The exhale releases life, in service to other life, or simply releases and discards.

7. HUE. There is a difference between humanity and mankind. Humanity carries the collective consciousness, the collective awakening, the very beginning and the very end, the Alpha and the Omega. Mankind is only the expression of human thought and feeling. It carries no memory; however, it carries the forgetting. Humanity has been brought forth to understand that the creative force, or God Force, works through all and is in everything that is. It is the beloved mighty I AM Presence that holds the continual form, or the continual shape, for all to express through.

Using the words, I AM THAT I AM, or I AM, we carry our Divine Blueprint as Divine Inheritors and Co-creators, expressing through the collective thought form of humanity. This carries the force for all, lifted from the stance of mankind, to be and become a member of the human race (humanity). It is through Divine Service that we step forth from mankind to humanity; for then, we see our Brother and our Sister as our self.

HUE is the sound vibration that carries within it the Pink and the Green Rays, and the Heart's Desire. The foundation blocks of love, wisdom, and power are applied through the HUE upon the Earth Plane and Planet. HUE comes forth to carry and to hold our Creatorship. If mankind is served, he will recognize that he is a member of this human race. The beauty of this and the expression of this is the joy of service; that all upon this planet can then, and only then, form one body of light; one body, united in service to the mighty I AM Presence, and held in continual and sustained form. We can light a candle in honor of the Light of God that Never Fails, knowing it is truly the light that will bring each man, woman, and child, upon this planet, home to their Source, the Source that we all share.

HOLY, HOLY, HOLY!
HUE, HUE, HUE,!
Almighty I AM, Almighty I AM, Almighty I AM.

8. Conception of Perfection. Desire is within the genetic coding, held within the heart, which strives to be ONE with perfection, removing the illusion of separation. Desire is that which comes from the Perfected Cell, the cell that duplicates throughout the system and allows one to perceive or even have the conception of perfection. Desire is a function of the Cellular Awakening, for the desire for perfection must be held. We cannot become perfect until we have the desire to be perfect. This desire is built upon the Eight-sided matrix of the Perfect Cell. The function of the Perfect Cell allows the body to accept the new energetic pattern of perfection. The rhythmic pattern of seven resonates to the harmonics of desire. Use the pattern of seven; seven times seven times seven.

This concept was held long in our own Immaculate Conception, the blueprint of perfection that we carry. This was always, and always shall be. The Immaculate Concept of perfection is the work of a heart, individualized, upon the Earth's Plane and Planet.

9. The Fifth Ray. For the completion of the work of the Fifth Ray upon the planet, information is gathered from the middle way. This is not only the quickest way, but also, in a sense, a conservative approach, for that which stands upon the edge always risks the crumbling of the earth beneath it. In the order and sequence of the Divine Plan, the work of the Fifth Ray draws its energetic work from that of the Sixth body. The work of the Fifth Ray comes from the beloved beings of light who have stepped forth to give their continuous radiance to that of the Earth Plane and Planet. They have, within themselves, ready access to the energetic readings of the Earth's layers.

Those who come forth on this Fifth Ray minister to mankind, give service to the health and welfare of mankind, and serve abundantly. They also represent the material Third Density expression of abundance, which is the abundance of choice. Individualization takes its Home, or House of the Father, into the expression of "Sol," the fifth tone in light and sound. The expression of light is the expression of thought, whereas the expression of feeling is the expression of sound. Reasoning is thought, thought is light, and the completeness of light is enlightenment. The completeness and thoroughness of this work also hinges upon the individualized focus of light and sound. The Green Ray represents the ministry of service and science to mankind and comes through the office of Archangel Raphael.

10. Energy Lessons. The ninth energetic body, anchored into and held by the Human Aura, attains our eternal freedom. This can be activated through breathing with the Earth. When breathing with, and working in service to the Earth, there is an energetic remuneration that manifests as a technique for healing, as follows.

In the second energetic field of the Earth, which is an emotional field, there are rainstorms and electrical storms. We can breathe with the Earth during these storms by grounding into her inner core and drawing this core energy up (expanding), then dispersing it (contracting) through our Heart Chakra into the atmosphere. Do this for approximately eighteen breaths, followed by the technique of the microcosmic orbit to revitalize and rejuvenate your electromagnetic field.

To orbit the breath, inhale from the perineum up the back of the spine, across the top of the head to the Third Eye, and exhale down the front, through your Heart Chakra, preferably, with the tongue to the roof of the mouth, to awaken the Eight-sided Cell of Perfection. The Eight-sided Cell of Perfection is held in a cradle within the heart and is the perfect child who longs to come out, who longs to express itself. It is ONE with I AM THAT I AM. This child can be awakened, held and cradled like a newborn, in perfection.

Within the core of the Earth is also the Eight-sided Cell of Perfection. The core energy of this planet continuously contracts and expands. Duplication comes forth with the expansion, and it is the Earth's spin that allows the sustaining and maintenance of perfection. The ability of this Cell to duplicate or replicate also depends on our ability to expand and contract our energetic consciousness in sync with the Earth. Consciousness is only an energy; it is the Heart of Desire that provides us with the choice to use this technique as a tool. Using this technique requires Will.

The Will is the basis of "breath," for breath determines the rate of spin. The amount of Will put forth with thoughts and feelings determines the amount of space that is expanded. Much work needs to be done on the planet to restore the Will. This requires Compassion. Compassion goes beyond the thought. Compassion is sound emotion, an emotion to carry thought at all times. Thought is that which is selected to act upon, but it is the emotion that carries it.

11. Cloak of Divinity. The Swaddling Cloak comes forth to hold us and to carry us. This is given to us by Mary, as a Cloak of Divinity, so that we will know that we are never alone. This serves as a connection to her heart and her vision of our perfection, given to each of us as our Immaculate Conception. This cloak will protect and assist us to carry this work and message forward. The geometric shape of the square also holds and carries space, like the cloak of protection. Just as with Ascension, it is not a matter of taking the light and holding the light, but of carrying the light and protecting that which comes forth from the mighty Logos, in the form of a cloak or square.

Many have been directed at this Time of Transition to return to areas of birth, not of the birth in this embodiment, but to areas where we have birthed many times. This is to re-collect or complete experiences through time compaction. Completion is a work of joy, for as we go to the top step of this work, we are ready for the next flight.

Declare: I AM THE FREEDOM OF THE ETERNAL GOD MADE MANIFEST NOW, and become the identity which you truly wish for. Individualization manifests as "To be or not to be?" You can step forth and be fashioned anew from the heart of the mighty Logos, streaming forth in the identity of eternal life, this which is the wellspring of All That Is.

That which holds or carries space is the perfect square; however, contained within the perfect square are the triangles, which come forth to duplicate energy, or replicate energy. As a perfect representation of what this energy should be, we can choose to absorb this duplication of energy, carry, or store it for future use. This is known as an identical, individualized energy, or the patterned energy. To carry or to hold energy is to bring light within its configuration.

Within the heart are the patterns that we hold and carry. The DNA coding within the Perfected Cell has enabled us to evolve. Close to the perimeter of this mighty Perfected Cell is the RNA coding of the double-helix. We are asked to see, surrounded by this Perfect Cell, six helixes, which come forth as the perfection of divinity.

12. Cosmic Service. The Beloved planet, Babajeran, is a Cosmic Being that offered itself and was created in Divine Cosmic Service. Creation only comes forth on the Expansive Ray, or that which manifests itself as the geometric language of the circle. What is known as service is founded on the law of seven times seven.

The Fifth Ray individualized itself in the form of plant and animal life upon the planet and the Devas, the Elementals, and the Elohim. The Elohim are the wind, rain, fire, and the earth; however, these four elements are embodied even further in refined, focused consciousness. Occasionally, there are those Elohim who step forth in human embodiment to bring the message forth of the Cosmic Being Babajeran.

Depending on how fast or how slow energy spins, corresponding spaces are created by choice, through the cooperation of light and sound. The Pink Ray, in the creation and formation of this world, compassionately offered to the rest of the universe, as a cosmic service, a home, or a creative, safe space for the Slows. The beloved

Will was then breathed into the Slows through the mighty I AM Presence and the Higher Self. And through this space, the language of the geometric shape was made manifest.

In the Alignment, as beings of light, we harken to the Heavenly Host and are held, as a mother holds her child to her breast. We have not only seven or eight energy bodies, but share with the Earth, Babajeran, collective bodies. This Ascension is not the end-all or the be-all, but the opportunity to create, not as an implosion or explosion, but as a peaceful, expansive wave. There is a prayer for service, healing, and the entry into the Golden Age:

Beloved being of light that I AM,
Stream forth these Golden Rays into my being.
I AM resonating with all my focus,
All that I AM into the golden light that streams from Divine Creation.
Together we dance in the joy of being ONE.

Babajeran has held up to fourteen genetic codings. This has been held, not only within the DNA, but within Divine Coding. We are part of Babajeran, and as part of her, we are the same Divine Creation and are also a Divine Inheritor of the cosmos. The Golden City Vortex is a good place to speak to Babajeran, for it serves as a great capillary of thought and is the most perfect place to usher in this Golden Age.

The Golden City of Gobean is also referred to as a "delivery system," for all that is touched there, all that is thought, all that is, can instantaneously be projected through the entire planetary system. The healing of our bodies is a collective momentum. Through this, healing travels back. and a continuous breath is then assured.

13. History of the Rays. The Fifth Ray, the Ray of Science and Healing, is the Ray that brings forth abstract thinking, that which breaks down and shows the structure of all that is among the planets and creation. There is truly no such thing as "spiritual," "etheric," or "physical." All is energy, and this energy rotates and accelerates in spin. This determines where energy shall be placed, qualified as light or thought, and as sound or feeling.

The Third Dimensional world is composed of three layers: the Elemental Life Force; that which is the thought and feelings; and the breath, or the aligned Will. The Fifth Ray serves as the dispensation, working with consciousness, or conscious thought, also seen as light.

The world of sound expresses the desire to achieve. Feelings are associated with pitch, which resonates to a desire within the thought itself, and provides the pattern to go forth and Co-create with that thought. Thought and feeling then proceed on to the world of the aligned Will. The focused Will streams forth into the Golden Age, the period of time where harmony and peace is sustained. The cooperative, collective effort and global Ascension come from aligning with the Divine Plan, as Babajeran aligns with the human plan. This work comes forth on the Fifth Ray for a sustained period of time within the Fourth Dimension of peace and harmony. Accepting our eternal freedom in the Ascension is the sustained energy of harmony and peace. Our world of thought and feeling, all that is continual movement and change, expands into a world of change that can also sustain the Divine Plan.

The first race to come to this planet was known as the Blues. They arrived when water covered the entire planet, with no land. The remnants of this great race and civilization of beings are the dolphins and whales. They carry a consciousness that supersedes the human. They offered themselves in service to the planet, to hold space for the restoration of Prahna.

The Yellow Ray was the second race to come forth. These beloved beings were known as the Golden Ray. A continuous body of land floated over the continuous body of water. Their body and energetic structure were built upon staying within the Light of God that Never Failed. The continuous cycle of sunlight into these bodies of light assured a continuous circulation into their system. Their expression of divinity became complete, and many ascended and continued their work as lifestreams upon other planets.

The great Creators decreed that the third race should stream forth the Pink Ray. This held, within the Ray, the continuous love of the heart. Through its Divine connection, Divine Compassion streamed forth upon the face of this planet. Other life streams, which were held in planets far away, cried to the planet to learn compassion. The noble Red Race, the third race, could not turn away their pleas, and they became the first race ever to walk upon land. As the others came and incarnated, the genetic mixture evolved into the physical body we currently know, and the beginning of our civilization. This is where we are now, at the end of an epoch.

The Fourth Race is ready to stream forth as the Fourth Ray of Resurrection and Purity, from Archangel Gabriel and Serapis Bey. This Ray shall stream forth upon the planet, for the work of this Pink Ray is soon to be complete. This great race of beings shall understand the purity of physical expression, the spiritual and physical immortality, and that life is only the movement of energy.

The Higher Self has been misrepresented as the I AM Presence. The Higher Self is connected to the I AM Presence, which is an ascended body, knowing no limitation of time. All the I AM Presence understands is creation. The Higher Self descends from the I AM Presence which then streams forth from its energetic fields, a space to create our embodiment. Through the I AM Presence, the energy of divinity is anchored at the center of the Heart Chakra.

14. The Cup. The work of Forgiveness upon the Earth Plane and Planet assures that love will stream forth into the hearts of men forever. When we release discrimination, and even doubt, it takes us away from that position called blame. To blame, it is necessary to judge. Mankind blames itself and must forgive itself its sins. It must release that, and realize its divinity in the expression of full creation. We raise the Cup that we may drink of joy and creation and never forget that we are ONE with I AM Presence. This is a time for celebration; for accepting the eternal freedom in the Light of God that Never Fails.

The Elixir within the Cup was originally brought from the Solar System of the Pleiades for longevity, and to hold a continuous state of joy and creation, to take us through the Ascension. When we touch the Cup, are we not then responsible for it? For every intake, there is the outtake. With the continuation of the cycle in this particular universe, there is a balanced exchange: as above, so below. As we give out, that is the measure in which we receive. That which is given with a pure Heart's Desire will return sevenfold. That is the nourishment of the Cup. It always has, and it always shall.

These are the eternal Laws of Creation that the universe was founded upon. This universe was created to have abundance and joy; this universe was created to have harmony and longevity. Ascension was brought to glorify creation, so that the greatest majesty of All That Is shines forth and expands into eternity. Ascension is expansion; it is nothing more, nothing less. It is as simple as that. Perfection is the most beautiful thought we can hold for ourselves.

The work of Ascension is not to become elitist; it is not for the few; it is to stream forth to the heart of all. The expansion of energy is the choice to continue to live. The beauty of Ascension is having the experience and understanding that each day is ours, and it is our choice to command each day with our divinity. We raise the Cup to never forget the divinity housed in the heart of service.

15. Discipline. The second layer of the first body of light is the weather layer and also the emotional layer, which is where the disturbances of the thunderstorms and the tornados occur, through the mighty Elohim Astrea. This layer disturbs harmony if the body and mind are unbalanced. Harmonization is the key to balanced Co-creation; that is, bringing the body and mind into a state of balance. Taming these disturbances, to result in a sound body and sound mind, is accomplished through discipline and diet.

The work of Ascension is the work for eternal freedom. Sweat and tears are part of the process. The end result is that we stand forth as a Creator. To come forth in perfection, the first step of responsible Co-creation, on the path of Mastery, is the purification of the body. There are essential dietary guidelines that must be adhered to in order for the body to sustain a hold on this process. The purification of the body through dietary intake is the first essential step to understand disciplines of energy.

To interfere, or to mix vibrations within the system with animal life that has held conscious form, scatters the coding of patterns. At no time should we judge an animal to be less. It holds universal principle and thought within its form. It will evolve to the point of the human, if it evolves upon this planet, through choice. It is treated as a seed and should be seen and held as such. Animals are Brothers and Sisters who have yet to increase the spin of subatomic particles around the Golden Thread Axis.

Also of concern are the intake of certain chemicals, and those which we allow to alter our perception, such as alcohol and drugs, even foods that have an opiate effect. Remove all substances that, through sense of separation or loss, have a tendency to bring on a stupor. List all substances of intake that are believed to be harmful, and abstain from then. Also list all harmful thoughts for six weeks. This will allow the body to become receptive to the idea that it can be patterned, and the thoughts behind the actions broken. Within this discipline is the joy of eternal freedom.

Air quality and intake pose yet another concern. Purification of the body must include continuous breathing exercises in the sunlight, away from pollution, in repetitions of twelve, or eight, if necessary. Before sleep, do the following exchange: cover one nostril, breathe for eight repetitions, then cover the other nostril and breathe for eight repetitions. If you are a male, begin with covering the right nostril; if you are a female, begin with covering the left. This sets up a succinct timing and delivery system and assists the body while it sleeps. It allows for an easier time to adjust to the rhythmic breath that comes forth from the beloved mighty I AM Presence, as the mental body separates during the hours of sleep.

Ideally, drink eight cups of liquid a day, but no less than two per day, of the clearest and cleanest possible water. The technique for clarification and purity through the Green and Gold Rays is woven through the ring finger of the left hand. Water, the Elixir of Life, should only be charged by the person who will drink the water.

Visualize the light of the Green and Gold Rays streaming through the ring finger of the left hand into the water. Use the command, I AM THAT I AM, to hold continuous, individualized focused patterns of clarity and purity. Drink the water. This creates the "Elixir of Light."

16. Ascension Alignment. To expand into the energetic bodies, we must be ready to use this energy to benefit all in constructive ways. The work of Ascension expands our energy into world service. We must move through the trial-by-fire of the eighth energetic body to evolve to the ninth energetic body.

A mighty violet cloak is a cloak of protection for exploring the world of the ninth energetic body. This ninth body was built upon the principles of the Trinity. Within the Trinity is also the duality and fear that we face during the trials of the eighth energetic body. Use the cloak to explore this duality and these fears. The ninth energetic body is an aligned body, used for Ascension.

The ninth energetic body is also known as the first collective body, which allows exchanges with the Beloved I AM Presence. These exchanges carry momentum, and the gathered thought and focus of the present create the space to fill this ninth energetic body. The ninth energetic body carries the purification of all the mental bodies carried from this and all previous incarnations. We have the choice to purify all thought gathered to us. This is possible with close union or contact with the mighty Beloved I AM Presence. The ninth energetic body allows the sustaining energy to stream forth between the Higher Self, in communication with the Beloved I AM Presence and our mental body. There, all thought is gathered, purified, and cleansed.

As a reference, the first eight bodies are gathered in a collective effort for the human. Entering into world service, the eighth energetic body is born. In the ninth energetic body, we are faced with all the duality that comes forth to all human embodiments. As a trial-by-fire, the most treacherous fears and doubts are presented to the mind for resolution and purification. While holding the eighth energetic body, we may live for five, six, seven, or even eight hundred years by following the dietary and breath requirements.

In the ninth collective body, the Mastery of thought begins. This Co-creative process is sustained and maintained by the purification of thought, taken from the eighth body to the ninth body. The ninth energetic body is a collective effort between the mighty Beloved I AM Presence and the individualization of that Presence.

Earth is meant to be the planet of love in action, action which comes truly from the forgiving heart. The victory of Ascension is assured through this action, for there is no finer victory than the freedom of life through a forgiving heart. This eternal victory comes forth from God, which is known as the eleventh body. It is, eventually, in this body, that one is able to break out of the atmosphere of gravitational pull, the electromagnetic current of the planet itself.

Energetic work is love in action. An energetic alignment pitch to the I AM Presence can be discovered by placing the palms of the hands on the temples. Humming this pitch aligns the Kundalini and one's system to the planetary system, calling to the beloved, mighty I AM Presence to come forth in perfection. A tingling sensation comes over the hands, into the throat, and down into the feet. The ninth energetic body exists approximately thirty-six feet around the human shell. It is through the beloved mighty I AM Presence that the ninth body pulls in tighter. At first, it holds the Golden Ray, but as it pulls closer to the body, it takes on a silvery-bluish sheen and is approximately two inches from the body. It comes forth from the decree of the Presence: I AM THE PRESENCE OF COLLECTIVE THOUGHT.

Three pyramids pull the focused thought, as one harmonic unit, even closer to the body. It is in the purification of thought that perfection streams forth, for the thought focuses the space and allows the love in action.

17. Disciplined Focus. The Ray that streams forth to begin the eighth sustaining period is the Golden Ray. When life feels complicated, find the stillness in the heart, which assures the connection to the beloved mighty I AM Presence. This Presence is always there, ever prevailing, ever Omnipotent. We are in the Seventh Cycle, the completion of all, and as we enter into the Eighth Energetic Cycle, we are assured that all shall finally be sustained and maintained. The Heart of Desire of Perfection finds an energetic resonance that can be fulfilled, sustained, and maintained.

To become responsible and to take world responsibility, stand as a pillar as one who is firmly attached to the foundation and focused, and yet as one who reaches to the sky. Become the pillar to assure that the foundation will be built and the structure will be maintained and sustained. For guidance, step back and ask for the I

AM Presence; for in that union, true guidance and Mastery expresses itself. Being in the image and likeness of God, the I AM THAT I AM, is the true joy of that space, that stillness.

In the path of Mastery and world service, there are certain agreements that must be made to fulfill material needs: decree daily for these fulfillments, and always carry the focus of what is truly desired clearly in the mind. Do not allow doubt, fear, or anger to ever come forward, for then the focus is clouded, and once it is clouded, that is what comes. On this path of Mastery, there are instantaneous effects. Call forth the Will into Divine Alignment and Service, then decree for what is desired and it will come forward. It is the Will that keeps the purpose.

When in doubt, fear, or anger, disturbances will be attracted to us electromagnetically. However, when focusing only on what is desired from the heart, disturbances will not be part of the expression or choice. It is a discipline to keep concepts pure, to hold a focus of the true Heart's Desire. Additionally, when we allow our thoughts to become focused on anger or fear, our metabolic rate tends to drop based on nervous system changes and consequent undisciplined dietary changes. In this slowing down of the rate of spin in each of the chakra centers, an energetic change in the body can occur.

Remedy this by purifying the body with water through bathing and breathing. Adding salt to a bath and/or breathing the air near salt water will help. Breathe into each of the chakra centers, and adjust the rate of spin through your breath. Decree to the mighty I AM Presence and demand and command, as noted earlier, to manifest perfection.

When stepping inside and calling to the I AM Presence, breathe ever so gently to be renewed. Being revitalized will carry this Immaculate Concept of divinity and joy forward. Others will desire the same radiance, and service will be in bringing this joy. Being excited and joyous is contagious, as is laughter. Creation will adjust itself accordingly. It is important to proceed without fear. This is our Divine Heritage.

We are all part of the great family of creation, part of the great family of service. We came here with the Immaculate Concept and the desire to bring forth service, so that the Transition will be completed in a manner of peace and harmony. This work of bringing forth the understanding of "the perfection that we truly are" is a great joy. Let this great joy well up in the heart. By utilizing the focus of the Immaculate Concept, all else will revel in the perspective of being a gentle breeze through the trees, on a soft spring day. All else will manifest in this joy. The true desire to create and share joy will bring in others who desire the same thing.

In summary, Co-creative energy balances thought, feeling, and will; thought being the light; feeling, the sound; the will, the action. There is compassion always. Decree by stepping back into the stillness and defining what is truly desired. Then come forth, decreeing in the name of the I AM THAT I AM that this be manifest, fulfilled, and sustained.

18. Awaken to a New Day. It is necessary to be aware of the state of the world and not try to escape, but it is also necessary to take responsibility for our choices. There is a way to do this; by following a guiding force and a guiding path, through the celebration of harmony and alignment, attuned with that of the mighty I AM Presence. We were brought here to Master the Earth Plane. What we think, we become, and our feelings are activated to protect the physical body. Each day we can say "I make the choice to be free, to be happy, to be in harmony," or we can choose to be in fear, in pain, in lack, and believe that we are abandoned and separated from our mighty I AM Presence. We can say "I will be in the glory of light. I will manifest harmony in my world and extend this to the world of those around me. I AM a force that is ONE with my Brother and I AM a force that is ONE with the mighty I AM Presence."

The celestial chorus awakens the Elemental Life Force in the early morning hours with the music of being. What is most important is to look within our hearts, follow our desire, and see ourselves as an extension of the Earth in the area where we live. We affect the vibration of the planet itself and she affects us. We need to work together as ONE. She offers herself as a nurturer and we too must respond as caretakers. It's time to open our eyes and awaken to a New Day.

19. Law of ONE. Choosing "All That Is" is the true being of the Source. As we seek our individuality, paradoxically, we search for the collective. The collective knows no boundaries, yet it is only through individualization that one understands the need to allow the larger Self to disseminate. This is called the Law of Oneness. This Law allows the Divine Will to stream forth into our hearts, softening them, so we will be willing to serve with Grace. Grace transmutes beyond all human creation into the heavenly realms. This Time of Grace, when it comes to the planet, will be a time when the collective shall beat to the heart of ONE great being.

The Law of Oneness is founded upon the principles known as the Jurisdictions, and the deeper reasoning of these leads us into harmony. The perseverance of the soul also comes from this great collective Source, as an out-breath. The time has come for the great in-breath, where we are brought back to that fiery Source of Helios and Vesta, the Source of all Sources for the creation of our universe. This Time of Transition is when we choose whether we will return to this Law of Oneness and allow our boundaries of individuality to dissipate, or allow a great Collective to supersede our higher consciousness. We truly are ONE and all it takes are two to pierce the illusion, to create heaven on Earth. To anchor in the Golden Cities of conscious light, we must be willing to consciously merge our being with that of the Earth Planet itself and find within, that great Pillar of Light that is anchored so firmly within the heart; this light can then be called upon in reservoirs.

In the collective forgetting, we proved that boundaries and separation could indeed exist; the individual could create a great mass ego; we could even produce such a sinister force, it could rule with much confusion. Now we need to prove, in this great in-breath, that we are a God-Free Creation, made in the image and likeness of light and sound. We have asked for our bliss and to follow our Heart's Desire. However, this time, bliss and desire come to the planet and to those who are "small." This, too, contain the inherent power of creation. We are brought here not only to Co-create but to disseminate and assimilate simultaneously. Disseminating the great Law of Oneness is through the goodness of the heart. Assimilating, in this great in-breath, is our method of collective spiritual contact. As we choose, we choose, too, for our Brother and Sister. Collective reasoning shows how collective thought is held. The great Law of Union and ONE works to bring eternal peace and gladness to every man, woman, and child upon the Earth Planet.

20. Come Forth in Your Light. Focus creates reality and focus is guided by intent. To those who behold dark, it is dark that they fear and see in everything. In the intent to eliminate the dark, the focus gives the dark a power that feeds the fear and doubt, and that focus is carried to all we contact. To those who behold light, the light begets light. In the intent to create light, the light is the focus and is expanded to all. By creating a focus of light, all focus of dark is excluded. Our feelings and actions are given power by our focus of thoughts, and our words create spaces for the actions to manifest. Our feelings intensify our words, which expand the space that, in turn, quickens the action. Personal peace and personal light are the Love of the Mother/Father God that Never Fails. The world is in need of our light and our love.

Index

About Lori and Lenard Toye

Lori Toye is not a Prophet of doom and gloom. The fact that she became a Prophet at all is highly unlikely. Reared in a small Idaho farming community as a member of the conservative Missouri Synod Lutheran church, Lori had never heard of meditation, spiritual development, reincarnation, channeling, or clairvoyant sight. Her unusual spiritual journey began in Washington State, when, as advertising manager of a weekly newspaper, she answered a request to pick up an ad for a local health food store. As she entered, a woman at the counter pointed a finger at her and said, "You have work to do for Master Saint Germain!"

The next several years were filled with spiritual enlightenment that introduced Lori, then only twenty-two years old, to the most exceptional and inspirational information she had ever encountered. Lori became a student of Ascended Master Teachings.

Awakened one night by the luminous figure of Saint Germain at the foot of her bed, her work had begun. Later in the same year, an image of a map appeared in her dream. Four teachers clad in white robes were present, pointing out Earth Changes that would shape the future United States.

Five years later, faced with the stress of a painful divorce and rebuilding her life as a single mother, Lori attended spiritual meditation classes. While there, she shared her experience, and encouraged by friends, she began to explore the dream through daily meditation. The four Beings appeared again, and expressed a willingness to share the information. Over a six-month period, they gave over eighty sessions of material, including detailed information that would later become the I AM America Map.

Clearly she had to produce the map. The only means to finance it was to sell her house. She put her home up for sale, and in a depressed market, it sold the first day at full asking price.

She produced the map in 1989, rolled copies of them on her kitchen table, and sold them through word-of-mouth. She then launched a lecture tour of the Northwest and California. Hers was the first Earth Changes Map published, and many others have followed, but the rest is history.

From the tabloids to the *New York Times*, *The Washington Post*, television interviews in the U.S., London, and Europe, Lori's Mission was to honor the material she had received. The material is not hers, she stresses. It belongs to the Masters, and their loving, healing approach is disseminated through the I AM America Publishing Company operated by her husband and spiritual partner, Lenard Toye.

Lenard Toye, originally from Philadelphia, PA, was born into a family of professional contractors and builders, and has a remarkable singing voice. Lenard's compelling tenor voice replaced many of the greats at a moment's notice—Pavarotti and Domingo, including many performances throughout Europe. When he retired from music, he joined his family's business yet pursued his personal interests in alternative healing.

He attended *Barbara Brennan's School of Healing* to further develop the gift of auric vision. Working together with his wife Lori, they organized free classes of healing techniques and the channeled teachings. Their instructional pursuits led them to form the *School of the Four Pillars* which includes holistic and energy healing and Ascended Master Teachings. In

1995 and 1996 they sponsored the first Prophecy Conferences in Philadelphia and Phoenix, Arizona. His management and sales background has played a very important role in his partnership with his wife Lori and their publishing company.

Other publications include three additional Prophecy maps, twelve books, a video, and more than sixty audio tapes based on sessions with Master Teacher Saint Germain and other Ascended Masters.

Spiritual in nature, I AM America is not a church, religion, sect, or cult. There is no interest or intent in amassing followers or engaging in any activity other than what Lori and Lenard can do on their own to publicize the materials they have been entrusted with.

They have also been directed to build the first Golden City community. A very positive aspect of the vision is that all the maps include areas called, "Golden Cities." These places hold a high spiritual energy, and are where sustainable communities are to be built using solar energy alongside classical feng shui engineering and infrastructure. The first community, Wenima Village, is currently being planned for development.

Concerned that some might misinterpret the Maps' messages as doom and gloom and miss the metaphor for personal change, or not consider the spiritual teachings attached to the maps, Lori emphasizes that the Masters stressed that this was a Prophecy of choice. Prophecy allows for choice in making informed decisions and promotes the opportunity for cooperation and harmony. Lenard and Lori's vision for I AM America is to share the Ascended Masters' prophecies as spiritual warnings to heal and renew our lives.

Books and Maps by Lori Toye

Books:

NEW WORLD WISDOM SERIES (*formerly New World Atlas Series*)

FREEDOM STAR: *Prophecies that Heal Earth*

THE EVER PRESENT NOW: *A New Understanding of Consciousness and Prophecy*

GOLDEN CITY SERIES
Book One: Points of Perception
Book Two: Light of Awakening
Book Three: Divine Destiny
Book Four: Sacred Energies of the Golden Cities

I AM AMERICA TRILOGY
Book One: A Teacher Appears
Book Two: Sisters of the Flame
Book Three: Fields of Light

Maps:

I AM America Map
Freedom Star World Map
United States 6-Map Scenario
United States Golden City Map

I AM AMERICA PUBLISHING & DISTRIBUTING
P.O. Box 2511, Payson, Arizona, 85547, USA. (480) 744-6188

For More Information:
www.iamamerica.com
www.loritoye.com

I AM America Online Bookstore:
http://iamamericabookstore.iaabooks.com

# About I AM America

I AM America is an educational and publishing foundation dedicated to disseminating the Ascended Masters' message of Earth Changes Prophecy and Spiritual Teachings for self-development. Our office is run by the husband and wife team of Lenard and Lori Toye who hand-roll maps, package, and mail information and products with a small staff. Our first publication was the I AM America Map, which was published in September 1989. Since then we have published three more Prophecy maps, nine books, and numerous recordings based on the channeled sessions with the Spiritual Teachers.

We are not a church, a religion, a sect, or cult and are not interested in amassing followers or members. Nor do we have any affiliation with a church, religion, political group, or government of any kind. We are not a college or university, research facility, or a mystery school. El Morya told us that the best way to see ourselves is as, "Cosmic Beings, having a human experience."

In 1994, we asked Saint Germain, "How do you see our work at I AM America?" and he answered, "I AM America is to be a clearinghouse for the new humanity." Grabbing a dictionary, we quickly learned that the term "clearinghouse" refers to "an organization or unit within an organization that functions as a central agency for collecting, organizing, storing, and disseminating documents, usually within a specific academic discipline or field." So inarguably, we are this too. But in uncomplicated terms, we publish and share spiritually transformational information because at I AM America there is no doubt that, "A Change of Heart can Change the World."

With Violet Flame Blessings,
Lori & Lenard Toye

For more information or to visit our online bookstore, go to:
www.iamamerica.com
www.loritoye.com

To receive a catalog by mail, please write to:
I AM America
P.O. Box 2511
Payson, AZ 85547

CPSIA information can be obtained
at www.ICGtesting.com
Printed in the USA
FSOW03n0058090816
23556FS

9 781880 050613